Origins and Destinations

Family, Class, and Education in Modern Britain

Origins and Destinations

Family, Class, and Education in Modern Britain

A. H. HALSEY
A. F. HEATH
J. M. RIDGE

CLARENDON PRESS · OXFORD
1980

Oxford University Press, Walton Street, Oxford OX2 6DP

OXFORD LONDON GLASGOW
NEW YORK TORONTO MELBOURNE WELLINGTON
KUALA LUMPUR SINGAPORE JAKARTA HONG KONG TOKYO
DELHI BOMBAY CALCUTTA MADRAS KARACHI
NAIROBI DAR ES SALAAM CAPE TOWN

*Published in the United States by
Oxford University Press, New York*

British Library Cataloguing in Publication Data
Halsey, Albert Henry
Origins and destinations.
1. Educational equalization – Great Britain
2. Educational sociology – Great Britain
3. Social classes – Great Britain
I. Title II. Heath, A.F.
III. Ridge, John Michael
370.19′341   LC213.3.G7   79–41031
ISBN 0-19-827224-3
ISBN 0-19-827249-9 Pbk

*Set by Hope Services, Abingdon
and printed in Great Britain by
Richard Clay (at The Chaucer Press) Ltd
Bungay, Suffolk*

Acknowledgements

All those who were connected in any way with the Oxford Social Mobility Project will know how much the success of the data-collection owed to Phyllis Thorburn, the Senior Research Officer. Her experience and organizing ability were vital.

As authors of this small part of the analyses in progress on the Project material we would like to thank Kenneth Macdonald of Nuffield College, for his many stimulating, albeit often gnomic, suggestions both for future research and clearer exposition.

Our early attempts to fit logistic curves by hand (and eye) were miserable failures. In despair of a solution, we had abandoned the attempt when Peter Clifford came to our rescue. The results of his help form the base of Chapter 7; the method he explains in Appendix III. We are very grateful to him.

We are indebted to Paul Duncan-Jones for the use of his data-handling procedures which contributed substantially to the efficiency of the data analysis. For most of the analyses reported here we used the SPSS system as implemented by Oxford University Computing Service on the ICL 1906A. We are grateful for the Service's ready response to our often enormous demands, and especially to Paul Griffiths for some vital modifications of SPSS.

Finally, it is a pleasure to acknowledge our great debt to Margaret Bett whose preparation of the typescript went a good way beyond the normal call of secretarial duty.

Contents

CHAPTER 1

Education and Political Arithmetic

We have set ourselves a question in this book which in its most general and deceptively simple form is whether education can change society. However, the context in which we ask this question modifies both its generality and its simplicity. We ask it particularly of England and Wales in the twentieth century, having at our disposal summary familial and educational biographies collected from a sample of 10 000 men living in these two countries in 1972.[1] We ask it still more particularly of the period since the Second World War and the Education Act of 1944, having in mind the assessment made in 1949 by Professor Glass and his associates at the London School of Economics of the relation between education and social selection in the generation preceding the War[2] and the 'welfare state' legislation which immediately followed it.

The theoretical simplicity of our question is also unavoidably complicated by this context. Its formulation and the data on which we rely were shaped by the requirements of a more general study of occupational mobility. For us this means that our approach to the relation between educational and social change is in the spirit and style of the political-arithmetic tradition in which Glass carried on his mobility research.[3] We recognize, of course, that there are other and legitimate interests in the study of mobility, not least the interest in class formation and class action which informs the other main book to appear to date on the national 1972 survey – John H. Goldthorpe, *Social Mobility and Class Structure*.[4] Nevertheless, the political-arithmetic tradition is apt for our purposes, enabling us to assess anew the part played by education as a channel of social selection for the last generation of Britons. It lacks the merit, if merit it be, of fashionability, and we hope to show that its power can be strongly reinforced from certain theoretical and methodological advances in America and France which we shall use in the body of the book. Meanwhile, by way of introduction, we would reassert the strength of this indigenous style of social science. It has a long and distinguished history. Its origins can be traced back at least as far as Booth and the Webbs, and perhaps earlier to Mayhew in the nineteenth century and William Petty in the seventeenth century.

These writers were concerned to describe accurately and in detail the social conditions of their society, particularly of the more disadvantaged sections, but their interest in these matters was never a disinterested academic one. Description of social conditions was a preliminary to political reform. They exposed the inequalities of society in order to change them. The tradition thus has a double intent; on the one hand it engages in the primary sociological task of describing and documenting the 'state of society'; on the other hand it addresses itself to central social and political issues. It has never, therefore, been a 'value free' academic discipline, if such were in any event possible. Instead, it has been an attempt to marry a value-laden choice of issue with objective methods of data collection.

The British political arithmeticians may be justly described as having held a position of cautious optimism on the question of the power of education to change society. Probably this reflects their close affinity to the liberal optimists whose policies of expanding opportunities within the given structure of education have dominated in capitalist countries since the last third of the nineteenth century.[5] Probably also it reflects an unresponsiveness to Marxism which in recent formulations, notably those of Bowles and Gintis, far from conceiving a causal role for education in social change, treats it as a dependent agency of social control, reproducing recruits to the class structure through pedagogical relations of authority which correspond to, and, for the child, anticipate, relations of authority in work.

The tradition we espouse does not, therefore, offer a decisive answer to the question we have set ourselves. If we look further to the literature of the sociology of education as a whole, the range of answers is wider. Indeed, the field is a battleground centred on this very issue. Our discussion of the general state of the debate can be brief, partly because our review of the sociology of education has recently appeared,[6] and partly because our formulation of the question is more profitably discussed in the context of the country and the period covered by our empirical data. Nevertheless, a sketch of the relevant literature may serve to clarify the scope and limitations of the contribution we intend to attempt.

Past writing has yielded two basic theories about education and social change. The first is that education is the rock on which a modern and prosperous civilization is built. It creates new knowledge, ensures that people can use advanced scientific cultures, and brings individuals into the jobs they are able to do well. Education is investment in human capital. As a leading proponent of human capital theory has put it,

labourers have become capitalists not from a diffusion of the ownership of corporation stock, as folk lore would have it, but from the acquisition of knowledge and skills that have economic value. This knowledge and skill are in great part the product of investment and, combined with other human investment, predominantly account for the productive superiority of the technically advanced countries. To omit them in studying economic growth is like trying to explain Soviet ideology without Marx.[7]

Some critics of this theory challenge the connection between education and economic efficiency. For example, Sir Keith Joseph, doubting the wisdom of rapid expansion of British universities since the Second War, suggested that 'the growth of the public sector in recent years had placed an undue strain on private industry' and that 'the decline of private enterprise in public esteem' was to be explained partly by misguided left-wing teachers 'who had between them helped to erode the will to work'.[8] Nor is this a new theme. In the nineteenth century the British business class sent twice as many of its sons to Cambridge as it received back into business careers and, accordingly, business leaders typically held an ambivalent and suspicious attitude towards the recruitment of graduates. Other critics, while accepting the close tie between education and the economy, criticize its nature. Thus Samuel Bowles writes, 'The record of educational history is . . . that schools have evolved in the U.S. not as part of the pursuit of equality, but rather to meet the needs of capitalist employers for a disciplined and skilled task force, and to provide a mechanism of social control in the interests of political stability'.[9]

Bowles's criticism brings us to the second theory, which is that education is essentially an organization of control by one generation over the next. Schooling is the major public instrument for the production of appropriate social person-alities. For Weber, the extended character training of the literati perpetuated the 'stucture of domination' in ancient China. For Durkheim, *l'éducation morale* was crucial to the social integration of the Third Repulic. But again, the hostile versions, whether from the pen of Ivan Illich or Bowles and Gintis, tell us that schools stupify the majority into acquiescence in the interests of the powerful, impoverishing the life of ordinary men. If men are to be free, to be creative and to be rich in the things that matter, they must rid themselves of the professional pedagogue and the oppression of organized educational bureaucracies which make them both revere false knowledge and spend ever-longer proportions of their lives in attempting to acquire it.

In Britain, both theories in various guises have played a prominent role in public debates on education. For example, in proposing an unprecedented expansion of higher education, the Robbins Committee laid weight on both industrial efficiency and education for democracy.

We begin with instruction in skills suitable to play a part in the general division of labour. We put this first, not because we regard it as the more important, but because we think that it is sometimes ignored or undervalued. Confucius said in the Analects that it was not easy to find a man who had studied for three years without aiming at pay . . . . And it must be recognised that in our own times, progress – and particularly the maintenance of a competitive position – depends to a much greater extent than ever before on skills demanding special training.

The Committee went on, however, to give equal stress to

a function that is more difficult to describe concisely, that is nonetheless funda-mental; the transmission of a common culture and common standards of citizenship. By this we do not mean the forcing of all individuality into a common mould: that would be the negation of higher education as we conceive it. But we believe that it is a proper function of higher education, as for education in schools, to provide, in partnership with the family, a background of culture and social habit upon which a healthy society depends.[10]

But if both economic efficiency and a common culture have been major goals of educational policy, most sociologists, and especially those associated with the political arithmetic tradition, have seen social inequality as a major barrier to their achievement. As R. H. Tawney put it in 1931, 'The hereditary curse upon English education is its organisation upon lines of social class.'[11] In consequence, as Harold Silver has shown, 'for most of this century the discussion of education in relation to such concepts as "equality", "equality of opportunity", "democ-racy" or "social justice" has focussed on the *structure* of the educational system, and *access* by children from different social groups to its different component parts'.[12]

For our part, then, the changing structure of British education and the social distribution of educational opportunity must be our principal descriptive tasks. In consequence we shall describe, in Chapter 2, the shape and scope of the educational system entered by the successive cohorts of boys which our 1972 sample enables us to identify, and we shall specify the categories and procedures we have used so as to place our respondents in the class structure and to measure the changing patterns of class chances for the various types and levels of schooling. On these definitions we shall then be able to trace the development or diminution of class inequalities as between state and private schooling (Chapter 3), selective and non-selective schools (Chapter 4), length of secondary schooling (Chapter 8), and post-secondary education (Chapter 10).

Class differences in access to the more advanced or more privileged sectors of education are, then, an abiding concern of the political arithmetic tradition in which we locate ourselves. They are attacked on the twin grounds that they hinder economic efficiency and that they represent a departure from social justice. Efficiency is diminished, it is argued, in that talented children from the working class are denied the opportunity to develop their abilities: 'wastage of ability' becomes a crucial educational issue. A classic statement of the problem comes from one of our immediate predecessors, J. W. B. Douglas:

In recent discussions there has been a tendency to assume that there is only a limited number of persons who can benefit from higher education and that there is a clearly defined 'pool of talent' on which to draw for university places. It has been said, however, that what is extracted from the pool depends much less on its content than on the effectiveness of the pump; it is clear from the present study that the pump is leaking badly at the points of secondary selection and early leaving. The pool of talent found at the end of the secondary school period is likely to be only a portion of that which would be found if it were possible to draw fully on potential rather than realised ability. Over a period of three years in the primary schools, there is a substantial loss of ability in the manual working-class children which could be prevented . . .[13]

On the side of the common culture and social justice, as opposed to economic efficiency, perhaps the most eloquent voice was Tawney's. Tawney was writing before the war when, as we shall see in Chapter 2, secondary education was yet to become universal and when only a proportion of places in the secondary schools awarded on the basis of competitive examinations was available for non-feepayers. Secondary education for all was Tawney's aim.

The goal to be aimed at is simplicity itself. The idea that differences of educational opportunity among children should depend upon differences of wealth among parents is a barbarity . . . . The primary school . . . should be, as in some countries it already is, the common school of the whole population, so excellent and so generally esteemed that all parents desire their children to attend it. It should, in short, be the preparatory school from which all children, and not merely a fortunate minority, pass on to secondary education, and which, since the second stage would then succeed the first, as a matter of course, when children were ripe for it, would be free from the present pressure to prepare them for a competitive examination affecting their whole future. A special system of schools, reserved for children whose parents have larger bank accounts than their neighbours, exists in no other country on the same scale as in England. It is at once an educational monstrosity and a grave national misfortune. It is educationally vicious, since to mix with companions from homes of different types is an important part of the education of the young. It is socially disastrous, for it does more than any other single cause, except capitalism itself, to perpetuate the division of the nation into classes of which one is almost unintelligible to the other.[14]

But economic efficiency and social justice tend to be uncomfortable bed-fellows and the particular conception of 'equality of opportunity' which came to dominate English education in the immediate pre-war and post-war periods owes perhaps more to the concern over wastage of talent than to Tawney's concern for a common culture. In this conception 'equality of opportunity for children of equal ability irrespective of their social origins'[15] was the desideratum. Class differences *per se* were not necessarily objected to; class differences among those with equal ability were what had to be eliminated. This conception of equality of opportunity, and its relation to economic efficiency, comes out clearly in a recent statement by Daniel Bell. The thesis is summed up in one word – meritocracy.

The post-industrial society in its initial logic, is a meritocracy. Differential status and differential income are based on technical skills and higher education. Without those achievements one cannot fulfil the requirements of the new social division of labour which is a feature of that society. And there are few high places open without those skills . . . . Thus, the university, which once reflected the status system of the society, has now become the arbiter of class position. As the gatekeeper, it has gained a quasi-monopoly in determining the future stratification of the society.
In the nature of a meritocracy, as it has been traditionally conceived, what is central to the assessment of a person is the assumed relation of achievement to intelligence, and of intelligence to its measurement on the Intelligence Quotient scale. The first question, therefore, is what determines intelligence. In the received social science and biology opinion, the number of talented persons in the society, as measured by IQ, is a limited pool; and this is reflected in the bell-shaped curve of a normal distribution of test scores in a particular age-category. By the logic of a meritocracy, these high scoring individuals, no matter where they are in the society, should be brought to the top in order to make the best use of their talents. This is the basis of the liberal theory of equality of opportunity and of Jefferson's belief in the 'natural aristoi' against the ascriptive nobility.[16]

It would be wrong, however, to suppose that meritocracy receives its justification only from its presumed relation with economic efficiency. Meritocracy also draws moral support from its position as the embodiment of the liberal principle of 'justice as desert'. As Miller puts it, 'Desert is a matter of fitting forms of treatment to the specific qualities and actions of individuals and in particular good desert (i.e. deserving benefit as opposed to punishment) is a matter of fitting desired forms of treatment to qualities and action which are generally held in high regard.'[17] In a society such as our own, ability is one of the things 'held in high regard'. To reward those with high ability by giving them access to the more prestigious forms of education, grammar schools or universities, is thus to ensure distributive justice according to the criterion of desert.
We should perhaps also note that the criterion of desert is one that tends to flourish in a liberal market society. It is far from being the only principle of justice but, as one of us has noted elsewhere, 'In an open, mobile society where

individual success depends, at least partly, on competition in a free labour market, desert offers the most fruitful source of legitimation to those who have succeeded. Success can be ascribed to effort and ability, and failure to incompetence and laziness. Both can accordingly be justified.'[18] While we would not, ourselves, wish to assent to the superiority of desert as a principle of justice, it is nevertheless important for us to consider just how far the British educational system has achieved its professed goal of meritocracy. Accordingly in Chapter 4 we introduce a meritocratic model of educational selection and use it in subsequent chapters to examine how far the various stages of education have approximated to the meritocratic ideal at different points of their development within the period covered by the experience of the adult British population in 1972. We shall pay particular attention to the consequences of the 1944 Education Act. How far did this measure, which represents the culmination of pre-war agitation for greater equality of opportunity, shift the balance of advantage away from the more privileged classes and permit a closer approximation to meritocracy? How far, too, does the continued existence of a private sector subvert this ideal? The 1943 White Paper on Educational Reconstruction asserted that 'A system under which fees are charged in one type of post-primary school and prohibited in the other offends against the canon that the nature of a child's education should be determined by his capacity and promise and not by the financial circumstances of his parents.'[19] Does the capacity and willingness of a parent to pay fees still secure for his child educational advantages that he would not have obtained within the state sector?

Meritocracy, then, is one yardstick by which to judge the performance of the British educational system and by which to gauge the effectiveness of social reform. But, meritocracy is by no means either unassailable, or unassailed, as an ideal. Indeed, it is the argument in favour of meritocracy, which Bell espouses, that was the object of Michael Young's lampoon in *The Rise of the Meritocracy*.[20] Young, at least in that particular book, articulates the discontent of egalitarians with the limitation of the concept of equality of opportunity to which the liberal tradition has been essentially confined. The emphasis shifts, therefore, from the notion of 'equal opportunity to be unequal' to inequality itself. It is therefore no surprise to find Michael Young as the author not only of the term meritocracy, which he attacks, but also the phrase 'positive discrimination' which he advocated in the Plowden Report.

Further attacks on the concept and practice of meritocracy have come from a number of directions. One influential criticism which sums up a growing body of work comes from the American writers Bowles and Gintis. They argue that in practice merit, as conventionally defined by IQ, has little to do with economic efficiency: meritocracy, rather, is an ideology which serves to justify existing inequalities.

The educational system legitimates economic inequality by providing an open, objective, and ostensibly meritocratic mechanism for assigning individuals to unequal economic positions. The educational system fosters and reinforces the belief that economic success depends essentially on the possession of technical and cognitive skills – skills which it is organized to provide in an efficient, equitable, and unbiased manner on the basis of meritocratic principle.

But [they continue] beneath the facade of meritocracy lies the reality of an educational system geared toward the reproduction of economic relations only partially explicable in terms of technical requirements and efficiency standards. Thus we shall first suggest that educational tracking based on competitive grading and objective test scores is only tangentially related to social efficiency. Then we shall confront the technocratic-meritocratic ideology head-on by showing that the association between length of education and economic success cannot be accounted for in terms of the cognitive achievements of students. Thus the yardstick of the educational meritocracy – test scores – contribute surprisingly little to individual economic success. The educational meritocracy is largely symbolic.[21]

We shall not, in the present volume, be able to examine the relation between test scores and individual economic success in Britain, although we hope to address this question in a later publication. However, there is a variant of Bowles and Gintis's position that we shall tackle directly. This is the argument of the French sociologist, Pierre Bourdieu. Bourdieu, like Bowles and Gintis, sees the school as essentially a conservative force and meritocracy as specious.

By giving individuals educational aspirations strictly tailored to their position in the social hierarchy, and by operating a selection procedure which, although apparently formally equitable, endorses real inequalities, schools help both to perpetuate and legitimise inequalities. By awarding allegedly impartial qualifications (which are also largely accepted as such) for socially-conditioned attitudes which it treats as unequal 'gifts', it transforms *de facto* inequalities into *de jure* ones and economic and social differences into distinctions of quality, and legitimates the transmission of the cultural heritage.[22]

The thrust of the attack here is on the liberal tradition of optimism. In so far as Bourdieu holds out any hope for educationally based egalitarianism, he does so through advocating that 'the educational system should have at its disposal the means to carry out systematic and widespread educational priority programmes of the kind that it can dispense with as long as it is aimed at children from the privileged classes.'[23] But more fundamentally, the call is for redistribution of what Bourdieu calls cultural capital, which determines access and achievement in schools. It is this theory of cultural capital which we shall attempt to test. Essentially, Bourdieu's argument is that the school, while ostensibly fair and meritocratic, does not give everyone an equal chance. The ones who can receive what the school has to give are the ones who are already endowed with the requisite cultural attributes – with the appropriate cultural capital.

What is being advanced here is a different and powerful objection to meritocracy. Bourdieu does not put it like this himself, but he, in effect, claims that the educational system is nominally universalistic but in reality particularistic; in theory it promises to reward 'IQ plus effort' (Michael Young's formulation of meritocracy), but in practice IQ plus effort are not on their own sufficient. The appropriate cultural attributes associated with middle-class families are necessary too. The nature of the handicaps which prevent individuals from achieving educational success must be a major concern for us throughout this book. Is it merely a matter of IQ? Or is culture more important still?

The arguments of Bowles and Gintis and of Bourdieu have by no means lacked their British exponents. But the main British battle which has set the defenders of meritocracy against the advocates of equality has been fought over the issue of comprehensive schools. This gives the British debate a curiously parochial character. Moreover, a necessary link of selective schools to meritocracy and of comprehensive schools to educational equality is far from self-evident. After all, if Bowles and Gintis are to be believed, America has long had a comprehensive educational system which has vigorously espoused an ideology of meritocracy. Again, the motivations behind comprehensive reorganization in Britain were by no means all anti-meritocratic. Some of the arguments could be seen as accepting meritocratic premises but arguing that a comprehensive system would better enable them to be realized than would a system in which selection for different forms of secondary education was carried out at the age of 11. For example, Young summed up a view of educational selection in the 1950s that 'the future development of children could not be accurately assessed at the tender age of eleven' and that 'once children were shepherded into separate pens it was too difficult for those who developed late to transfer from one to another.'[24] But the main argument, as Young makes clear, was not educational but social; it was a reiteration of Tawney's plea for a common culture. '[The] chief interest was not, however, so much educational as social; the left-wingers claimed that to segregate the clever from the stupid was to deepen class divisions. They proposed that all children, irrespective of sex, race, creed, class . . . *or* ability, should be lumped together.'[25]

Nevertheless, the attack on comprehensive schools in Britain has largely concentrated on the alleged obstacles to meritocracy which they provide. The Black Paper writers are the best-known example of this attack.[26] They generally condemn comprehensive schools on the alleged grounds that they produce a specious equality at the expense of the liberty of the minority of the academically-gifted children. In their 1975 paper, they drew ten 'basic' educational implications, including:

(i) without selection the clever working-class child in a deprived area stands little chance of a real academic education;
(ii) you can have equality or equality of opportunity; you cannot have both. Equality will mean the holding back (or the new deprivation) of bright children;
(iii) if the non-competitive ethos of progressive education is allowed to dominate our schools, we shall produce a generation unable to maintain our standards of living when opposed by fierce rivalry from overseas competitors.

Underlying these educational implications are genetic and cultural theories of the learning potential of different groups. One variant which has added much passion to recent debate is the genetic. The American psychologist, Arthur Jensen, is perhaps the outstanding voice,[27] and Professor Hans Eysenck has published vulgarizations of the same argument in Britain.[28] On this view, though the freedom of individuals to seek self-fulfilment is regarded as sacred, the social distribution of capacity to do so is held to be predominantly determined by genetic constitution. Various environmental, including educational, inferences are then drawn. For Richard Herrnstein the implication for education appears to be that of a vehicle which runs solely under the dictates of an ineluctable genetic force leading towards a rigid hereditarian meritocracy. He sees

a future in which social classes not only continue but become ever more solidly built on inborn differences. As the wealth and complexity of human society grow, there will be precipitated out of the mass of humanity a low capacity (intellectual and otherwise) residue that may be unable to master the common occupations, cannot compete for success and achievement and are most likely to be born to parents who have similarly failed.[29]

For Eysenck, the implication for education is that progressivism and comprehensive schooling are a departure from social justice and the need is to return to IQ testing as the basis for educational selection.

For many years [he writes] I.Q. tests were instrumental in securing a better education for [the bright working-class child] than they would otherwise have been able to obtain; the elimination of such tests by left-wing governments is still one of the least intelligible actions taken in the name of advancing the status of the deprived child. As we have seen, I.Q. tests are not entirely measures of innate ability; the correlation between genotype and phenotype is only 0.9 or thereabouts. But this correlation is close enough to make the I.Q. test a genuine instrument of social progress; it depends far, far less than any alternative measure on social factors which would give unfair advantages to the middle-class child . . . . For all those who wish genuinely to restore to bright working-class children the best opportunities for an education appropriate to their talents, the restoration of I.Q. tests to their rightful place seems the best, if not the only way.[30]

For Jensen, 'The problem of Negro-White inequality in educability is thus essentially the problem of Negro-White differences in intelligence.'[31] The educational implications, as Jensen sees them, are three. First, there is the search for different methods for different children to enable them to move towards the same educational goals. Second, he advocates more research on learning readiness and anticipates that 'the more or less uniform lock step sequencing of educational experiences may have to be drastically modified for the benefit of many children.' But third and most important, he infers the need for a greater diversity of curriculum goals. What he means is made clear by his remark that 'the purely academic goals of schooling have been so strongly ingrained in the thinking and in the values of our society that radical efforts will probably be called for to modify public education in ways whereby it can more effecitvely benefit large numbers of children who have limited aptitudes for traditional academic achievement.' On any interpretation this must mean the educational institutionalization of inequality.

In addition to these genetic theories in defence of IQ testing and selection, there is also an interesting cultural version of the defence of institutionalised inequality. The theory is a curious one, for in many ways it duplicates the left-wing anti-meritocratic arguments of Bourdieu. It runs as follows:

The implication of the sociologists is that there are numerous children who, for reasons of class, are being unfairly inhibited from going on to the education they deserve. My point is that many of these children are, for cultural reasons, likely to be inhibited from gaining the best of what is offered them even if they were to be offered 'chances' in these terms; and this because they have already been formed by historical socio-cultural forces which makes the segment of 'high' culture put before them pretty meaningless – even their range of linguistic capacity inhibits them . . . . The mere indication of higher I.Q. does not, in itself, indicate ability to benefit from what is, in effect, for many children a foreign cultural experience. A great deal of social mobility has already been achieved so that class barriers no longer constitute the inhibiting factors they once did; anyone of real ability can now make the grade, if that is the term for it. But an *excessive* concern for such opportunities may well be against the true educational interests of children of lesser, though still of good, ability, who may, at the moment, seem to be stigmatised as 'social waste'. Their satisfactions may spring out of a fuller exploitation of such cultural possibilities as form part of their world rather than an attempt to afford them 'opportunities' via an unpalatable higher culture they cannot really assimilate . . . . The most that can be expected is a reasonable degree of mobility – and this, at least, has been achieved. Anything more is likely to meet simply the stubborn imperfectibility of human institutions; no human problem of this nature can be reduced below a certain level simply because it is a required and irreducible characteristic of complex societies. Indeed, in so far as class divisions lead to cultural heterogeneity, some degree of class division may be said to enrich the State.[32]

What Bourdieu castigates, Bantock would seem to praise. They seem agreed on the factual issues but bitterly divided on the ideological. To settle the ideological issues is beyond the scope of this book, and indeed of any book, but we can check the factual basis of some of the assertions made by Bantock and Bourdieu. Again, we cannot hope to resolve the arguments for and against comprehensive schools. Quite apart from the ideological issues involved, the data and indeed the realities of the British educational system do not yet permit a proper assessment of comprehensive reform in Britain. Selective grammar schools still exist in considerable numbers and many of the comprehensive schools that currently exist still show the stigmata of their grammar or secondary modern predecessors. Another generation will have to pass before we can embark on any thorough evaluation. Nevertheless, we can offer an empirical appraisal of the waning selective, tripartite system and by comparison with the American comprehensive experience we can offer some guesses about the consequences of comprehensive reform for the attainment of goals such as equality of opportunity.

Finally, the American experience and debates indicate another set of questions to which we must address ourselves. As we have pointed out, the American debates over equality and equality of opportunity have taken a distinctly different direction from the British. Since America has long had a comprehensive system, the conception of equality of opportunity has taken, according to Coleman, a distinctive form.[33] It has contained, he claims, the following four elements:

1. providing a *free* education up to a given level which constituted the principal entry point to the labour force;
2. providing a *common curriculum* for all children, regardless of background;
3. partly by design and partly because of low population density, providing

that children from diverse backgrounds attend the *same school*;
4. providing equality within a given *locality*, since local taxes provided the
   source of support for schools.

In this American conception, then, equality of opportunity requires *all* children
to be exposed to the same curriculum in the same schools. Equal opportunities
are thus realized by virtue of exposure to equal educational inputs.

A major challenge to this position came from Coleman's research com-
missioned after the Civil Rights Act of 1964. The Act required the Commissioner
of Education to assess the 'lack of equality of educational opportunity' among
racial and other groups in the United States. It was widely expected that the
study would show glaring inequalities between black and white schools and that
differential scholastic achievement by race could be substantially explained by
these differences. Coleman's findings, however, were that black and white school
characteristics were surprisingly equal and that family background was much
more important than school characteristics in explaining differential achievement
among school children.

Coleman, then, showed that there was relative equality of educational *inputs*
but inequality of educational *results*. As he puts it,

By making the dichotomy between inputs and results explicit, and by focussing
attention not only on inputs but on results, the Report brought into the open
what had been underlying all the concepts of equality of educational opportunity but had remained largely hidden: that the concept implied *effective*
equality of opportunity, that is, equality in those elements that are effective for
learning.

In American thinking, then, there has been a shift to equality of results, and
some of the consequences of this shift can be seen in the policies of affirmative
action. Thus it is not sufficient, as in Britain, to remove legal disabilities on
women, blacks, or other disadvantaged groups. This makes equality of opportunity purely formal. What is demanded instead is that the members of these
groups should have the same effective chances of attending university or securing
well-paid employment as white males.

Making use of much of Coleman's results then came Jencks's well-publicized
work *Inequality*.[34] Jencks's very first chapter warns the reader

that we are primarily concerned with inequality between individuals not inequality between groups . . . there is always far more inequality between individuals than between groups. It follows that when we compare the degree of
inequality between individuals, inequality between groups often seems relatively
unimportant. It seems quite shocking, for example, that white workers earn
50 per cent more than black workers. But we are even more disturbed by the
fact that the best-paid one-fifth of all white workers earns 600 per cent more
than the worst-paid one-fifth. From this viewpoint, racial inequality looks
almost insignificant.
    Our decision to emphasize individual rather than group differences was made
on political grounds. We would, of course, like to see a society in which everyone's opportunities for advancement were equal. But we are far more interested
in a society where the extremes of wealth and poverty are entirely eliminated
than in a society where they are merely uncorrelated with skin colour, economic
origins, sex, and other such traits.

Jencks's work, then, is largely concerned with *within-group* differences rather than the between-group differences of the British tradition. He tells us, for example, that 'there is nearly as much income variation among men who come from similar families, have similar credentials, and have similar test scores, as among men in general'. He concludes that equalizing educational opportunity would do very little to make adults more equal and that reformers should therefore concentrate firstly on reducing adult income inequalities directly rather than indirectly via educational reform, and secondly on treating schooling as an end in itself rather than a means to some other end:

Some schools are dull, depressing, even terrifying places, while others are lively, comfortable, and reassuring. If we think of school life as an end in itself rather than a means to some other end, such differences are enormously important. Eliminating these differences would not do much to make adults more equal, but it would do a great deal to make the quality of children's (and teachers') lives more equal.[35]

With Jencks we come back full circle to the question with which we started. Can education change society? And Jencks gives us a resounding No. 'There is no evidence that school reform can substantially reduce the extent of cognitive inequality, as measured by tests of verbal fluency, reading comprehension, or mathematical skill. Neither school resources nor segregation has an appreciable effect on either test scores or educational attainment'.[36] Moreover, 'We cannot blame economic inequality on differences between schools, since differences between schools seem to have very little effect on any measurable attribute of those who attend them.'

Raymond Boudon, in his *Education, Opportunity and Social Inequality*[37] returns a verdict which is essentially similar to that of Jencks. Like his compatriot, Bourdieu, he notes that the correlation between a privileged family background and educational achievement continues to be reported by sociologists in many countries despite educational expansion. He draws the general conclusion

that society rather than school is responsible for inequality of educational opportunity. More explicitly, we have seen that even if schooling were highly effective in reducing cultural inequality (which it is not), a high amount of inequality of opportunity probably would still be observed. Even if grade school education were so effective that achievement at its completion were independent of social background, the probabilities of a lower-class youngster attending college and *a fortiori* of attending a prestigious institution of higher education would probably remain much lower than that of an upper-class youngster . . . . School systems can be changed much more easily than stratification systems. But a policy of economic and social equality might contribute towards reducing the effects of stratification.[38]

Boudon, besides endorsing pessimism as to the limits of educationally promoted equality, is introducing here a sociological sophistication into the relation between class origins and educational attainment which we shall try to take further in Chapter 8 below by developing an exponential model of secondary-school survival which might explain the history of differential drop-out from different types of school at different periods among boys of different class origin.

We shall not, in this volume, look at the relation between schooling and adult inequality, but we shall look at some educational inequalities and the effects that school reforms might have on them. Do we have to accept Jencks's negative conclusions or are there, in the British context, reforms that have been, or could be, effective? We must confess that we shall not be able to judge these reforms by tests of verbal fluency, reading comprehension, or mathematical skill, but measurable consequences of some kind we shall demand. Our aim is to describe and test empirical relations, although like our predecessors in the political-arithmetic tradition, we choose those relations to be tested according to their social and political significance. Let us then recapitulate the questions to which we hope to bring forward relevant empirical results.

1. *What have been the class differences in access to education?* How does the private sector compare with the state sector, and grammar schools with secondary modern schools? How do the class differences in access to the selective secondary schools compare with those in access to the sixth form? And how have these class differences been changing over time? Can it be concluded that educational expansion leads to equality of class chances for education?

2. *How far has the British educational system achieved its professed goal of meritocracy?* How does access to selective schools, to the sixth form, and to the university look when judged by the yardstick of meritocracy? How far does the continued existence of a private sector subvert the ideal of meritocracy, and how far did the 1944 Education Act promote progress to this ideal?

3. *What are the handicaps which prevent individuals attaining educational success?* What is the relative importance of IQ, social class, and cultural capital? Does the educational system merely reproduce the distribution of cultural capital, or does it offer genuine opportunities to those who lack initial capital?

4. *What are the likely consequences of comprehensive reform for the achievement of goals such as equality of opportunity and equality of results?* What are the consequences of replacing the waning tripartite system with comprehensive schools on the American model?

5. *Is the structure of the educational system important?* Does it matter what type of school one attends? Does attendance at grammar or independent schools affect one's educational career, or does Jencks's conclusion that 'differences between schools have very little effect on any measurable attribute of those who attend them?' apply to Britain as it does to America?

NOTES

1. The research team was chaired by A. H. Halsey and included Jean Floud, John Goldthorpe, Keith Hope, K. I. Macdonald, R. Martin, John Ridge, Phyllis Thorburn, Jenny Barton, Antoinette Cook, Sarah Graham, and Catriona Llewellyn. We wish to acknowledge the important contribution made to our work by Profession Graham Kalton in providing the design of the sample; and also the collaboration of Mary Agar Field Services Ltd., who undertood the interviewing programme with great efficiency. Full details of the sample design and survey research procedure, written by Phyllis Thorburn, may be obtained from the Social Survey Archives at the University of Essex.
2. D. V. Glass (ed.), *Social Mobility in Britain,* (Routledge and Kegan Paul, 1954). At an earlier point in our work we contemplated the phrase 'another generation' as an appropriate title for this book, but we concluded that this would be a more apt description of the work of the Oxford Mobility study as a whole.
3. Glass was conscious of his debt to Lancelot Hogben whose *Political Arithmetic*, (Allen & Unwin, 1938) was an influential contribution to that tradition between the wars. The earlier work in the political-arithmetic tradition was concerned with poverty and the reform of social security. In education the first major work was Kenneth Lindsay's *Social Progress and Educational Waste* (Routledge, 1926). The crucial political issue in education at this time was the position of the bright boy who was prevented by financial pressure from continuing his education at secondary school. Lord Birkenhead had claimed that 'There is now a complete ladder from the elementary school to the university, and the number of scholarships from the elementary to the secondary school is not limited, awards being made to all children who show capacity to profit.' Lindsay's work, and that of Gray and Moshinsky, 'Ability and Opportunity in English Education', in L. Hogben (ed.), op. cit., demolished this particular illusion and helped pave the way to the 1944 Education Act which made secondary education free within the state sector.
4. A list of publications emanating from the Oxford Mobility project appears below at Appendix II.
5. One of us has discussed this tradition of thought elsewhere (A. H. Halsey (ed.), *Educational Priority*, vol. 1, HMSO, 1972, chapter 1); and with particular reference to Alfred Marshall's classical formulation (A. H. Halsey, 'Sociology and the Equality Debate, *Oxford Review of Education*, (1975), 9-23).
6. See J. Karabel and A. H. Halsey (eds.), *Power and Ideology in Education* (Oxford University Press, New York, 1977), and A. F. Heath, 'Significant Developments in the Sociology of Education?', *Oxford Review of Education*, 4. 1 (1978), 95-110.
7. Theodore W. Schultz, 'Investment in human capital', *American Economic Review*, 51. 1 (1961), 1-17.
8. Sir Keith Joseph in the *Times Higher Education Supplement*, 28 June 1974.
9. Samuel Bowles, 'Unequal education and the reproduction of the social division of labor', in *Review of Radical and Political Economics*, Vol. 3, Autumn 1971.
10. Committee on Higher Education Report, 1963, Cmnd. 2154, pp.6-7.
11. R. H. Tawney, *Equality* (Unwin Books, 1931), p.142.
12. H. Silver, *Equal Opportunity in Education* (Methuen, 1973), p.xi.
13. J. W. B. Douglas, *The Home and the School*, (MacGibbon and Kee, 1964), pp.127-8.
14. R. H. Tawney, op. cit., Fourth Edition, (1964), p.145.
15. This is the definition used by Floud and Halsey in their studies in the 1950s.
16. D. Bell, *The Coming of Post-Industrial Society* (Basic Books, Inc., 1973), pp.410-11.
17. D. L. Miller, *Social Justice* (Clarendon Press, 1976), p.85.
18. A. F. Heath, *Rational Choice and Social Exchange* (Cambridge University Press, 1976), p.143.
19. Cmd. 6458.
20. M. Young, *The Rise of the Meritocracy* (Thames & Hudson, 1958).
21. S. Bowles and H. Gintis, *Schooling in Capitalist America* (Basic Books, Inc., 1976), p.103.

22. P. Bourdieu, 'The school as a conservative force', in John Eggleston (ed.), *Contemporary Research in the Sociology of Education* (Methuen, 1974), p.42.
23. Ibid., p.42.
24. M. Young, op. cit., p.33.
25. Ibid.
26. C. B. Cox and R. Boyson, *Black Paper 1975* (J. M. Dent & Sons, 1975). G. H. Bantock, *Freedom and Authority in Education* (Faber, 1966), and *Education and Values* (Faber, 1965).
27. See his 'How much can we boost I.Q. and scholastic achievement?', Harvard Educational Review, 39 (Winter 1969), 1–123. See also his *Educability and Group Differences* (Methuen, 1973), for a later, more general, and more carefully guarded exposition.
28. H. Eysenck, *Race, Intelligence and Education* (Temple Smith, 1971), and *The Inequality of Man* (Temple Smith, 1973).
29. R. J. Herrnstein, *I.Q. in the Meritocracy* (Allen Lane, 1973).
30. H. J. Eysenck, (1973), pp.224–5.
31. A. R. Jensen, op. cit., p.355.
32. G. H. Bantock, *Education and Values* (Faber & Faber, 1965), pp.150–1.
33. J. S. Coleman *et al.*, *Equality of Educational Opportunity* (Harvard University Press, 1969), pp.13 ff.
34. C. Jencks, *et al.*, *Inequality: A Reassessment of the Effect of Family and Schooling in America* (Basic Books, Inc., 1972).
35. C. Jencks, op. cit., p.256.
36. C. Jencks, op. cit., p.8.
37. R. Boudon, *Education, Opportunity and Social Inequality* (John Wiley, 1973).
38. Ibid., p.114.

CHAPTER 2

Classes, Cohorts, and Educational Development

Given the problems of educational opportunity and attainment and the theoretical and historical context in which we want to tackle them, we must now specify how in research practice we define classes and how we shall use a survey in 1972 to reconstruct the education experienced by children passing through schools and colleges in England and Wales as they have developed since before the First World War.

From the fairly lengthy interview schedule[1] a skeletal reproduction of the life histories of men living in England and Wales in 1972 is available to us. But it must be emphasized that the content of the interview was dominated by the decision of the research team to replicate as far as was practicable the questions asked by David Glass and his associates at the London School of Economics in their pioneering survey in 1949. At the same time the team also attempted a similar replication of the American study by Blau and Duncan carried out in 1962.[2]

Our task, then, in this book is to adapt the material from a survey conducted for the general purposes of mobility enquiry so as to focus on to our particular concerns. These, we must repeat, were part of those of a larger project, and the information was not, and could not, be collected with solely our own interests in mind. The 'political arithmetic' tradition is only one of several possible approaches to the study of mobility.

THE SAMPLE

The design and construction of the 1972 sample as a whole has been well summarized by John H. Goldthorpe.[3] Here we need only repeat that the stratified two-stage design produced a largely self-weighting sample of men aged between 20 and 64 resident in England and Wales in early summer 1972.

From this set of 10 309 interviews, we have selected a smaller 'educational history' sub-sample consisting of 8529 interviews only. This sub-sample is defined by two additional criteria:

(a) men aged 60 and above are excluded;

(b) those not resident in England or Wales at age 14 are excluded. Both restrictions are imposed by the specifically educational concerns of the present volume. The oldest men had been educated at a time when the legal minimum school-leaving age was not clearly specified, and before the pattern of elementary and secondary schooling had settled into the form described below as characteristic of England and Wales between the two World Wars. Those who were living outside England and Wales at age 14 are more obviously inappropriate members of a sample designed to illuminate the working of the educational system of England and Wales.

Direct comparisons between our results and those reported by Goldthorpe must always be qualified by these differences in the basic samples. The age-limit in particular means that our ten-year age-groups, discussed below, do not correspond to Goldthorpe's. Table 2.1 is an exception. Here we report results for the whole sample: thus the reader can more easily appreciate the impact of the minor modifications we have introduced into the basic class schema used by Goldthorpe. The distribution of our 'educational history' sub-sample on our modified schema appears as the overall percentages of Table 2.2: percentages in the text description of our eight classes also refer to this sub-sample.

CLASSES

Schemes of social division derive from many different conceptions of society in both social science and common language. We were anxious to avoid implicating ourselves in a conception of stratification in Britain as a monolithic hierarchy or a 'layer-cake' of strata. Similarly, we would emphasize that the schema we have adopted is not to be identified with a scale of prestige or socio-economic status. In Table 2.1 the social-class classification which we shall be using in the analysis of our data is set out. This classification derives from the Hope-Goldthorpe social grading of occupations.[4] It follows the scheme used by Goldthorpe in his *Social Mobility and Class Structure*, but also differs from it. The degree of differentiation provided by the Hope–Goldthorpe categories in terms of both occupation function and employment status enable us to bring together, within the eight occupational groups and the three broader social classes we distinguish occupations whose incumbents will typically share in broadly similar *market* and *work* situations – which, following Lockwood,[5] we take as the two major components of class position. It should be noted, however, that we have modified the sevenfold schema of occupational groups used by Goldthorpe in that we have separated agricultural labourers and small-holders into an eighth category. We use this eightfold scheme throughout the book and also a further combination of it into three social classes. The labelling of these three social classes has caused us difficulty and hesitation but, while conscious of the linguistic inelegance and logical impurity of terms in common use, we have, with John Goldthorpe, adopted the labels 'service class', 'intermediate class', and 'working class'. A more detailed description of our eightfold classication follows.[6]

Class 1[7] (H–G categories 1, 2, 3, 4, and 7): all higher-grade professionals, whether self-employed or salaried; higher-grade administrators and officials in central and local government and in public and private corporations (including company directors); managers in large industrial establishments; and large proprietors. Class I might thus be taken as largely corresponding to the higher and intermediate echelons of what Dahrendorf, following Karl Renner, has termed the 'service class' of a modern capitalist society – the class of those exercising power and expertise on behalf of corporate 'authorities': plus such elements of the classic bourgeoisie, independent business men, and 'free' professionals, as are not yet assimilated into this new formation.

Class II (H–G categories 5, 6, 8, 9, 10, 12, 14, and 16): lower-grade professional and higher-grade technicians; lower-grade administrators and officials; managers in small business and industrial establishments, and in services; and supervisors of nonmanual employees. Class II could then be seen as complementing

Table 2.1

A Social-class Classification

Eight Classes		Percentage	Three Classes	Percentage
I.	Higher-grade professionals, administrators, managers, and proprietors.	7.7	S E R V I C E	
II.	Lower-grade professionals, administrators and managers. Supervisors, and higher-grade technicians.	6.0		13.7
III.	Clerical, sales and rank-and-file service workers.	7.4	I N T E R M E D I A T E	
IV.	Small proprietors and self-employed artisans. The 'petty bourgeoisie'.	12.6		31.4
V.	Lower-grade technicians and foremen. The 'aristocracy of labour'.	11.3		
VI.	Skilled manual workers in industry.	27.2	W O R K I N G	
VII.	Semi- and unskilled manual workers in industry.	22.6		54.9
VIII.	Agricultural workers and smallholders.	5.1		
All		100		100

Note: The percentages in the table differ slightly from those of Table 2.2 because the latter does not include the oldest members of the sample, nor those resident outside England and Wales at age 14.

Class I in comprising the subaltern or *cadet* positions of the service class. Putting Classes I and II together, we have formed a social class, amounting to 13.4 per cent of our respondents by origin (i.e. classified by their father's occupation when they were aged 14) which we refer to as the *service* class.

Class III (H–G categories 21, 25, 28, and 34): routine nonmanual – largely clerical – employees in administration and commerce; sales personnel and other rank-and-file service workers. In contrast to the service class, Class III covers essentially subordinate positions whose incumbents could perhaps be taken as forming a nonmanual labour force.

Class IV (H–G categories 11, 13, 19, 29, and 36): small proprietors, self-employed artisans; and all other 'own-account' workers apart from professionals. Class IV may thus be equated with that of the petty bourgeoisie.

Class V (H–G categories 15, 17, and 20): lower-grade technicians whose work is to some extent of a manual character; and supervisors over manual workers. This class might be seen as constituting a latter-day 'aristocracy of labour', or 'blue-collar élite'. Putting Classes III, IV, and V together we have formed an *intermediate* class constituting 30.8 per cent of our respondents by origin.

Class VI (H–G categories 18, 22, 23, 27, and 30): skilled manual-wage workers in all branches of industry, including all who have served apprenticeships and all those who have acquired a relatively high level of skill through other forms of training.

Class VII (H–G categories 26, 32, 33, and 35): all manual workers in industry in semi-skilled and unskilled grades.

Class VIII (H–G categories 24 and 31): agricultural workers, including small-holders. Taken together, we have termed these groups the *working class*. Constituting 55.7 per cent of our respondents by origin, they are mainly composed of the industrial working class, but also include the agricultural workers.

It should be clearly recognized that the aggregation of the Hope–Goldthorpe categories to form either the eight- or the threefold classification we use in this book was carried out without reference to the position of categories in the ordering of the scale, which its authors would interpret as one indicative of the 'general desirability' of occupations (but which could also be taken as one of occupational prestige or even, perhaps, as proxy for one of socio-economic status). The rank order of the H–G categories is such that our eight occupational groups, as well as the three social classes, overlap (though only slightly in the case of the service class) in their 'general desirability'. This means, therefore, that the classifications cannot be regarded as having, nor should they be expected to have, a consistently hierarchical form.

Our choice of these classifications rather than scale values, apart from consistency with the larger study of mobility of which our work is part, follows from the interest we share with John Goldthorpe in exploring the class structure of modern Britain, rather than occupational attainment and its determinants in family and education. The use of scale values, though appropriate to the type of multiple-regression analysis used by Blau and Duncan, implies a one-dimensional continuum of occupations which in our view misrepresents the class structure of Britain.

COHORTS

The limitations of a single survey for our purposes are familiar. It gives us information collected from individuals at one point of time in 1972. Apart from the fact that women are excluded, the men concerned were at different points in the life cycle: they had in other words incomplete familial, educational, and occupational biographies. Nevertheless we can still use this information, collected at one point of time, to reconstruct the experience of those who entered the social and educational structure of British society at various dates from early in the century till the early post-war years. The simple technique of analysing the data by cohorts enables us to do this. Our cohorts and their social class origins are displayed in Table 2.2.

That the survey was confined to males is a major limitation to our purposes.

Table 2.2

Social-class Origins of Men Born 1913–1952 Resident
in England and Wales at age 14[1]

	Father's Class[2]									
	I	II	III	IV	V	VI	VII	VIII	All	(N)
1913–22	5.2	4.7	6.1	13.9	10.8	29.4	23.7	6.3	100	(1881)
1923–32	5.8	5.3	6.5	12.2	10.9	29.1	25.2	5.0	100	(1901)
1933–42	6.9	5.9	8.0	11.3	11.9	28.3	24.2	3.5	100	(1894)
1943–52	10.8	7.7	9.5	8.6	13.5	24.9	22.5	2.5	100	(2353)
ALL	7.4	6.0	7.6	11.3	11.9	27.7	23.8	4.2	100	
(N)	(591)	(481)	(611)	(909)	(955)	(2228)	(1913)	(341)		(8029)

Notes

1. This subset of the Oxford 1972 sample is as noted on p.16 above, the basic 'educational history' sample used throughout this book, unless otherwise stated. There are 8529 respondents in this sample: the base of this table (8029) reflects that inevitable feature of survey analysis, the absence of information on some variables for some informants.

2. 'Father's class' throughout this book refers to the report by the informant for the time when he was aged 14 of the occupation of the head of his family. This was normally his father, but the decision was left to the informant. In the 1972 sample as a whole, some 8 per cent of informants reported that their mother was head of the family at this time: this group were particularly likely to be unable to report a 'father's occupation' (e.g. 'housewife'). The data have been organized so that these informants appear not to have reported on any characteristics of their mother: in fact, these variables are all labelled as characteristics of their non-existent father.

Of course it must be borne in mind that, given the unavoidable historical character of mobility studies, male occupations were the major articulation between on the one hand nuclear families and on the other the class and status structure of Britain in the period with which we are concerned. Nevertheless it followed from our decision to replicate the Blau and Duncan study that we should confine ourselves to males. Had we been designing a questionnaire solely for our own purposes and concentrating on the educational experience of Britons, the omission of women would have been quite unjustifiable.

A second limitation resides in the fact that the material with which we have to work is 'external' rather than 'internal', or 'objective' rather than 'subjective'. We have, in other words, familial, educational, and occupational information about the circumstances of individuals and not data on psychological attitudes or attributes. Thus when we come to discuss such concepts as meritocracy we are limited so far as the survey is concerned, to evidence which does not include, for example, measured intelligence. And when we consider the determinants of educational attainment, quite apart from the restricted range of circumstantial characteristics of our respondents, we have no direct means of measuring such variables as ambition or drive. However, the need to gather reliable external data on our respondents' biographies had already stretched the questionnaire to the limit of practicality.

Information of this kind is, of course, available in *longitudinal* studies like those by Douglas,[8] or the National Children's Bureau,[9] which chart the progress of a given cohort through the educational system as it is during a particular period. In our case, however, we did not wish to duplicate these studies, but to carry out a different enterprise that was not possible for the longitudinal studies, namely to look at the changes that have taken place in the educational system (most notably, of course, the 1944 Education Act and the establishment of the tripartite system) over a longer time span, and to look at the effects of these institutional changes on the experience of succeeding cohorts of pupils. Ours, then, is in a sense an exercise in social history and, while grasping the advantages, it must also accept the limitations of such a focus.

Cohort analysis of our survey material enables us to look at successive waves of children growing towards adulthood under an evolving educational system. But cohort analysis also has its limitations when applied to survey data. Because of mortality the older cohorts especially are not strictly speaking random samples of the children and young people they are made to represent. There are in any case doubts about the validity of the data on age of school-leaving in the case of the oldest members of the sample, who went to school when the statutory leaving age was ill defined. We have, therefore, excluded those aged 60-64 at the time of the survey, and used four decennial birth cohorts throughout our analysis, i.e. 1913-22, 1923-32, 1933-42, and 1943-52. Thus the oldest of our cohorts entered the schools just after the First War and the youngest experienced the beginnings of the transformation of secondary education to a comprehensive system.

But we can say little with certainty about those in our sample who attended comprehensive schools. Their numbers are small, their representativeness suspect, and our knowledge of the organization of their secondary schools at a time when comprehensives were in an early stage of development is inadequate. In any case we are limited by the 'historical' character of a snapshot survey in that we cannot bring into view the full impact of secondary-school comprehensivization or the expansion of higher education during the 1960s. Professor Glass remarked in the introduction to his book on the 1949 survey that the effects of the Education Act of 1944 would not be fully discernible before the passage of thirty or forty years. We and our successors will always have to make the same remark about recent changes with implications for the future of opportunity, mobility, and inequality in society. Another generation will have to pass before a full evaluation of comprehensive reform can be offered, and in the meantime the hasty conclusions of 'Black Paper' writers, as well as of those who hold the comprehensive movement to be an unambiguous success, must be read with scepticism.

A further limitation on our cohort analysis of educational experience must again be emphasized. The original sample is one of men resident in England and Wales in 1972, and these were asked where they lived at age 14. A small proportion were then elsewhere than in England and Wales, and we have eliminated them from the analysis. Others, of course, who had been educated in England and Wales had eliminated themselves by emigration.[10]

We have stressed these various limitations of our survey material. Nevertheless and in our view more important, the 1972 survey affords the possibility of tracing the impact of a long period of educational expansion and change on the fortunes of the successive generations of children who have passed through the schools, and this is our major purpose.

EDUCATIONAL CATEGORIES

In the text and, more especially, in the tables thoughout this volume, we use summary labels to refer to the variety of educational institutions and outcomes that our informants encountered. The exact reference of these labels is not always self-evident. It is therefore important to define them formally, so that the operational categories of our analysis can be related to the brief outline of the development of the more complex reality, given in the final section of this chapter.

Questions on education were asked in a standard format in the interview schedule, whether referring to the informant, his father, mother, brother, or wife. Thus we have reproduced in Appendix I only the questions (3a–i) asked of the informant himself. Questions g and h were asked only of the informant: the set was otherwise repeated identically for other family members.

Primary schooling: private primary schooling is defined as any attendance at a private fee-paying school before age 11 (whether the informant actually paid fees or not). This includes 'preparatory' schools (normally attended until age 13), as well as the now extinct 'junior' departments of grammar schools. *State* primary schooling includes state primary and (earlier) elementary schools, as well as denominational schools 'maintained', 'aided', or 'controlled' by local education authorities.

Secondary schooling: school attendance after age 11, which may have meant no change of school for those at the (pre-1944) elementary schools, and initially for those at private preparatory schools. In coding responses, allowance was made for up to four different types of secondary schooling. The variable we use in our analyses refers to the 'highest' type attended, if more than one, on the following scale:

1. Secondary Modern – this includes codes 01, 02 (Elementary), 04 (All-age school) and, of course, 05; also codes 14 (Special schools), 15 (Foreign – not relevant in our sub-sample), and 16 (Other: a very small group including state boarding schools and army schools). '

2. Comprehensive – code 06, which includes multilateral and bilateral schools as alternative names of early comprehensives.

3. Technical – here, the time-reference is important. Code 03 (Central and other similar types) is essentially a pre-1944 category, developed to very different extents, and with various teaching aims, by different local authorities Code 07 (Technical) is essentially post-1944 in reference: schools in this category were more uniform in aim and, probably, in degree of development than their pre-war counterparts.

4. Local Authority Grammar School – in coding this and the remaining school types a more complex procedure was followed. Pilot surveys had confirmed our belief that the precise status of a selective secondary school was not always known even by the informant who had himself attended it. Interviewers were therefore instructed *always* to note the name and location of such schools,

as well as circling one of the pre-coded categories. Coders then used lists of Direct Grant schools and Headmasters' Conference schools (GBGSA for women) to determine the precise category of a named school; lists were prepared for 1931, 1951, and 1961, and the nearest in time used as appropriate. 'Grammar School' in our analyses indicates that codes 08 or 09 had been ringed (i.e. the school was not independent), and that the named school was not on the Direct Grant list for the nearest time-point.

5. Independent: non-HMC – if the interviewer had circled code 10, 'Independent (fee-paying) school', the coder searched for its name in the temporally appropriate Headmasters' Conference (GBGSA) list. If not found, it was deemed to be Independent, non-HMC.

6. Direct Grant – as for Grammar School, but the school's name did occur in the appropriate Direct Grant list.

7. Independent: HMC – as for category 5, but the school's name did occur in the appropriate HMC/GBGSA list.

School-leaving Age: rather than have interviewers and informants make guesses, a box was provided for cases where the informant was sure only that school attendance had stopped as soon as legally possible. For the informant, such responses have been converted to ages 14 or 15, depending on whether he was born before or after 1933. Difficulties of interpretation, and a comparison with official figures are discussed in detail in Chapter 7.

School Examinations: in the present volume, we are concerned only with codes 02–06, that is, Ordinary School Certificate and (later) O-Level GCE passes and Higher School Certificate and (later) A-Level GCE passes. Although matriculation was technically distinct from the School Certificate, we have not made the distinction in our analyses.

Further Education and Qualifications: sections f and i of question 3 had to be explicitly linked by the interviewer (thus, for every qualification coded and described in part i, there had to be a corresponding, labelled code and description in part f). Recording and coding both proved to be difficult and time-consuming. In the present volume, we are mainly concerned with attendance at futher and higher education institutions, not with the actual attainment of qualifications, so our task is simpler. However, the coding frame for qualifications has to be used to establish the type of institution attended. Thus:

University – formally defined as 'Full-time' training (part f) leading to (successfully or not) a qualification (part i) included in level 'a' in the Classification of Qualifications in *Qualified Manpower Tables, Sample Census 1966, Great Britain* (HMSO, 1970), Appendices B and C.

College of Education/Teacher Training – 'Full-time training associated with a qualification (whether gained or not) carrying the occupational tag "teaching"' (Occupation Unit Group 193; *Classification of Occupations* (HMSO, 1970, p.xxxiv).

Part-time Further Education – pre-codes 04, 05, or 06 on part f: that is, day- or block-release, sandwich course(s), other part-time vocational training (e.g. evening classes). Note that on this definition apprenticeships, articled clerkships, in-firm training, and correspondence courses have *not* been considered as further education, unless associated (as the first two often are) with day-release or other courses pre-coded as 04, 05, or 06.

Age, origin class, and education are by no means the only variables we use in the rest of this volume. However, they are crucial, and the two latter at least require explicit definition. Other variables will be defined as they are encountered in the text. We can now elaborate the relation between cohorts and educational categories by sketching the development of the institutions.

EDUCATIONAL DEVELOPMENT

The development of education in western industrial countries may be summarized as having characteristically three stages. In the first stage primary education is universalized and is terminal for the majority with a minority going on to secondary and tertiary education. In the second stage secondary education is universalized, the primary schools are transitional to the secondary schools and a minority go on to tertiary institutions. In the third stage the secondary schools became transitional to a system of mass higher education. Martin Trow has discussed the growth of education in America within this framework.[11] Britain has yet to traverse the full course of this process of educational expension but the history of its educational system in general and the experience of our four cohorts in particular may be discussed as phases within Trow's stages. The great landmark of the first stage in Britain was the Education Act of 1870 which laid the foundation for universal schooling at the primary level, i.e. children aged 5 to 11. The contemporaneous term was 'elementary' and the state elementary schools were not in principle confined to primary education. As the elementary system developed, administered through local education authorities under the Elementary and Technical Code, more children gradually attended more regularly and to a greater age until, in 1921, the statutory school-leaving age was fixed at 14 years. Meanwhile, various forms of 'higher-grade' and 'central' schools had introduced schooling beyond the primary level. In effect, therefore, the second of the three stages of educational modernization, which was heralded in Britain by the 1902 Education Act, overlapped with the first. The 1902 Act provided for a national system of state secondary schools, partly from central and partly from local funds, but administered by local-education authorities. Pupils transferred at age 11 on the basis of competitive examinations. A majority of children, however, varying according to local provision, stayed in elementary schools to the statutory leaving age of 14.

Thus by the time our first (1913-22) birth cohort entered school there was a universal primary system still under the shadow of the terminal character of the primary schools in Trow's first stage, but with a small ladder at age 11 to secondary schools including grammar schools (which also took private fee-payers), technical schools, and central schools. The second cohort (1923-32) started to enter the primary schools in 1928. The ladder to selective secondary education had slowly broadened for them and the last of them just missed the formal introduction of universal secondary education through the Education Act of 1944. Our third cohort was the first to pass through primary schools which were clearly transitional to secondary schools. That transition continued to be dominated by tests of attainment and intelligence at 11-plus, which determined the kind of secondary school into which primary leavers would go and for those who went to secondary modern schools the course was still typically a short one, ending at the school-leaving age of 14.

For the fourth cohort (1943–52) the primary to secondary transition was modified in two ways. The secondary course was elongated with the raising of the statutory leaving age to 15 in 1947 and the beginnings of comprehensive-school reorganization (through which grammar, technical, and secondary modern schools began to be amalgamated) altered the prospects of children in some localities and eliminated the significance for them of the 11-plus examination which had hitherto dominated the curriculum and life of primary schools.

It follows that our first and second cohorts are relatively clearly distinguished from the third and fourth by the development of the secondary system of schools through which they passed. Nevertheless, it should be appreciated that our *first* cohort belonged to a generation which saw itself as having entered, in the aftermath of the 1902 Act, into a new world of educational opportunity by comparison with the previous generation. Writing in 1923 as one not likely to be complacent about inadequacy in education, R. H. Tawney summed up the recent history of English secondary education as follows. 'The number both of pupils and school places in 1922 is . . . all too small. But, inadequate as they are, they represent something like an educational revolution compared with the almost complete absence of public provision which existed prior to 1902.'[12]

The 1907 free-place regulations, made under the 1902 Act, gave a powerful stimulus to the local authorities to provide free secondary education. The Board of Education required that,

as a condition of the receipt of higher rate of grant, in all schools where a fee is charged, arrangements must be made . . . securing that a proportion of school places shall be open without payment of fee to scholars of public elementary schools who apply for admission, subject to the applicant passing an entrance test of attainments and proficiency . . . . The proportion of free places thus required will ordinarily be 25 per cent.'[13]

The number of free places rose, in subsequent years, at a faster rate than fee-paying places until the introduction of the 'special place' regulations in 1933.[14] A few months before the introduction of the 1907 Regulations, less than a quarter of the pupils in English secondary schools held free places from the elementary schools. By 1931 the percentage had risen to 45. Seven years later it had dropped to 42.8 but against this must be set a 6 per cent rise in the number of ex-elementary pupils paying part fees.

This growth in the supply of free education in selective secondary schools was constantly rendered inadequate by an even more remarkable increase in the aspirations of parents towards places for their children in the secondary schools. The demand for scholarship opportunities and the willingness of parents to purchase admission to a grammar school wherever possible was partly, if not mainly, due to an accurate assessment of the occupational advantages thereby obtained.[15] The national system of grammar schools was consequently 'built principally upon the aspirations of the wage-earning classes, and the determination of those in receipt of small salaries themselves to equip their children to earn larger ones'.[46]

Demand in the sense of a school place for everyone up to the statutory leaving age was always met. But the demand resulting from the continuing revolution in the parental aspirations for places in selective secondary school was never fully satisfied. An official inquiry in 1920 showed that large numbers of children were being refused admission to secondary schools.[17] In 1919 to 1920, 9271 children were excluded from English secondary schools for lack of accommodation and a further 8780 because, although they reached the standard required, there were not sufficient free places to make it possible to take them in.[18] In consequence, the selection of children for free places in state secondary schools became a competitive examination rather than an assessment of individual fitness for secondary education. Thus the special place examination taken at age 10 or 11 became the crucial instrument of academic selection.

Official policy in the early years of the development of a national system of secondary education was explicitly aimed at equalizing access to the grammar schools between classes and between districts and regions. This was the clear intention of the 1907 Regulations and was frequently reiterated during subsequent years. The attitude of the Board of Education to recalcitrant local authorities was exemplified in their Report for 1926/7.[19] The Board stated that

the object of the free place requirement was not, as is sometimes supposed, to open the door of higher education to elementary school children of exceptional promise, but rather to bring the advantages of such education as far as the limited funds at the Board's disposal would permit, within the reach of the poorer classes and to place them on the same footing as pupils whose parents were not in a position to pay the school fees.

Our first two cohorts therefore passed through a developing system of secondary-education entry to which was governed by parental means and academic tests. Though the academic criteria slowly gained ground over the parental purse in the later inter-war years, the scholarship ladder remained a narrow one. The major efforts of the egalitarian movement in this pre-war period were directed towards the broadening of access to the opportunities offered by grammar-school education and to the transfer of the burden of selection from parental capacity and willingness to pay to some more objective and socially acceptable measure of ability. Success in these endeavours varied from area to area but in general after 1902, though the educational ladder was broadened, the dual system of entry by scholarship and by fee-paying remained. Rather more than half of those attending grammar schools in 1939 did so as fee payers. Moreover, the very limited extent to which the children of manual workers benefited was becoming known. On Merseyside, for example, 'barely half those who received free education in secondary schools came from working-class homes.'[20]

Dissatisfaction with official policy in matters of secondary education was widespread especially among trade unionists and the supporters of the Labour Party. During the 1930s and especially in the upheaval of war conditions after 1939, the demand for universal compulsory secondary education was vigorously renewed. By 1944 the strength of these demands carried them through to the statute book.[21] Secondary education became every child's birthright to be entered automatically after the primary stage and fee-paying was abolished in all maintained schools. It was laid down in the Act that 'the statutory system of public education shall be organized in three progressive stages to be known as primary education, secondary education and further education.'[22]

THE EDUCATION ACT OF 1944

The 1943 White Paper, *Educational Reconstruction*, had found some serious defects in the pre-war arrangements for transmission from primary schools to the various forms of secondary or post-primary education.

The conditions attending the admission of children to the various forms of post-primary education present some disquieting features. It has been noted that the children who are most successful in the examination taken at 11 secure places in secondary schools, but this is not to say that all the places in secondary schools are filled by the ablest candidates for admission. The Board's Regulations do not do more than require that 25 per cent of the yearly admissions should be confined to pupils whose admission is independent of their ability to pay the prescribed fee, and though this percentage is very often greatly exceeded, it remains true that many children get the benefit of secondary education owing to the ability of their parents to pay fees. Seeing that these fees represent only a proportion (on the average about one-third) of the cost of the education given in the secondary schools, it follows that a parent by paying only one-third of the cost of education can buy a place in a secondary school for his child, possibly to the exclusion of an abler child whose parent is not in that position. A system under which fees are charged in one type of post-primary school and prohibited in the other offends against the canon that the nature of a child's education should be determined by his capacity and promise and not by the financial circumstances of his parent. (paras. 17 and 20)

The 1944 Act was aimed at radical change, first by trying to secure that *all* children should move on at 11 to one or other form of secondary school rather than remaining where they were, and second by trying to change the principles on which the decisions about secondary schooling were to be made. 'The keynote of the new system', said the White Paper, 'will be that the child is the centre of education and that, so far as is humanly possible, all children should receive the type of education for which they are best adapted' (para. 27). Within the state-maintained sector of education, therefore, all places were to be free and the financial circumstances of the parent would no longer limit the opportunities available to the child. Furthermore, the Special Place examination was to be abolished and instead children would be classified 'not on the results of a competitive test, but on an assessment of their individual aptitudes largely by such means as school records, supplemented, if necessary, by intelligence tests, due regard being had to their parents' wishes and the careers they have in mind' (para. 27). To suit the variety of different aptitudes that children might exhibit and the variety of careers they might have in mind there were to be three types of secondary schooling, of diversified types, but of equal standing.

First, there was to be the grammar school. But the White Paper had reservations about the number of children for whom this would be the appropriate form of schooling.

An academic training is ill-suited for many of the pupils who find themselves moving along a narrow educational path bounded by the School Certificate and leading into a limited field of opportunity. Further, too many of the
nation's abler children are attracted into a type of education which prepares
primarily for the University and for the administrative and clerical professions;
too few find their way into schools from which the design and craftsmanship
sides of the industry are recruited. If education is to serve the interests both of
the child and of the nation, some means must be found of correcting this bias
and of directing ability into the field where it will find its best realization.
(para 28)

Accordingly the White Paper had great hopes of the other two types of school,
the secondary modern[23] and the technical. Of the former the White Paper said:

Lacking the traditions and privileged position of the older grammar school they
have less temptation to be 'at ease in Zion'. Their future is their own to make,
and it is a future full or promise. They offer a general education for life, closely
related to the interests and environment of the pupils and of a wide range
embracing the literary as well as the practical, e.g. agricultural sides. (para. 29)

Finally, there were the technical schools.

Planned to give a general education associated with preparation for entry to one
or other of the main branches of industry or commerce they have grown up in
close relation to local needs and opportunities of employment. But their
progress in numbers has been comparatively slow and their chances of attracting
the most able children vis-à-vis the Grammar Schools have been adversely
affected by the fact that they normally recruit at the age of 13. With altered
conditions, and with a more rapid development in the future, they hold out
great opportunities for pupils with a practical bent. (para. 30)

Despite all these great hopes, it must have been clear from the outset that the
Act could never achieve all its different aims simultaneously. It left the independent sector of education quite untouched, and so the English educational
system was bound to continue to offend against the canon that 'the nature of a
child's education should be determined by his capacity and promise and not by
the financial circumstances of his parent.' Furthermore, the White Paper failed
to deal with the potential conflict between parents' wishes and their children's
aptitudes, and the potential conflict between both of these and the scarcity, and
inflexibility, of the resources used in any educational system. To our knowledge,
no study was every undertaken by any Local Authority (with whom the duty of
implementing the Act lay) to discover the nature and distribution of children's
aptitudes or parents' wishes and so to provide the different types of secondary
school in the numbers that would balance demand and supply for places. Instead
the supply of places was determined largely by historical accident and partly by
current policy leading to a wide variety in the standards and types of provision
in different areas, a variety that could not conceivably be related to the distribution of parental wishes, much less children's aptitudes, in the different areas.
    Given this imbalance of demand and supply a system of rationing was
inevitable, and the chosen method was the 11-plus examination, a competitive
examination remarkably similar to the old Special Place examination. It was in

intention a meritocratic system of selection which allocated the ablest children to the academically most demanding (and occupationally most rewarding) grammar-school places. Meritocracy was thus to take precedence over democracy or plutocracy. The great majority of parents had no choice as to the form of their children's education. True, the small minority who were allocated grammar-school places could always opt for a technical or modern school, but the converse was not true for those allocated a modern school (although some limited choice was available *within* categories of schooling). The only really effective choices lay with those parents who were sufficiently well off to be able to choose between the state and the independent systems of education. Within the state system affluence was to be irrelevant and meritocracy was to reign supreme. We shall see in the chapters that follow what difference this made to the social composition of the intake to the grammar schools.

Both before and after the 1944 Act controversy centred on the competing principles of tripartitism and the multilateral comprehensive schools.[24] As we have seen, the Education Act of 1944 did not itself specify a particular structure for secondary education; it simply directed the education authorities to provide their pupils with 'such variety of instruction and training as may be desirable in view of their ages, their abilities and aptitudes, and of the different periods which they may be expected to remain at school, including practical instruction and training appropriate to their respective needs'.[25] Such a formula avoided the controversy but in fact official policy, until 1955, supported tripartitism.

Tripartitism, however, always had its opponents, and by 1951 the comprehensive school had been fully adopted as the secondary-education policy of the Labour Party.

The tripartite system, it was claimed, rested upon, and indeed perpetuated, those class distinctions which the Labour movement was pledged to destroy. The aim of the common school has accordingly been envisaged as the promotion of social unity and the destruction of class barriers — it is hoped that the creation of the common school will promote equality within the social as well as the educational system, and so prevent the new aristocracy of brains which . . . threatens to supercede the aristocracies of wealth and birth.[26]

None the less, opposition to the comprehensive school remained widespread among teachers, educational administrators, and even within the Labour Party itself: fears for the traditional standards of scholarship associated with the grammar school were particularly stressed.[27] With the notable exception of London and some special areas like the Isle of Wight or Anglesey, very few plans for comprehensive schools were made[28] until the Labour Party came into office in 1964 and the Secretary of State, C.A.R. Crosland, called for submission of plans by all local authorities in his Ciruclar 10/65. The small proportion even of our youngest cohort who attended comprehensive schools reflects this slow development.

PRIVATE SCHOOLS

So much, then, for the evolving structure of state secondary education. Finally, we must complete our account of the school system through which our four cohorts passed by describing the private sector. In this, of course, we turn from the vast majority to a minority of roughly 6 per cent who attended proprietary, preparatory, and 'public' schools. Given our interest, however, in both equality and mobility we shall have to examine this minority private sector, partly because it always had a social importance out of all proportion to its numerical place in the education system as a whole, and partly because of its implications for later educational and occupational placement.

We look at private primary schooling in Chapter 3. Meanwhile, we should note the variety of these schools. They are mainly day schools, but some are residential, taking children, mostly boys, at age 7 or 8 to prepare them for the 'public' secondary schools. They vary also in quality. Before the 1944 Act the Department of Education and Science had minimal powers over private schools. They simply had, if they were not in receipt of a state grant, to supply a brief description of the school. Under the 1944 Act registration was introduced but not enforced till 1957. Since that time, all private schools have been inspected by HM Inspectors before being registered.

In addition to being registered a school may also apply to be recognized as efficient. In 1965 out of some 2762 independent primary and primary and secondary schools in England, 1188 held this status.

At the secondary level the social significance of the private sector has been carried by the 'public' schools. These establishments have no statutory definition but are normally defined as those whose heads are members of the Headmasters' Conference. They have maintained a steady position throughout the period in which we are interested as places of high educational privilege to a small minority, bestowing not only a general social cachet but, more specifically, superior chances of obtaining university education. The HMC schools have traditionally required relatively high standards both academically and financially, and have normally taken children at the age of 13, mainly from the linked system of 'preparatory' schools, on the basis of performance in their common-entrance examinations.

In addition to the 'public' schools there is also to be distinguished (and we have done so in our analysis) a wide range of non-HMC schools with rather lower academic and financial standards. These are a very heterogeneous category, but many of them accepted children at 11 and provided something akin to a grammar-school education for those children of the affluent who had failed to secure a grammar-school place on the basis of the 11-plus. Then, apart from these two fully private types of secondary school, there were the anomalous Direct Grant grammar schools which retained a place on the boundary between the state and the private sector of education. They received a grant from central government directly (rather than through the local authorities as was the case with ordinary grammar schools) on condition that they supplied a number of free places to children who had been to state primary schools. The remaining places either went to fee-payers or were taken up by the local authorities, which could thus use the Direct Grant school as a source of additional grammar-school places. Some authorities, such as Lancashire, made great use of this and their Direct Grant schools seem to have 'creamed off' many of the ablest boys from the state system. In our analysis below we sometimes distinguish and sometimes combine the public schools and the Direct Grant schools (some Direct Grant schools in any case belong to the HMC) and these together accounted for 6.5 per cent of our sample as a whole - a proportion which slowly increased in successive birth cohorts. For the first cohort (1913-22) it was 5.0 per cent and for the last 7.4 per cent.[29]

FURTHER AND HIGHER EDUCATION

In Chapter 10 we shall be dealing with the experience of our four cohorts in post-secondary institutions of education. In Britain a distinction is usually made between higher and further education. Higher education includes the universities and colleges of education (formerly teacher-training colleges). Most work in these institutions has been full-time. Further education includes a wide range of colleges under the control of local-education authorities offering full- and, more typically and more often, part-time, courses in commerce, art, crafts, and professional training. Higher education and further education have always somewhat overlapped, with a general tendency for the latter to aspire to the status of the former. Thus in the period relevant to our fourth cohort some technical colleges became colleges of advanced technology and finally technological universities, and polytechnics have developed though still staying under the control of local authorities. Nevertheless, the development of the two systems may most conveniently be treated separately.

When our first cohort came to the relevant age nearly all full-time higher education was provided in universities as a three-year degree course while the courses then given in teacher-training colleges involved two years of study. In 1924-5 there were 42 000 university students and 16 000 teacher trainees. By the end of the inter-war period in 1938-9 there were 50 000 university students and 13 000 teacher trainees. The comparable figures to represent the opportunities available in universities and teacher training institutions for our third cohort were those of 1954-5 - 82 000 and 28 000 respectively. For our fourth cohort (1943-52) the 1962-3 figures showed a marked increase to 118 000 and 55 000 respectively.[30]

NOTES

1. The section on education and qualifications is reproduced as Appendix I. Copies of the complete schedule may be obtained from the Social Science Research Council Survey Archive, University of Essex.
2. See D. V. Glass (ed.), op. cit., and P. Blau and O. D. Duncan, *The American Occupational Structure* (John Wiley & Sons, Inc., 1969).
3. J. H. Goldthorpe, op. cit.
4. See J. H. Goldthorpe and K. Hope, op. cit. (1974).
5. D. Lockwood, *The Black Coated Worker* (George Allen & Unwin, 1958).
6. Cf. J. H. Goldthorpe and C. Llewellyn, *Sociology* (1977).
7. The following five paragraphs are a modified version of J. H. Goldthorpe and C. Llewellyn, op. cit., pp.259-60. The H-G categories in brackets are a 36-fold combination of the H-G classification. We have further had occasion to use the 36-fold H-G scheme to separate the self-employed from the salaried elements in the service and intermediate classes. These groups we have termed the 'entrepreneurs' and the 'salariat'. Details of the groupings appear below in Chapter 3.
8. J. W. B. Douglas, *The Home and the School* (MacGibbon & Kee, 1964).

9. Ronald Davie, Neville Butler, and Harvey Goldstein, *From Birth to Seven* (Longman, 1972).
10. There were 242 men in the sample who were resident in the UK but not in England or Wales at age 14, and 565 who were overseas or unascertained at age 14.
11. See Martin Trow, 'The Second Transformation of American Secondary Education', in J. Karabel and A. H. Halsey (eds.), op. cit. (1977), pp.105–17.
12. R. H. Tawney, *Secondary Education For All* (Allen & Unwin, 1922), p.20.
13. Regulations for Secondary Schools (Board of Education) 1907.
14. These introduced the test of parental ability to pay fees among those selected from the public elementary schools. The Board recommended, as the limit for complete exemption, £3 to £4 per week per family with one child. See Regulation 1421 (Board of Education).
15. The results of the LSE 1949 study demonstrated over the period before 1949, the overwhelming occupational advantages resulting from attendance at selective secondary schools.
16. G. A. N. Lowndes, *The Silent Social Revolution* (2nd edn., Oxford University Press, 1969), p.125.
17. Report of the Departmental Committee on Scholarships and Free Places, 1920.
18. R. H. Tawney, op. cit., chapter 2.
19. Cmnd. 3091, p.23.
20. D. Caradog Jones, 'Social Factors in Secondary Education', in D. C. Jones (ed.), *The Social Survey of Merseyside*, vol. 3 (Hodder & Stoughton, 1934), p.29. See also Kenneth Lindsay, *Social Progress and Educational Waste* (Routledge, 1926).
21. For a full account of developments during the Second World War, see P. H. Gosden, *Education in the Second World War* (Methuen, 1976), especially chapter 3.
22. Education Act 1944, Section 7.
23. The best account of the subsequent history of this type of school is William Taylor, *The Secondary Modern School* (Faber & Faber, 1963).
24. For a full treatment of the history of the controversy see Olive Banks, op. cit., chapter 10.
25. Education Act 1944, Section 8, para. 1(b).
26. O. Banks, op. cit., p.283.
27. Ibid., pp.294–9.
28. There were sixteen comprehensive schools in England and Wales in 1954. For a short account of the comprehensive-school movement in the period covered by this study, see D. Rubinstein and B. Simon, *The Evolution of the Comprehensive School 1926–66* (Routledge & Kegan Paul, 1969).
29. A useful account of the public schools is to be found in Graham Kalton, *The Public Schools: A Factual Survey* (Longmans, 1966). See also the Newsom Report, *The Public Schools Commission First Report*, vol. i (HMSO, 1968), and for the direct grant schools see the Donnison Report, *The Public Schools Commission Second Report* (HMSO, 1970).
30. These figures for university and teacher-training numbers apply to Great Britain, i.e. to Scotland as well as England and Wales.

CHAPTER 3

State or Private Primary School?

In Chapters 1 and 2 we have set the sociological and historical contexts of the present enquiry, documenting the various issues that divide sociologists, introducing the questions to which we hope to provide answers and describing the major changes in British education which will have affected the experience of our respondents. Moving now to empirical results, we shall follow our respondents' educational careers from primary school to secondary school and then, for the fortunate minority, to further education and university.

EDUCATIONAL PATHWAYS

One way in which to conceive of these educational careers is as a set of routes or pathways which divide (or, more rarely, rejoin) at various points.[1] At each of these points the respondent had to choose, or a choice had to be made for him, and the choice will have had important implications for the paths along which he was able to travel later. A simple map of this set of pathways might be as follows: at the beginning of his school career the individual's parents chose whether to send him to a state primary or a private preparatory school. If they chose the former, the pupil was now also propelled towards the state system of secondary education, and found it harder to reverse his direction at a later date and move back into the private sector. Conversely, the pupil who was sent to a private preparatory school could then more easily go on to 'public' school since he received, unlike his state-sector contemporary, preparation necessary for success in the 'Common Entrance' examination.

A second crucial choice in the individual's educational career came, for a growing minority in each successive cohort, at the age of 11. Here, for our first two cohorts (1913–32), the educational decision-makers chose whether the pupil was to continue in his elementary school or be transferred to a free place in one of the forms of selective secondary school. From 1932 these scholarships were means tested and called 'special' instead of 'free' places. After the 1944 Act (i.e. for our second two cohorts) fees were abolished and the decision was one of allocation between grammar, technical, and secondary modern schools, the first choice setting him on a route that kept open his prospects of a university education and a professional job thereafter, the second directing him more towards the 'non-academic' sector of further education and technical qualifications like the OND and HND, and the third typically heading him towards direct and early entry into the labour market. Further choices had then to be made, by or on behalf of all pupils, at the age of 15 (or 14 before 1947) when the option of leaving school first became available. These choices stayed open through the remainder of the individual's school career, and the decisions reached doubtless reflected another set of crucial decisions – whether or not to take School Certificate examinations (or their equivalent after 1950 – GCE O-Level) and, still more important, whether to enter the sixth form of the grammar school and take Higher School Certificate (GCE A-Level after 1950). Finally came the decision, for those who stayed on into the sixth form, whether to seek a place in a university or teacher-training college, or to enter for one of the competitive examinations such as those used to select recruits to the Civil Service.

This of course is a highly simplified map of the educational system. If we drew it to a larger scale we would find many other 'decision points' or 'branching points' as Boudon describes them, but the ones we have described are the major ones defined by our *formal* educational institutions: the individual must *legally* be in an approved educational institution, either state or private, at the age of 5; the 1944 Education Act abolished the all-age elementary schools and the individual therefore was *legally* required to transfer to a secondary school. Again, the date at which leaving school becomes an option is defined by law. True, the actual outcomes at each of these branching points may be the result of a long process of drift and indecision rather than a single conscious decision, but outcomes there must certainly be, and these we can study.

Our first task, then, is to look at the outcomes and to see how frequented were the different paths on our map. How many chose private primary education: how many then moved back into the state system? How many were chosen for grammar and technical rather than elementary or secondary modern schools? When did they leave, and what examination successes did they have? Perhaps more interestingly we can look at the way in which the flows along the different paths have changed over time. We can compare the experience of our older cohorts who were educated before the war with that of the younger ones and we can see, for example, whether the 1944 reforms made it easier (or rather, strictly speaking, more common) for people to transfer between one type of secondary school and another as had been intended.

A second task is to look not at how *many* but at what *kinds* of respondents trod these different paths. Most obviously, we must look at the proportion of respondents from different social classes who took the different routes, and so reassess the classic issue of class differentials in access to selective secondary schools and universities. We need not restrict oursleves to social classifications by father's occupation since we have substantial information about our respondents' social backgrounds. We know, for example, whether our respondents came from an 'educated' home (educated in the sense of having one or both parents who had received a selective or university education); and we know something about the material as well as the 'cultural' conditions of the home.

In looking at the proportion of respondents from different social origins who, for example, attended grammar school (that is, at the 'class chances' of getting to grammar school), we are making use of what the student of social mobility calls an *outflow* table. But we must also look at the *inflow* tables, and these will tell us the social composition of the different types of school, state and private, primary and secondary. The two types of analysis enable us to tackle rather different types of question; the first tells us about class chances and inequalities of opportunity; the latter begins to tell us something about the cultural and social experience obtained within the different types of institution. It is the egalitarian question that has most often exercised sociologists of education, but the 'social mix' of pupils at a given type of school is also a matter of concern to those such as Tawney who have attacked the socially divisive character of British education. It is one thing to show that children from the middle class have substantial advantages in the competition for grammar-school places; it is quite another to show that pupils at grammar schools are predominantly drawn from the middle class. In popular discussion the two statements have too often been equated.

So far our primary tasks are descriptive. We must show what flows there have been along the various educational pathways, what kinds of people have trodden them, and what changes have occurred over time. But we also want to go beyond the descriptive and to start to *explain* the observed regularities and changes. In this and later chapters the explanations will often take the form of tests of the many theories discussed in Chapter 1. Not all can be tested: some in principle, others because we lack the necessary data. Nor, of course, do we limit ourselves so strictly. In some cases the data lead us into relatively uncharted areas; in some cases we offer fresh explanations of relatively familiar observations.

Let us turn now to the data. The first major, institutionally defined, decision facing the parent is the choice between state and private primary school. Of course, there are many earlier decisions that parents will have made – whether to send their son to nursery school, for example. What we call the decision between state and private primary school may itself be the outcome of a whole sequence of decisions in which options gradually became closed off until no real choice was left. Or indeed it may never have occurred to many parents that any choice was available. Financial constraints or class assumptions or local conditions may have settled the matter as far as they were concerned. But at any rate, whatever the precise processes involved, by the age of 5 the children will have been attending either a state school or one of the vast variety of private proprietary or preparatory schools.

The flows into these two main types of institution are straightforward enough to describe. In our oldest cohort, born between 1913 and 1922 and thus entering school for the first time between 1918 and 1927, a meagre 5.2 per cent entered the private sector. In the following cohort this was effectively unchanged at 5.1 per cent, both figures doubtless being affected by the conditions of the depression years. Certainly the recovery from the depression was marked by an upsurge with 7.1 per cent of those born between 1933 and 1942 attending private primary schools, a large increase proportionately although small in absolute terms. But even this increase was not maintained in the post-war period. There was a drop to 5.7 per cent of our youngest cohort starting school life in the private sector.[2]

SOCIAL CLASS AND PRIVATE PRIMARY SCHOOLING

Who then are this tiny minority of parents who opt out of the state system? It will come as no surprise that those most likely to do so are members of what we have called the service class. Table 3.1 makes the picture clear. Using our eightfold classification of social classes we see that it is Class I – the higher grade professionals, administrators, managers, and proprietors – who are by far the most likely to send their children to private primary schools; almost one-third of our respondents from Class I origins started their school career in private schools.

A clear picture emerges too if we look more closely at the occupational groups which make up Class I. Of the five occupational groups comprising this class it is the self-employed professionals (doctors, lawyers, and accountants, for example) who are most likely to send their children to the private primary schools; 55 per cent of our respondents from these origins received private primary schooling, by far the highest percentage recorded for any group. Next come large proprietors with 38 per cent, followed by the salaried professionals (30 per cent), higher-grade administrators (25 per cent), and managers in large industrial enterprises (23 per cent). These five groups are heavier users of these schools than any of the other thirty-one occupational groups that make up the collapsed Hope-Goldthorpe scale.[3] It is noteworthy that they are led by the two self-employed groups of self-employed professionals and large proprietors. Similarly we see from Table 3.1 that within the intermediate classes it is Class IV, the petty bourgeoisie, which is the heaviest user of private primary schools. And within Class IV we find that the only really significant users are the small proprietors (13 per cent) and the farmers and farm managers (12 per cent). While there are, then, gross class differentials in the use of private primary schools, the differences *within* classes are almost more interesting. There is a strong connection between self-employment or private enterprise and the private schools, and we may guess that this will be reflected in the values and cultures of these, so to say, 'entrepreneurial' schools.

Table 3.1

Attendance at Private and State Primary Schools
(percentages)

Respondent's Primary Schooling	Father's Class								
	I	II	III	IV	V	VI	VII	VIII	All
Private	32.7	14.3	6.9	10.3	2.4	1.1	0.9	0.3	5.8
State	67.3	85.7	93.1	89.7	97.6	98.9	99.1	99.7	94.2
	100	100	100	100	100	100	100	100	100
(N =)	(591)	(481)	(611)	(909)	(955)	(2228)	(1913)	(341)	(8029)

To explore this guess we turn from an outflow to an inflow analysis and find that a majority (56 per cent) of our respondents who attended private primary schools had Class I and II origins. Most of the others came from the intermediate classes (34 per cent), and only a tiny minority were working class (9 per cent). Perhaps a little surprisingly, in view of the outflow data, the proportion who came from entrepreneurial backgrounds (that is, whose fathers were self-employed professionals, large proprietors, or came from the petty bourgeoisie)[4] came to only 35 per cent of the total, but the explanation for this is that, while the self-employed are heavy users of private education, they comprise only a small and shrinking part of the population. Even so, the fact that one-third of the children at private primary schools came from these backgrounds suggests

Table 3.2

Attendance at Private Primary Schools by Birth Cohorts and
Father's Class
(percentages)

Father's Class	1913–22	1923–32	1933–42	1943–52	All
I, II	26.5	25.7	27.1	21.1	24.4
	*338**	*416*	*271*	*315*	
III, IV, V	6.9	6.4	8.5	4.4	6.4
	204	*277*	*155*	*159*	
VI, VII, VIII	0.9	0.4	1.8	0.9	1.0
	0	*0*	*0*	*0*	
All	5.3	4.9	7.2	5.8	5.8
(N =)	(1881)	(1901)	(1894)	(2353)	(8029)

*Figures in italic give log distances (see below).

that their influence on the character of these schools will have been substantial, although not perhaps overwhelming.

We may now explore changes over time by tabulating the outflow (Table 3.2) and inflow (Table 3.3) along the path to the primary school for each birth cohort. Table 3.2 shows the outflow from each of the three social classes to have been relatively fairly stable, the proportions from each class attending private primary schools rising and falling together. We can measure relative class chances more precisely by computing disparity ratios, that is, the ratio of the percentage from any two classes attending private primary schools.[5] The service class (I and II)/working class (VI, VII, VIII) disparity ratio was 30:1 for the 1913–22 cohort. It was smallest in the 1933–42 cohort when it fell to 15:1, and it then rose again to 23:1 in the youngest cohort. But we can draw no safe conclusion from this pattern. Given the virtual non-use of private primary schools by the working class, small percentage changes can give rise to large, but sociologically insignificant, changes in the disparity ratio. The advantages of the disparity ratio are its 'natural' interpretation (one group has twice, three times, etc., the chance of another group . . .) and ease of computation. But given its disadvantages, we have adopted a suggestion made by K. I. Macdonald[6] and preferred to use what we shall call the 'log distance' measure. Simply, this is the disparity ratio, but calculated between log frequencies: thus the ratio P_{ik}/P_{jk} is converted into the distance measure $\log_e P_{ik} - \log_e P_{jk}$.

The main advantage of the log distance measure is that whatever category one uses as the 'base', the distances between categories are unaffected. The categories can be represented as points on a line, with arbitrary origin and scaling. One thus has at a glance (or by a simple subtraction) the distances among all categories, not just that from each category to the base. For convenience in presentation, we normally take the bottom category as the base (with a distance of zero from itself), and simply give the distances of each category from it. We use natural logarithms (base e), and multiply by 100, rounding to the nearest integer.

In the case of Table 3.2 we thus have a service- to working-class distance of 338 in the 1913–22 cohort, and an intermediate- to working-class distance of 204: the service to intermediate distance is thus 134 (the arithmetic difference). Thereafter, the service- to working-class distance jumps to 416, falls to 271 in the 1933–42 cohort, and rises again to 315, while the service to intermediate distance stays relatively constant at 139, 116, and 156. The relative constancy of the service–intermediate distances is now more obvious, and justifies our distrust of conclusions based solely on disparity ratios computed from a small base.

While these movements were taking place in the relative chances of private primary schooling for boys of different social origin there was a trend in the social composition of these schools which can only be seen through an inflow table (Table 3.3). With a special interlude in the years of recovery from slump after 1938, they became increasingly service class, decreasingly intermediate class, and remained negligibly working class. In part, the explanation is to be found in the changing class composition of the supply of children which we traced in Chapter 2.[7] The service class increased its contribution to births in each successive cohort, the intermediate class contribution remained virtually constant, and the working class declined as a source of children. Given the fairly constant pattern of relative class chances which we saw in Table 3.2, the net result was that the private schools became more than ever service class in their clientele.

Table 3.3

Class Composition of Private Primary Schools by Birth Cohort
(percentages)

Father's Class	1913–22	1923–32	1933–42	1943–52	All
I, II	49.5	57.4	49.3	67.6	56.5
III, IV, V	40.4	38.3	36.8	24.3	34.3
VI, VII, VIII	10.1	4.3	14.0	8.1	9.3
	100.0	100.0	100.1	100.0	100.1
(N =)	(99)	(95)	(134)	(136)	(464)

The changing class structure has also affected the proportion of children at these schools who come from entrepreneurial backgrounds. The proportion of large proprietors, small proprietors, farmers, and farm managers among our respondents' fathers in the 1943–52 cohort was effectively half what it was with the 1913–22 cohort, while the proportion who were self-employed professionals has shown no increase. It is the salariat that has been expanding, and accordingly it is children from the salariat who have come to dominate in the private schools.[8] Thus whereas for the sample as a whole a third of the children at private primary schools came from entrepreneurial backgrounds, in the earliest of our four cohorts it was 39 per cent and for the most recent it was only 28 per cent. These changes in the occupational structure and its associated demography, therefore, may have been slowly changing the character and ethos of the schools. By the time of our youngest cohort a clear majority (58 per cent) came from what we term the salariat.

PARENTAL EDUCATION AND PRIMARY SCHOOLING

While it is undoubtedly important to look at the social-class origins of the pupils at private primary schools, this is clearly by no means the whole story. Perhaps equally important, if we are to understand what kind of family used these schools, is to look at the educational experience of the parents, and particularly at their own experience of private schooling. Which of the parents, it may be asked, had themselves been to private primary schools? Table 3.4 gives the answer.

Table 3.4

Primary Schooling and Parental Education
(percentages)

Respondent's primary schooling	Neither parent attended private primary school	Mother (but not father) attended	Father (but not mother) attended	Both parents attended private primary school
Private	3.5	35.3	44 4	75.5
State	96.5	64.7	55.6	24.5
	100.0	100.0	100.0	100.0
(N = 8529)	(8100)	(167)	(160)	(102)

This shows a relatively strong association between the type of primary school attended by parents and the one to which they sent their son. Where both parents attended a private school, the respondent was himself highly likely to attend one; where neither parent did so, the respondent had a negligible likelihood of doing so. Interestingly, respondents with a mother who had attended private primary school were somewhat less likely than those whose father had attended to go to a private school themselves, and to have had *both* parents at a private school doubled the probability. It might be guessed that the father's educational experience would have been decisive, given the common assumption that, at least in the period we are considering, the man had greater power within the family and will therefore have taken the major decisions. Alternatively, of course, it might be argued that mothers take a greater interest in their children's education. However, our results confirm neither of these extreme positions, but show rather a balanced situation where the paternal influence seems (on average) to be greater than the maternal, but not overwhelmingly so.

THE RELATIVE INFLUENCE OF CLASS AND PARENTAL EDUCATION

No one will be surprised to learn that the education of the child tends to resemble that of the parent, and that those who obtained privileged forms of education themselves are also more likely to secure it for their children. There are, however, a number of different mechanisms which might account for 'educational inheritance' One might be economic: private-school fees, even at the primary level, have never been negligible, and 'educational inheritance' might simply reflect inheritance of positions of economic privilege from one generation to another. Put somewhat differently, the 'effect' of parental education on respondent's education may prove to be spurious once we control for parental social class. Alternatively, there is a possible cultural argument: those parents who have themselves been through the private sector of education may be expected to have been socialized, through that educational experience, into a preference for private as against state education and a belief (whether justified or not) in the superior virtues of the private system. It would be surprising if this were not the case to some degree. Those who attend such schools will be exposed to the influence of parents and teachers who, by their very choice of these institutions for their children or for their own careers, must be assumed to prefer it to the state system. And everything we know about socialization suggests that these will be powerful influences. On this line of argument, in its strong form, parents who have been inculcated into the value of private education will be more willing to make financial sacrifices on behalf of their children's education and the 'effect' of parental education will thus remain even when we control for financial circumstances.

In the 1972 survey, we did not attempt to secure information on parental income and so we cannot control for financial circumstances in any strict way. But we can cross-tabulate respondent's primary education by parental education and parental class, and this is done in Table 3.5.

Table 3.5

Attendance at Private Primary Schools by Father's Class and Parental Education
(percentages)

| Parental Education | Father's Class | | | | | | | | |
	I	II	III	IV	V	VI	VII	VIII	All
Neither parent attended private primary school	19.2	8.1	5.7	6.8	2.1	1.0	0.9	0.3	3.5
One or both parents attended private primary school	73.0	50.0	25.7	56.9	13.0	9.1	3.8	0.0	48.3

Table 3.5 in fact lends support to both arguments. There is both a social-class and a parental-education 'effect'. Children from the service or intermediate classes were more likely to attend private primary schools than were working-class children, but even controlling for social class origins we see that children whose parents attended private primary schools were substantially more likely to do so themselves than those whose parents did not.

More interestingly, we see that the 'effects' of these two variables are not 'additive'. In Classes I, II, and IV we see that the respondent's likelihood of attending a private primary school was about 50 percentage points higher if either or both his parents attended one; but in Classes VI and VII the increase is negligible. The explanation follows from the two arguments already advanced. In order to obtain a private education for one's children it is not enough to want it, as we have assumed our privately educated parents did; the parent also has to have the capacity to pay for it, and this will be greatly reduced at lower social-class levels. Among those who do have the capacity to pay, however; parental values (rooted, presumably, in their own experience of private education) will be an important discriminator between the users and the non-users.

MULTIPLE SOCIAL INFLUENCES ON PRIMARY SCHOOLING

From this point we could go on to further contingency tables relating additional background factors such as parental secondary education to the respondent's primary education, but instead and more parsimoniously we have recorded only the correlations between the following variables:

Respondent's Private Primary Schooling (RPP): if the respondent attended a private primary school he scores 1; otherwise 0.

Father's Private Primary Schooling (FPP): scored similarly to RPP.

Mother's Private Primary Schooling (MPP): scored similarly to RPP.

Father's Private Secondary Schooling (FPS): if the respondent's father attended a Direct Grant or Independent School (either HMC or non-HMC) he scores 1; otherwise 0.

Mother's Private Secondary Schooling (MPS): scored similarly to FPS.

Father's Higher Education (FHE): if the respondent's father obtained a degree from a University or a higher-level qualification[9] from another institution he scores 1; otherwise 0. (Since only about 2 per cent of the respondents' mothers obtained such qualifications we have not constructed a corresponding variable for mothers.)

Father's Class (FC): this uses the eightfold classification of social classes described in Chapter 2. Class I scores 1, Class II scores 2, and so on.

We would remind the reader here that this eightfold classification of social class is not claimed to have any necessarily consistent hierarchical form and is not to be understood as a scale of occupational status of the kind used by Blau and Duncan.[10] Ideally, therefore, we should have represented the classification by a set of seven binary variables. But this would have been extremely cumbersome and we decided that the interests of economical exposition outweighed those of theoretical purity.[11]

Domestic Amenities (DA): this is a composite variable taking values from zero to 4. The respondent scores 1 for each of the following amenities which he reports to have been present in his home at the time when he was aged 14: fixed bath or shower, refrigerator, telephone, indoor WC.

Owner Occupation (OO): the respondent scores 1 if, at the time he was aged 14, his father was an owner-occupier; otherwise zero.

Council House Tenancy (CH): the respondent scores 1 if, at the time he was aged 14, his father was a council-house tenant; otherwise zero. It follows that a score of zero on both variables OO and CH indicates that the respondent was living in private rented accommodation.

Number of Siblings (NS): number of brothers and sisters born alive, including step, half-, and adoptive siblings.

Table 3.6

Correlations among Background Variables and with Respondent's Primary Education

	RPP	FPP	MPP	FPS	MPS	FHE	FC	DA	OO	CH
FPP	.388									
MPP	.348	.364								
FPS	.351	.552	.274							
MPS	.294	.309	.458	.368						
FHE	.240	.207	.169	.201	.165					
FC	−.320	−.231	−.210	−.232	−.200	−.321				
DA	.276	.180	.164	.191	.172	.190	−.408			
OO	.232	.150	.146	.160	.152	.155	−.326	.340		
CH	−.125	−.075	−.080	−.092	−.072	−.083	.173	.093	−.398	
NS	−.123	−.038	−.050	−.055	−.070	−.083	.230	−.206	−.215	.125

Note: The definitions and scorings of the variables appear in the text.

Table 3.6 shows that the correlations are in general rather low. However, this need not in most cases surprise us. Only a very small proportion of our sample attended private primary schools and the distribution of scores on variable RPP is accordingly highly skewed. If we now correlate primary schooling with a variable which has a less skewed distribution the correlation will necessarily be less than one. For example, even if father's class has the strongest possible association with primary schooling, such that all places at private primary schools are filled by children from the highest social class, there will still be some boys from this class who are unable to find places.[12] But this is not to be regarded as some kind of 'mere' statistical artefact or as a 'mere' product of our classification system. The fact that primary schooling is highly skewed in its distribution while social class is much less so is, we would claim, a characteristic of the real world and not an artefact. It is, furthermore, a sociologically important point that primary schooling cannot, because of this difference in the distributions, be predicted accurately from a knowledge of the respondent's social-class origins alone. This is the point that the low value of the correlation coefficient makes, and it is a useful one.

Given this point about the distributions of scores on our variables, it may be anticipated that some of the highest correlations are between those variables that have the most similar distributions. Of course, the fact that two variables have similar distributions does not entail that they will correlate highly; it merely determines the maximum *possible* size of their correlation. Accordingly, high correlations must reflect sociological processes. In fact, private education at the primary level correlates highly with private education at the secondary level for both mothers and fathers; in addition the type of education that mothers and fathers have had tends to be similar and to correlate relatively well with the respondent's primary education.

A second group of variables which correlate relatively highly are Father's Class, Owner Occupation, and Domestic Amenities. This is a group of what we might call 'material factors' which correlate moderately well with the education-background factors and with the respondent's primary schooling. Again there is nothing in this to surprise us or to modify the picture we had already drawn on the basis of the contingency tables.

A further step is to group the variables together and calculate the multiple correlation coefficients. Doing this first for the education group of variables (i.e. FPP, MPP, FPS, MPS, FHE) we obtain a coefficient of 0.491. Comparing this with the simple correlation of 0.388 when we correlate respondent's primary schooling with father's primary schooling alone, we see that the addition of the extra education variables has not increased out predictive power by very much. Next, taking the 'material' group of variables on their own (FC, DA, OO, CH plus NS)[13] we obtain a multiple correlation coefficient of .377, and comparing this with the figure of −.320 when we correlate primary schooling with father's class we are again struck by the small increment resulting from the addition of the extra variables. Finally, putting the two groups of variables together the multiple correlation coefficient still comes to only .534.

These are rather striking results. Adding variables, or even whole groups of variables, does not increase the multiple correlation coefficient much above the level of the simple correlation of respondent's primary schooling with father's primary schooling. It suggests that the picture obtained by cross-tabulating primary schooling against social-class origins and parental primary schooling will not be much changed by adding further variables. This is an important point which is surprisingly often forgotten. We could have presented a long series of contingency tables showing that parental secondary schooling, higher education, domestic amenities, and so on were all quite good discriminators between the users and non-users of the private sector in primary education. The temptation then is to infer, rather in the way that some writers on the 'vicious cycle of poverty' were led to do by analogous results, that there was some kind of *cumulative* advantage gained by the privileged and a *cumulative* disadvantage experienced by the underprivileged.[14] But the multiple correlation coefficient shows clearly that this is not so. The reason can be found in Table 3.5. This shows that Class I families where one or both parents had attended private primary schools were highly likely to send their sons to private primary schools. But these families will also tend to be the ones who had private secondary education, who are owner occupiers and have plenty of domestic amenities. Our series of contingency tables would merely be isolating the same small set of families over and over again, and we would not be gaining new information since we *already* knew from our first few tables that they were heavy users of the private sector. Similarly, at the other extreme, it is clear that Class VII or VIII families are most unlikely to use the private sector, and since the probability of their doing so is already effectively zero their handicap can hardly be increased however many different variables we introduce. To obtain new information, therefore, from our additional variables we need to turn to the *middle ranges* where the first variables do not discriminate well between the users and non-users (and of course it is in the middle ranges that most of our respondents lie). Again, what we have learnt from the multiple correlation coefficient is that the addition of extra background factors does not much help to discriminate here. There is no surprise, and accordingly no disappointment. To discriminate well at this level we would almost certainly need to know more not about the families' social position and educational experience, but about the particular situation confronting them: how close did they live to the different types of primary school, how good were these schools, where did their friends send their children? We would be surprised if these factors were not important, but they were not ones that we could capture in the survey on which we are relying.

The likely importance of these factors does not mean, however, that the background variables which we have been able to study are of no interest. Indeed, it is a matter of considerable theoretical and practical concern to see how their effect has changed over time, and it is to this that we now turn. First, the multiple correlation coefficient for our whole set of variables has declined fairly steadily. For the 1913–22 cohort it was 0.569; it then fell to 0.567, 0.554, and finally and more dramatically to 0.505 with the 1943–52 cohort. This means that primary schooling has become substantially more random with respect to social origins and parental education in the post-war period. One might thus be tempted to say that there has been increasing equality of opportunity of access to private primary schools. But this would be misleading. When we talk of equality of opportunity we usually have in mind the opportunities open to members of different classes, and our analysis of the contingency tables has already suggested that inequality in this sense has not changed substantially. Confirmation is offered by the correlation coefficient; it has barely fallen from −0.316 in the earliest cohort to −0.308 in the most recent. A number of other correlation coefficients have, however, fallen quite appreciably. The biggest changes are in the case of Domestic Amenities (from 0.318 to 0.261), Father's Private Primary Education (from 0.416 to 0.322), and Mother's Private Primary Education (from 0.402 to 0.332). These are the falls that account for the decline in the multiple correlation coefficient.

The decline in the correlation between Primary Schooling and Domestic Amenities is readily explicable. Ownership of consumer durables and of telephones has increased enormously over the forty years covered by our study, and standards of housing have also increased greatly. This means, of course, that the distribution of scores on this variable has changed dramatically. In the case of the 1913–22 cohort 54 per cent of the families had none of the four amenities, and only 1 per cent had all four. But in the case of the 1943–52 cohort only 9 per cent had none, and the percentage with all four had climbed to 19 per cent. Our earlier point about the distribution of scores on the different variables and the size of the maximum possible correlation between them is clearly relevant here; Domestic Amenities could have been quite a good predictor of Private Primary Schooling among the earliest cohort since the distribution of scores was highly skewed, and skewed in the same direction as scores on the primary-schooling variable (maximum possible value = 0.93). But since then the distribution of scores has become, first, less skewed, and then actually skewed in the opposite direction. We cannot expect it to be as good a discriminator now (maximum possible value = 0.84). But there is also the equivalent sociological point that, for example, the advantaged families who have all four amenities are nothing like as 'select' a group as they were before. Previously possession of all four would have indicated a quite unusually affluent family, doubtless with sufficient resources to afford private education. Now it does nothing of the sort.

Less predictable, however, have been the declining correlations between the respondents' primary schooling and their parents'. The variables have very similar distributions and they have shown very little change over time. In the oldest cohort 5.2 per cent of our respondents went to private primary schools, and 5.1 per cent had one or both parents who had done so; in the youngest cohort the comparable figures were 5.7 per cent and 5.4 per cent respectively. We must therefore look elsewhere for the explanation. One possibility is that there has been a weakening in the strength of the cultural tradition through which parents educated in private schools come to value the same kind of education for their children. There was no general weakening of preference for private education; the proportion of parents sending their children to private secondary education did not fall off in the final cohort as it did at the primary level (the percentage of respondents attending private secondary education in the four cohorts being 5.0, 5.4, 7.5, and 7.3). Nor does the correlation between respondents' and parents' experience of the private sector show any attenuation at the secondary level. It would seem more plausible to explain the change as a response to the enhanced esteem of state primary schools which have gained an international reputation for quality in this century and have become attractive to middle-class families. Alternatively, it may be that the rise of Direct Grant schools has encouraged some educationally ambitious parents, who might otherwise have chosen private primary schools, to send their children to the state sector in the hopes of winning free places at the prestigious Direct Grant schools. At all events, this interpretation is consistent with the data available.

CONCLUSION

Our discussion of the first formal decision along the pathway of an educational career, though it raises some methodological issues, is substantially a simple one. The initial decision is for the great majority no decision at all. Ninety-five out of every 100 children have entered the primary stage of their educational journey through the gates of a state school. Expansion and change has affected pre-primary schooling in recent years and the secondary and tertiary stages throughout our period. The state primary schools have, by contrast, been stable institutions in the sense of retaining the steady loyalty of most parents. In so far as they changed it was in the direction of increasing their attractiveness to the middle classes, although as we have suggested, their attractiveness may have lain in the convenient course which they provided to free places in the Direct Grant schools.

Nevertheless, for a 5 or 6 per cent minority there have been various kinds of private primary schools. They have always been used by a minority (roughly one-quarter) of service-class and especially entrepreneurial service-class families; and hardly at all by working-class people. Accordingly their social composition has been dominantly service class, and increasingly so. The social selection for private primary schooling of the minority from the service class then turns essentially on the educational experience of the parents and especially of fathers. These two factors, social-class origins and parental experience of private schooling, prove to be our best predictors of who will and who will not take the private road into an educational career. Further refinement of class 'indicators', at least from the survey information available to us, adds little to the accuracy of our predictions. Thus class and its conventionally associated upbringing in the parental generation are established at the outset as major influences on the educational pathways of the filial generation.

We must now trace these influences into the secondary schools.

NOTES

1. This model of the educational system as a set of branching pathways is very like that of Raymond Boudon, *Education, Opportunity and Social Inequality* (John Wiley, 1974).
2. These percentages differ from those in the bottom row of Table 3.2 because they are based on all 8529 members of our 'educational history' sample, whereas in Table 3.2 we necessarily exclude the 500 of them who could not be assigned to a social class at age 14. The differences are, however, trivial.
3. J. H. Goldthorpe and K. Hope, op. cit., p.134: see also Chapter 2 above, p.17.
4. Entrepreneurs are thus taken to consist of those in H–G categories 1, 7, 9, 11, 13, 19, 29 and 36. See Chapter 2, p.17.
5. The disparity ratio is a straightfoward measure of the relative probability of being in (column) category k, given (row) category i rather than j: that is, P_{ik}/P_{jk}. In terms of counts rather than frequencies, this can be expressed as

$$DR_{k/(i:j)} = (n_{ik}/n_{i.})/(n_{jk}/n_{.j}).$$

6. Personal communication for which we are grateful.
7. See Table 2.2 above, p.22.
8. By the salariat we refer to the following categories of the collapsed version of the Hope–Goldthorpe scale: salaried professionals, higher grade (2) administrators and officials, higher grade (3); industrial managers, large enterprises (4); administrators and officials, lower grade (5); technicians, higher grade (6); industrial and business managers, small enterprises (8); salaried professionals, lower grade (10); supervisors of nonmanual employees, higher grade (12); managers in services and small administrative units (14); supervisors of nonmanual employees, lower grade (16); nonmanual employees in administration and commerce (21). See J. H. Goldthorpe and K. Hope, *The Social Grading of Occupations: A New Approach and Scale* (Clarendon Press, 1974), p.134.
9. Degrees and higher-level qualifications are defined as those assigned to level 'a', 'b', or 'c' in Appendix B and C of *Qualified Manpower Tables, Sample Census 1966, Great Britain* (HMSO, 1970).
10. See Chapter 2 above, p.19.
11. In the case of Father's Class and Number of Siblings we tested the effect of using a categorical representation by dummy variables. The increases in variance accounted for were negligible, justifying our preference for simplicity in exposition.
12. On this assumption the maximum possible value for the correlation is -0.567. This is the appropriate 'ceiling' with which to compare the observed value -0.320.
13. It seems sensible to include Number of Siblings in the material group of variables since it can to some extent be taken as a measure of overcrowding in the home. It also correlates more highly with the members of the 'material' group than with those of the education group.
14. For a discussion of the cycle of poverty which seems to fall into this trap, see F. Field, *Unequal Britain* (Arrow Books, 1974); and for a discussion which lucidly describes the nature of the trap see O. D. Duncan, 'Inheritance of Poverty or Inheritance of Race?', in Daniel P. Moynihan (ed.), *On Understanding Poverty* (Basic Books, Inc., 1968), pp.85–110.

CHAPTER 4

From Primary to Secondary School

We come now to the transition from primary to secondary school, a point of fateful importance for children in selective educational systems and therefore especially so during the period of our study. For the earliest birth cohort (1913–22), as we described in Chapter 2, most children in fact stayed in the same elementary school with an increasing minority 'winning the scholarship' at 11-plus to go across to the separate selective secondary schools. Another, but decreasing minority, took the same path as fee-payers, and a still smaller minority passed from private primary schools to private secondary schools at age 13 via a 'Common Entrance' examination run by the private schools.[1] We saw too in Chapter 2 how the Education Act of 1944 legislated for a new system of 'secondary education for all' which was available to our third and fourth birth cohorts, mainly in the form of a tripartite division, but with some beginnings of comprehensive organization.

In theory the Education Act of 1944 eliminated from the state schools all inequalities of opportunity due to differences in financial circumstances. Accordingly, most commentators expected that the class chances of securing a grammar-school education would become more equal between children of different classes. One of our concerns, therefore, is to investigate the social effects of this deliberate move towards meritocracy.

TRANSFER FROM PRIMARY TO SECONDARY SCHOOLS

Before looking at the effects of the Act, however, we begin by looking at the pattern of transfers between the state and private sectors and at the overall pattern of entry to the different types of secondary school.

As at the primary level of education, the private sector caters for only a tiny proportion of the school population: 5.8 per cent of our sample had attended private primary schools, and 6.5 per cent attended private secondary schools. And of those who had started their school career in private schools, 57 per cent continued at the secondary level within the private sector. This may seem a surprisingly small proportion, although doubtless it partly reflects the hetero-geneity of the private sector at both primary and secondary level. Very far from all private primary schools in fact prepare children for the Common Entrance examination to 'public' schools, some being geared instead to success in the state system's 11-plus examiation. Conversely, the Direct Grant schools were required, as a condition of their status, to give free places to a proportion of children from state primary schools. A certain amount of interchange between the state and private systems was therefore to be expected, and we might further expect there to be the strongest link between private primary and secondary schooling in the case of the 'public' or HMC independent schools, and the weakest in the case of the Direct Grant grammar schools.

The pattern is easiest to discern if we look at the outflow from the two types

Table 4.1

Destinations[1] of Respondents from State and Private Primary Schools
(percentages)

	Secondary Modern	Comprehensive	Technical	Independent Non-HMC	Grammar	Direct Grant	Independent HMC	All
Private Primary (N = 465)	16.6 (0.3)[2]	0.4 (0.3)	5.2 (0.4)	19.6 (7.9)	20.9 (1.2)	9.0 (5.6)	28.4 (11.9)	100.1
State Primary (N = 7546)	66.4	1.5	12.1	1.4	16.7	1.2	0.8	100.1
All (N = 8011)	63.5	1.5	11.7	2.5	16.9	1.6	2.4	100.1

[1] See Chapter 2 for details of our classification of secondary schools.
[2] Figures in brackets give the ratio of 'observed' to 'expected' value.

of primary schooling to the various forms of secondary schools, and if we compare these 'observed' flows with those which would be expected on the basis of completely random allocation of primary-school children to secondary schools. Table 4.1 confirms our prior expectation. Children from private primary schools had almost twelve times the expected chance of going on to HMC schools, but less than six times the expected chance of admission to Direct Grant schools. Given these figures it is inevitable that these privately educated children would be unlikely to go to secondary modern schools or their pre-war equivalents, but it is perhaps surprising that the number going into the state grammar schools was not greatly above the chance expectation. This is in part, however, a statistical artefact. The ratios of the 'observed' to the 'expected' figures are not independent of the marginal distributions.[2] More specifically, the maximum possible value of the index of association (as the ratio is often known) is limited by the size of whichever marginal total is the larger. Thus in the case of the HMC schools the larger marginal total is the row total (the 5.8 per cent of respondents from private primary schools) and the maximum possible value is thus 100/5.8 = 17.2. In the case of grammar schools the larger marginal is the column total (the 16.9 per cent of respondents who attended grammar schools) and the maximum possible value is thus 100/16.9 = 5.9.[3]

This property of the index need not, however, worry us too much in the present case. In the first place, its maximum possible value is the same for the HMC, non-HMC, and Direct Grant schools, and so the differences between these three types of school are unambiguous. The link between the HMC schools and the private primary schools is clearly the strongest, and that with the Direct Grant schools is the weakest of the three. Secondly, despite the fact that there were a much larger number of places available at grammar schools than at the HMC schools, a smaller *absolute* number of boys from private primary schools went on to them. So again there is no doubt that the link with the HMC schools is by far the strongest.

There is, then, a relatively strong link between private primary and secondary education, especially in the case of the HMC schools. However, in emphasizing the very real differences in the typical destinations of children from state and private schools, we should not ignore the frequency of switching between sectors that has taken place as well. There are marked differences *between* categories in their typical destinations, but there are also large differences *within* categories. Both are important phenomena.[4]

SWITCHING BETWEEN THE STATE AND PRIVATE SECTORS

The extent of switching is clearly revealed by inflow analysis. Thus Table 4.2 shows that only 32 per cent of entrants to Direct Grant schools came from the private sector compared with 46 per cent of entrants to the non-HMC schools, and 70 per cent of entrants to HMC schools themselves. Even this last figure seems surprisingly low when compared with the ideal-typical progression from preparatory school to 'public' school via the common entrance examination. It probably reflects a certain heterogeniety even within this pretigious group of HMC schools. In fact the Conference includes the heads of both boarding schools like Eton and Winchester who accept children at 13, and also of some

Table 4.2

Primary School Origins of Respondents at Different Secondary Schools
(percentages)

	Secondary Modern	Comprehensive	Technical	Independent Non-HMC	Grammar	Direct Grant	Independent HMC
Private Primary	1.5	1.7	2.6	46.2	7.2	32.1	69.8
State Primary	98.5	98.3	97.4	53.8	92.8	67.9	30.2
	100.0	100.0	100.0	100.0	100.0	100.0	100.0
(N = 8011)	(5084)	(118)	(937)	(197)	(1355)	(131)	(189)

urban day schools which take children from 11. Of course, if schools like Eton probably recruit more than 70 per cent of their pupils from private preparatory schools, then other HMC schools must recruit less than 70 per cent from the private sector.[5]

Table 4.3

Attendance at Private Primary and Private Secondary Schools
(percentages)

Respondent's Schooling	Father's Class								
	I	II	III	IV	V	VI	VII	VIII	All
Private Primary	32.7	14.3	6.9	10.3	2.4	1.1	0.9	0.3	5.8
Private Secondary[1]	35.7	15.6	7.2	11.2	1.1	1.3	0.9	1.1	6.5

[1] Private secondary schools are defined as independent HMC, Direct Grant, and independent non-HMC schools.

While the amount of switching may be somewhat surprising, the class composition of those making the transfers is more predictable. Working-class children are more likely to leave the private sector than are service-class children, and service-class children are more likely to switch the other way than are working-class children. The guess might then be made that there would be an even closer correlation with class at the secondary level of the private sector than at the primary level. But Table 4.3 in fact shows that the associations are virtually the same. The explanation, however, becomes clear when we look at the actual numbers involved rather than at the percentages. Using our eightfold classification of classes, of the 193 respondents from Class I backgrounds who attended a private primary school, 51 (that is, 26 per cent) transferred to state schools at secondary level; and of the 18 respondents from Class VII backgrounds, 15 (83 per cent) transferred. These respondents who left the private sector were then replaced by very similar numbers from the state sector. Sixty-nine Class I respondents (17 per cent of those who started in state primary schools) and 14 Class VII respondents (0.7 per cent of those who started) transferred from state primary schools. Thus, despite a substantial interchange of boys the social composition of the state and private sectors remained much the same.

SOCIAL CLASS AND SECONDARY SCHOOLING

However, while switching may hardly have changed the social composition of the private sector as a whole, at secondary level we must still expect to find differences between the private schools in their social composition. Just as the HMC schools recruit more heavily from the private primary schools, so we would also expect them to recruit more heavily from the service class. Table 4.4 confirms that this is so in the case of access to the HMC schools, and the inflow Table 4.5 shows that these schools take over 90 per cent of their pupils from the service or intermediate classes, while nearly 70 per cent are indeed of service-class origin. The 'public' schools are remarkable in their social homogeneity.

Table 4.4

Attendance at Secondary Schools
(percentages)

Father's Class	Secondary Modern	Comprehensive	Technical	Non-HMC	Grammar	Direct Grant	HMC	All
I, II (N = 1072)	26.6 / -103*	1.5 / -6	10.2 / -11	8.8 / 287	35.1 / 115	6.2 / 252	11.8 / 367	100.2
III, IV, V (N = 2469)	59.1 / -23	1.3 / -21	12.9 / 12	3.3 / 189	19.6 / 57	1.8 / 128	2.1 / 195	100.1
VI, VII, VIII (N = 4470)	74.7 / 0	1.6 / 0	11.4 / 0	0.5 / 0	11.1 / 0	0.5 / 0	0.3 / 0	100.1
All (N = 8011)	63.5	1.5	11.7	2.5	16.9	1.6	2.4	100.1

* Figures in italic give log distances (see Chapter 3, p.37).

Table 4.5

Class Composition of the Different Types of Secondary School
(percentages)

Father's Class	Secondary Modern	Comprehensive	Technical	Non-HMC	Grammar	Direct Grant	HMC
I, II	5.6	13.6	11.6	47.7	27.7	50.4	66.7
III, IV, V	28.7	26.3	34.0	41.1	35.7	33.6	27.0
VI, VII, VIII	65.7	60.2	54.3	11.2	36.5	16.0	6.3
	100.0	100.1	99.9	100.0	99.9	100.0	100.0
(N = 8011)	(5084)	(118)	(937)	(197)	(1355)	(131)	(189)

The Direct Grant and the non-HMC schools by contrast recruit more widely, but the social experience they offer is still overwhelmingly service class. Given that the Direct Grant schools were required to recruit in part from the state primary sector, and did in fact recruit substantially more from the state sector than did the lesser 'public' schools, it is worth noticing that their pattern of social-class recruitment was none the less closely similar to that of the non-HMC schools. As we have suggested in Chapter 3, some service- and intermediate-class parents used the state primary schools to enable them to secure free places for their children at the Direct Grant schools.

A further significant difference between state and private secondary schools, analogous to that between state and private primary schools, appears when class recruitment is examined using our distinction between the salariat and the entrepreneurial elements[6] of the service and intermediate classes. Of the thirteen service- and twelve intermediate occupational groups, as defined in the Hope-Goldthorpe thirty-six categories, none has sent more than a modest minority of its sons to private secondary schools with the exception of the self-employed professional (H–G Category 1) who sent 65 per cent of their boys in the period we are considering, and the large proprietors (H–G Category 7) for whom the comparable number was 47 per cent. Moreover, the pattern of recruitment as between entrepreneurial and salariat families may be seen from an inflow analysis (Table 4.6) to distinguish the social composition of the different types of private

Table 4.6

Entrepreneur and Salariat Origins of Boys in Various Types of Secondary School
(percentages)

Family Background	Non-HMC	Grammar	Direct Grant	HMC
Entrepreneur[1]	37.1	15.1	24.4	37.1
Salariat[2]	44.2	33.4	50.4	51.3
Other	18.8	51.6	25.2	11.6
	100.1	100.1	100.0	100.0
(N = 1872)	(197)	(1355)	(131)	(189)

[1] Includes H–G Categories 1, 7, 9, 11, 13, 19, 29 and 36.
[2] Includes H–G Categories 2, 3, 4, 5, 6, 8, 10, 12, 14, 16, and 21.

secondary schools. In all four types of school there is a greater proportion of boys from salariat families (reflecting their dominance in the occupational structure as a whole), but the balance in favour of the salariat is greater in the Direct Grant schools than in any of the others, while it is smallest in the case of the non-HMC schools. The actual proportion of both groups is relatively high in the HMC schools, but this is because of the low proportion of other elements of the inter-mediate and working classes who are absorbed into them.

While the private schools represent one continuing form of selection, the developing state system was applying another. It may therefore be useful at this point to compare class differentials in access to state and private secondary schools. The most striking feature of these class differentials, which appear in Table 4.4, is how much smaller they are in the selective state schools than in the private sector. While grammar schools were socially selective in favour of the service- and intermediate-class groups, they were much less so than the private schools; and the Technical schools were recruiting boys almost proportionately from the different class origins. Thus the service-/working-class log distance is greatest in the case of the HMC schools, while in the technical schools it is very close to zero. In terms of chances of access to grammar schools, the service class is about as far from the working class as it is in the case of the secondary modern schools, but in the opposite direction. The patterns of recruitment were, of course, reflected in the social composition of the schools (Table 4.5): technical schools (and comprehensive schools) approximate to a representative cross-section of the population as a whole, and, while the grammar schools are certainly skewed towards the service class, their position is intermediate between that of the technical schools and that of the private schools. At the other extreme the service class is heavily under-represented in the secondary modern schools. The social composition of these schools is a mirror image of the HMC schools. Two-thirds of the HMC boys are of service-class, and two-thirds of the secondary modern boys are of working-class origin.[7]

However, while it is true from the participants' point of view that class chances really do become more equal as we move down the academic hierarchy, it does not necessarily follow that the selection procedures of the lower-prestige institutions are any less class biased than those of the high-prestige institutions. The size of the different institutions, and their place in the pecking order rather than different selection procedures may be what determines class chances of access. This important point about class selection through a varied but stratified educational system must be validated. We must demonstrate why unequal class chances do not *necessarily* entail the existence of different selection procedures, and then test the null hypothesis that there are *in fact* no such differences.

A MODEL OF THE SELECTION PROCESS

To achieve these objectives we have constructed a highly simplified model of the selection process. First we assume that the school population is divided into three classes, a service class of 1072 people, an intermediate class of 2469, and a working class of 4470 (the actual numbers in our sample). Second, we assume that the various educational institutions are arranged in a hierarchy of academic prestige, the most prestigious selecting the most able pupils, the next most prestigious selecting the next-ablest pupils, and so on, ability being defined as measured intelligence. Finally we assume that measured intelligence is normally distributed within each class, the average IQ of the service class being 109, that of the intermediate class being 102, and that of the working class 98 (with a standard deviation of 14 points in each case).[8] If, then, each educational institution selects pupils solely on the basis of their measured intelligence, we have a meritocratic selection procedure as conventionally defined.

The working of the model can be followed with the aid of Figure 4.1. For the sake of argument we suppose that the HMC schools are placed at the top of the academic hierarchy. They have 189 places available, and therefore choose the

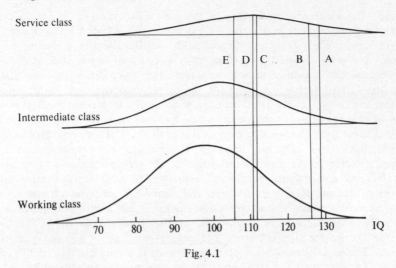

Fig. 4.1

189 ablest pupils irrespective of their social origin. To do this would be to select all pupils with IQs of 129 or more, that is, all those pupils to the right of the line A in Figure 4.1. The Direct Grant schools come next in the hierarchy. They have 131 places available, and can fill these if they take all the remaining pupils who have IQs of 126 or more, that is, all those between lines A and B. Grammar schools follow and, having a much larger quota of places to fill, have to take everyone to the left of line B and to the right of line C. This means that, to fill their places, they have to accept children with IQs down to 112. The independent non-HMC schools come next with a threshold IQ of 111, and the technical schools with 106, leaving the non-selective state schools to accept the remaining children at the back of the queue. Table 4.7 shows the proportion of each class which would be selected for the different types of school on these assumptions. It shows a marked class differential in access to the HMC schools, a somewhat less marked one in the case of the Direct Grant schools, and very little class differential in technical schools. It also shows that a negligible proportion of working-class children would go to the public and Direct Grant schools, but over 10 per cent would go to grammar schools.

It emerges, therefore, that on the assumptions of our model, a strictly meritocratic selection procedure could lead to a pattern of class chances not unlike that observed in the real world. The various educational institutions may, therefore, be employing selection procedures which are (in their different ways) all equally meritocratic (or unmeritocratic). The crucial question, however, is whether the model mirrors the real world. Can it be used to account for the *actual* pattern of access to the different types of school? As we saw in Chapter 2, selection on the basis of competitive examination has been an important feature of admission to all but the secondary modern, elementary, and comprehensive schools throughout our period. Even the 'public' schools have employed an ostensibly meritocratic examination (the Common Entrance) as the major means

Table 4.7

Predictions of the Meritocratic Model
and Comparisons with the Real World[1]

(percentages)

Father's Class	Average[2] IQ	Non-Selective	Technical	Non-HMC	Grammar	Direct Grant	HMC
I, II	109	42.1/28.1	14.1/10.2	3.4/8.8	29.4/35.1	3.9/6.2	7.1/11.8
III, IV, V	102	61.8/60.4	12.5/12.9	2.8/3.3	18.7/19.6	1.7/1.8	2.5/2.1
VI, VII, VIII	98	72.1/76.3	10.6/11.4	2.1/0.5	13.0/11.1	1.0/0.5	1.2/0.3
IQ Threshold[3]	—		106	111	112	126	129

[1] Percentages to the right of the diagonal lines are the corresponding 'real world' figures from Table 4.4.
[2] Standard deviation = 14.
[3] For explanation, see text.

of selection. True, intelligence tests themselves have never been the sole basis of selection even within the state system, but they have undoubtedly been a major element in the post-war period, and it is likely that the other tests used correlate quite highly with the results of IQ tests. Our assumption that schools select on the basis of measured intelligence is therefore one which accords reasonably well with the actual procedures used. In addition, intelligence has been commonly used as a yardstick by which to judge how closely selection approached meritocracy. Our model therefore provides a standard against which to judge how far the British educational system has realized its own professed ideals.[9]

Among the contentious assumptions involved here is that relating to the academic hierarchy. Within the state sector of education, there can be little doubt that grammar schools stood above technical schools in prestige, and the latter above secondary moderns, and it is also clear that something closely approximating to the 'creaming' procedure assumed by our model has operated in the state system.[10] The place of the private schools is more doubtful. The Direct Grant schools recruited a proportion of their pupils by 'creaming' from the state system, and it is therefore more realistic to place them above rather than below the grammar schools. In terms of prestige, too, it is probably reasonable to place the HMC schools at the head of the hierarchy. On the other hand, it is clear that they do not cream off all the ablest pupils in the age group. One possibility would be to exclude them from the model altogether, and it is a straightforward, if tedious, task for the reader to make the appropriate recalculations if he wishes. However, by including the HMC schools in the model we can make an estimate of the *maximum* possible extent to which the class differentials in access to these schools can be accounted for by the principle of meritocracy. Putting them at the top of the hierarchy will maximize the correspondence between the predictions of the model and the observed events of the real world. The discrepancies between predictions and observations consequently give a minimum estimate of the extent to which non-meritocratic factors must be included to account for the observed class differentials.[11] Finally, we have placed the non-HMC schools below the grammar but above the technical schools because we suspect them to be most often used by parents who wish their children to have a 'grammar' education but who cannot secure places for them at one of the more prestigious institutions. We shall present some evidence on the examination success rates of these schools in Chapter 7 which is consistent with this assumption. Again, we should note that moving the non-HMC schools up or down the hierarchy will change the predictions of our model, and it is easy for the reader to make the appropriate adjustments.

Turning, then, to the discrepancies between the predictions of the model and the real world, Table 4.7 shows that all three categories of private school and the grammar schools in fact take more service-class pupils than the model predicts, while technical schools and non-selective schools accept less. Meritocratic selection is modified by class bias. Working-class pupils are conversely distributed, while the proportions of intermediate-class pupils accepted are very close to those predicted, though still with some class bias. This pattern is not in itself surprising. If some institutions take more service-class pupils than predicted, others must take fewer. On the other hand, we might not have guessed that there would be a 'shortfall' of service-class pupils in the technical as well as in the non-selective schools, but we should not jump to the premature conclusion that the technical schools are therefore less biased towards the service class than are, say, the grammar schools.

The best method of estimating departure from meritocracy is to calculate the degree to which the lines A, B, C, D, and E have to be tilted away from the vertical in Figure 4.1 in order to secure complete agreement between the model and the real world. This is done in Figure 4.2. These lines thus become very like

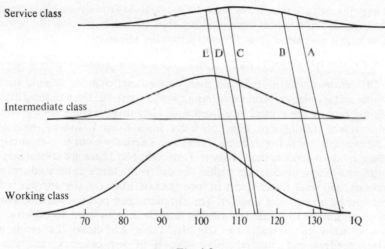

Fig. 4.2.

the economist's indifference curves. They show, for example, that grammar schools are indifferent between, say, a service-class boy of average intelligence and a working-class boy of higher intelligence. It can again be seen that, if the different educational institutions follow equally discriminatory procedures as indicated by identical slopes to the lines A, B, C, D, and E, the same general pattern as before will be generated, with the most unequal class chances occurring in the case of access to the HMC schools and a much more even one with technical schools. In other words, if the technical schools have a more representative intake, it could be purely because they come last in the queue, not because their allocation procedures are any fairer. They have so few service-class children simply because most of them have already gone to higher prestige institutions.

Consider, therefore, the HMC schools. In the real world they gave places to 11.8 per cent of the service-class respondents in the sample. If they were selecting only the ablest service-class boys, they could have secured this result by taking all those respondents from the service class who had IQs of 126 or more (compared with the threshold of 129 predicted by the meritocratic model). Conversely, they gave places to only 0.3 per cent of working-class boys in the real world, and to secure this result they would have had to raise the working-class threshold to 137, giving an overall service-class/working-class handicap of 11 IQ points. As we move down the academic hierarchy we find that the handicap is 10 points for the Direct Grant schools, 7 points for the grammar schools, 9 points for the non-HMC schools, and 7 points for the technical schools. The state-selective schools thus emerge as equally unmeritocratic, although they are at the same time substantially more meritocratic than any of the types of private school. Among the three types of private school we see that the higher their assumed prestige the more unmeritocratic they are, although we should remember that this result is particularly sensitive to the order in which we arrange the institutions. If we were to move an institution *up* the hierarchy, we would *reduce* the service-class/working-class IQ handicap, and the converse would be true if we moved an institution down the hierarchy.

WITHIN-CLASS DIFFERENCES

From differences between classes in their educational chances we now turn to differences *within* classes. Again we find a familiar pattern. Despite the different educational fate of the typical boy from each class there is still a wide scatter in the educational destinations even of boys from Class I. Indeed, to take a dramatic example, more respondents from Class I actually went to elementary or secondary modern schools than went to HMC schools. There are several ways of measuring the extent of variation within the different classes in their educational destinations, and since the choice is to some extent arbitrary, our answers will to some extent be a statistical artefact. The simplest, and perhaps most defensible procedure is simply to divide the sample into those who went to selective and those who went to non-selective schools. Table 4.8 shows the result with secondary modern and comprehensive schools in one category, and private, grammar, and technical schools in the other.

It can be seen that, with this classification, maximum concentration occurs at the two extremes of the class structure and maximum scatter among the intermediate classes III and IV. Thus 77 per cent of Class I go to selective schools, while 77 per cent of Class VIII go to non-selective schools. In contrast with this homogeneity at the extremes, the respondents from Class III divided 55:45 between non-selective and selective schools. Intermediate-class children fan out into a variety of educational destinations, from which we may suspect that they will fan out still further to a variety of occupational destinations ranging widely across the class structure. The picture is even more striking in the case of Class V. Their educational destinations almost exactly mirror the educational structure of the system as a whole (although with some under-representation in the private sector). It is as though boys from Class V are randomly shuffled across the educational spectrum. Thus, while it is true that Class V as a whole enjoys advantages compared with the working classes, the individual in Class V can hardly be said to be participating in a system which gives him unfair advantages. He would be no worse off with a system that allocated places on the basis of chance alone.

Table 4.8 also shows the distributions for a more elaborate division into non-selective, state-selective, and private schools. Again this seems a reasonable

Table 4.8

Attendance at Private, State-Selective, and Non-Selective Schools
(percentages)

	Father's Class								
	I	II	III	IV	V	VI	VII	VIII	All
Private (HMC, Direct Grant, and Non-HMC)	35.6	15.6	7.2	11.2	3.1	1.5	0.9	1.5	6.5
Grammar and Technical	41.0	50.5	38.4	30.9	30.2	23.1	22.0	21.1	28.6
Non-selective	23.4	33.9	54.3	57.8	66.7	75.5	77.1	77.4	65.0
	100.0	100.0	99.9	99.9	100.0	100.1	100.0	100.0	100.1
(N =)	(591)	(481)	(609)	(907)	(953)	(2220)	(1909)	(341)	(8011)

Combined Private + Grammar/Technical (bracketed): I = 76.6, II = 66.1, III = 45.6, IV = 42.1, V = 33.3, VI = 24.6, VII = 22.9, VIII = 22.6, All = 35.1

division since these three types of school did offer substantially different educational experiences. But now the class with the greatest heterogeneity (as measured by the variance, non-selective schooling receiving a score of 1, state-selective a score of 2, and private a score of 3) becomes not Class III but Class I. In other words, on this view respondents from the highest class are most dissimilar in their educational destinations. And indeed the dissimilarity of their destinations becomes very close to the maximum possible. The maximum would occur when one-third of the class went to each of the three destinations.[12] In fact, 23 per cent went to non-selective, 41 per cent to state-selective, and 36 per cent to private schools.

It might be objected at this point that there is a substantial arbitrary element in our calculation. While the division between these three types of schooling may be sensible enough, it is not self-evident that the 1, 2, 3 system of scoring is satisfactory. We might reasonably claim that the educational experiences offered by grammar schools is much closer to that of the independent schools than to that of secondary moderns. But if we try a somewhat different scoring system, for example scoring 1 for secondary moderns, 2 for technical, 3 for grammar, and 4 for independent, we again get a similar result. The class with the highest variance is still Class I. Of course, this is in no way to gain-say the fact that members of Class I as a whole have substantially better educational opportunities than members of other classes, but it does highlight the point that to an *individual* in Class I the nature of his secondary education is a matter of very considerable doubt.

TRENDS IN CLASS MERITOCRACY AND SECONDARY SCHOOLING

So far we have been making generalizations about the experience of the whole sample of men in England and Wales in 1972. The question arises, however, of whether there are trends in class experience of educational opportunity over time. And here we can look particularly for the effects of the 1944 Act. One of the main objectives of the Act was, by making secondary education free, to enable selection to take place on more meritocratic grounds. In terms of our earlier discussion, this means that the lines C and E in Figure 4.2 should be tilted much less away from the vertical in the post-war period in order to align the model with the real world: the service-class/working-class IQ handicaps should become smaller. Conceivably we might also expect to find that class chances of entry to the independent schools would become even *less* equal, as the service-class parents of less able children, who would previously have bought places for their children at grammar schools now had to buy places for them in private schools.

As a first view of what actually happened, Table 4.9 shows the changing class chances of access to selective schools (defined to include the technical and grammar schools of the state sector as well as all schools in the private sector). The picture has an unexpected feature. Chances of admission to selective schools generally increased at all levels of the class structure in the case of the 1923–32 and 1933–42 cohorts, but then actually fell back again in the case of the 1943–52 cohort to levels very like those, in most cases, of a generation earlier. For example, the likelihood of a service-class child receiving a selective education in

Table 4.9

Attendance at Selective Schools by Birth Cohort
(percentages)

Father's Class	Birth Cohort				
	1913–22	1923–32	1933–42	1943–52	All
I, II	69.7 *124**	76.7 *108*	79.3 *107*	66.4 *112*	71.9 *111*
III, IV, V	34.9 *55*	44.0 *52*	43.3 *47*	37.1 *54*	39.6 *51*
VI, VII, VIII	20.2 *0*	26.1 *0*	27.1 *0*	21.6 *0*	23.7 *0*
All	29.6	37.0	38.8	34.8	35.0
(N =)	(1873)	(1897)	(1890)	(2351)	(8011)

*Figures in italic give log distances (see Chapter 3, p.37).

the mid-fifties and 'sixties was no higher than it had been for his parents' generation thirty years earlier. Moreover, the log distance measures display a similar pattern. The service-class/working-class distance fell in the first two cohorts from 124 to 108. It remained constant at 107 in the third cohort, but then widened in the final cohort to 112.

These results are so surprising, and so depressing from the point of view of the educational reformer, that we must examine them in some detail. First it is fairly clear that many of the observed changes can be accounted for in terms of the changes in origins and numbers of children and the development of schools which we found in Chapter 2. Throughout our period there has been a fairly steady increase in the supply of places at selective schools. Thus 555 members of our oldest cohort received places at selective schools, and this figure increased successively to 702, 734, and 818 for the youngest cohort. At the same time, however, two changes of considerable importance were taking place on the demand side. First, the relative size of the service and intermediate classes was increasing, the percentage of our sample that had these class origins being successively 40.6, 40.6, 44.0, and 50.1 in the four cohorts. In addition, and perhaps more important, the birth-rate increased sharply in the late 1940s, and the number of respondents in each of our cohorts was thus successively 1873, 1897, 1890, and 2351. These three changes in the conditions of supply and demand for school places are such that together they could have generated the observed trends in class chances. The expansion of selective school places relative to both the middle classes and the population as a whole in the 1923–32 cohort enabled higher proportions of all classes to attend; in terms of our Figure 4.1 this meant that the line E moved to the left, leading to more equal class chances. In the following (1933–42) cohort the expansion of places was roughly matched by the relative expansion of the middle classes, so that class chances relative to each other remained much as they were before. And in the final cohort (1943–52)

64   *Origins and Destinations*

the expansion of places was much less than that of the school population, and so differential class chances increased once more.

More rigorously, we can compare the actual trends with those predicted by the 'meritocratic' model under these changing supply and demand conditions. We assume that the average measured intelligence, and the standard deviation, were the same as in the earlier model and that they do not change over time, that the sizes of the classes, and the number of places at selective schools changed in the way that they actually did, and that meritocratic selection procedures remained in force throughout the period.

Table 4.10

Attendance at Selective Schools:
Predictions of the Meritocratic Model over Time
and Comparisons with the real world[1]
(percentages)

| Father's Class | Birth Cohort | | | | |
	1913–22	1923–32	1933–42	1943–52	All
I, II	52.8/69.7	60.4/76.7	62.0/79.3	55.3/66.4	57.9/71.9
III, IV, V	33.5/34.9	40.7/44.0	42.3/43.3	35.8/37.1	38.2/39.6
VI, VII, VIII	23.8/20.2	30.1/26.1	31.6/27.1	25.8/21.6	27.9/23.7
IQ threshold[2]	108	105	105	107	106

[1]   Percentages to the right of the diagonal lines are the corresponding 'real world' figures from Table 4.9.
[2]   For explanation, see text.

The model (Table 4.10) gives results which, compared with the real world (Table 4.9), are similar. The model predicts, as in the real world, that class chances increase at all levels in the 1923–32 cohort and become more equal, that there is a further very slight improvement with the 1933–42 cohort, and a fall-back with the 1943–52 cohort to the levels of the earliest one. There are only two differences of any note between the real world and the model. First, as with our earlier application of the model, Classes I and II consistently get more places than the model predicts, and Classes VI, VII, and VIII consistently get less. Meritocracy, as we remarked earlier, is modified by class bias. But second, in the real world Classes I and II secured *fewer* selective places in the 1943–52 cohort than they did in the earliest cohort, whereas our model predicts the reverse. This suggests that selection procedures may actually have become more meritocratic in the youngest cohort. An alternative view, however, and one which we think more plausible, is that the average IQ of the service class fell. Over the period of the four cohorts respondents from the service class expanded from 10 per cent of the sample to 18 per cent, and it is highly unlikely that the average measured IQ of respondents from the expanded service class would have been as high as that of respondents from the original service class. The point is simply that the average IQ of the cleverest 18 per cent of the population is bound to be lower than that of the cleverest 10 per cent. We do not for one moment suggest that there is anything like a perfect correlation between social class and measured intelligence, but to the extent that there is a correlation we would expect a similar phenomenon to occur.

Our view that there was little real change in the degree of meritocracy is confirmed if we compute the IQ handicaps. In the 1913–22 cohort the service-class/working-class handicap was 7 IQ points. In subsequent cohorts it was 8, 9, and finally 6 IQ points. The drop in the final cohort is quite dramatic, but as Table 2.2 indicates, it was precisely in this cohort that most of the expansion in the service class took place. In contrast the size of the intermediate class remained fairly constant throughout our period, while the proportionate (but not absolute) change in the size of the working class is not large. We would not, therefore, expect the relative mean IQs of these classes to change by very much, and it is interesting to find that the intermediate/working-class IQ handicap remains relatively constant too. In the earliest cohort it was 2.5 points, and it was subsequently 2.9, 2.1, and 2.4 points. There was no movement towards meritocracy here. We illustrate a method of checking this argument in Chapter 5 (p.79). Unfortunately, the data that we make use of there are not amenable to similar treatment here. But it is clear that a decline in the IQ handicap of the magnitude we have noted in the case of the youngest cohort could be accounted for by demographic changes.

So far, then, it appears to be the case that the observed changes in class chances could be explained purely in terms of class structure and fertility, and that there are few grounds for supposing that the selecting procedures became any more meritocratic in the post-war period. There are, however, two possible objections to this claim which must be met. First, it could be that by combining both state and private selective schooling we have obscured two trends working in opposite directions, the state schools becoming more meritocratic but the independent schools less so. In fact this cannot have been the case. When the private and the state sectors are analysed separately in the same way as we have shown for selective schools, it turns out that the patterns follow a similar sequence. There was, in both the state selective and the private schools, a modest trend towards equalization of class chances throughout the first three cohorts, followed by a reversal among our post-war cohort.

A second objection is that we have ignored comprehensive schools and that, if these were included or taken into account, the decline in educational chances for all social classes in the 1943–52 cohort would be less dramatic. In fact comprehensive schools made an impact on the youngest cohort only. If we were to regard all places at comprehensive schools as offering an educational experience of similar standing to that offered in technical and grammar schools, 'class chances' would certainly be increased at all levels. But the proportion even of our youngest cohorts attending comprehensive schools is so small that the effective change is really very little. With this new and extremely generous definition of selective schools 70 per cent of children from the service class in the 1943–52 cohort, instead of 66 per cent with the earlier definition, attended selective schools, and 27 per cent in place of the previous 22 per cent from the working class. This does mean that on the new figures class chances became more equal rather than less equal in the youngest cohort, but this is exactly what we would expect to find if a representative cross-section of the population attends comprehensive schools. It does not, of course, require us to assume that selection procedures for the grammar and technical schools were in any way changed.

Granted, then, that our 'supply and demand' explanation for the observed trends is sound, how do we reconcile our results with the picture customarily portrayed, namely that there has been some continuing, albeit slow, decline in class differentials? And how do we account for the failure of the 1944 Act to produce any significant changes in class differentials? Let us consider first the customary view. Little and Westergaard (1964)[13] provide the standard account, and it is, of course, important to remember that the data they had available to them covered a slightly earlier period than ours, taking them as far only as the immediate post-war period. Their data are presented in Table 4.11. It shows a

Table 4.11

Percentage of Pupils from Different Social Origins and Years of Birth Attending Grammar Schools: Little and Westergaard's Results[1]

Father's Occupation	Before 1910	1910–19	1920–29	1930 and After
1. Professional, managerial	37	47	52	62
2. Other nonmanual	7	13	16	20
3. Semi-skilled or unskilled worker	1	4	7	10
All	12	16	18	23

[1] *Source:* A. Little and J. Westergaard, 'Trends of Class Differentials in Educational Opportunity in England and Wales', *British Journal of Sociology*, 15 (1964), 301–15.

steady increase throughout the whole of their period in the proportion of children attending grammar schools, an increase that occurs at all of the three social class levels which they distinguish. It also shows that the *rate* of increase was highest in their Class 3, and hence that there was a decline in class differentials, but that the *absolute* gains were greatest in their Class 1. As Boudon summarizes it,

from the point of view of individuals, the probability of attending grammar school has increased in the period more rapidly – indeed, much more rapidly – for lower-class than for higher-class boys. But from the point of view of social groups, from the beginning to the end of the period, 100 higher-class people have been able to send an additional 25 boys to grammar schools, whereas this additional number is 9 for the lower group.[14]

These results differ from the ones we have presented so far in one main respect. Ours showed a negligible increase in the proportion of each class attending selective schools in the 1933–42 cohort whereas Little and Westergaard's post-1930 cohort showed a substantial increase. (Of course, ours also show a decline in the 1943–52 cohort, but Little and Westergaard's data do not come as far forward as this.) Part of this difference is almost certainly due to the different time spans covered by cohorts, but another important source is that we have included technical schools in our analysis whereas Little and Westergaard omitted them. When we look at grammar and technical schools separately we find importantly different trends occurring. These are shown in Table 4.12. This shows that the proportion of children attending *grammar* schools increased throughout our period, including even the 1943–52 cohort. Even in this latest cohort the supply of grammar-school places managed to keep pace with the growth in total population, although not with the growth in the middle classes. Thus the proportion of children from all three classes attending grammar school increased substantially right up until the 1933–42 cohort, the rate of increase being higher in the working class but the absolute increase being greater in the service class just as in the case of Little and Westergaard's results. Thereafter, in the 1943–52 cohort, the working class managed to protect its gains while the now expanded service class lost some of theirs, but by no means fell back to the position of a generation earlier. As far as grammar-school places go, then, there were for most groups substantial gains throughout the period and a steady narrowing of class differentials. Here, our picture is much more like that given by Little and Westergaard.[15]

When we turn to technical schools, however, the picture is very different. As the White Paper *Educational Reconstruction* had suggested, there was a steady development in the number of children they took in the pre-war period, but contrary to the great expectations of the White Paper there was a sad decline thereafter. Nor is this merely a result of errors in nomenclature and changes in classification. The decline is most marked in the post-war period when no nomenclature had settled down. What this means, then, is that the expansion of the grammar schools in the post-war period was largely at the expense of the technical schools. This is all the more ironic in view of the White Paper's claim during the war years that

too many of the nation's abler children are attracted into [grammar shools] which prepare primarily for the University and for the administrative and clerical professions; too few find their way into [technical] schools from which the design and craftsmanship sides of industry are recruited. If education is to serve the interests both of the child and the nation, some means must be found of correcting this bias.

But the means were not found. Whether or not it was for the best interests of the children and the nation, what seems to have happened is that local authorities, perhaps as the result of political pressures from parents, expanded the prestigious grammar schools, and allowed the technical schools to wither. The result was an increase in equality of opportunity which was more apparent than real. What the working class gained through the expansion of the grammar schools they very largely lost through the decline of the technical schools. Thus over the period of our study 100 working-class families sent an extra eight boys to grammar school, but they also sent eight fewer to technical schools.

We return, therefore, to a crucial question. Given that the 1944 Act and its associated reforms attempted to make access to technical schools as well as to grammar schools more meritocratic, why does there seem to have been no effective change in class differentials in the post-war period? A number of

Table 4.12

Attendance at Grammar and Technical Schools by Birth Cohort
(percentages)

Father's Class	1913–22		1923–32		1933–42		1943–52	
	Grammar	Technical	Grammar	Technical	Grammar	Technical	Grammar	Technical
I, II	27.0	16.2	32.4	17.1	42.1	7.9	35.9	5.5
III, IV, V	14.9	12.8	17.3	20.3	22.1	13.2	23.0	7.1
VI, VII, VIII	6.2	13.5	8.7	16.3	14.8	10.0	14.6	5.9
All	10.9	13.6	13.9	17.6	20.6	10.7	21.2	6.2

answers to this are possible. One is simply that the selection procedures used post-war involved the same degree of class bias as the pre-war procedures despite their heavier weighting towards financial criteria. Put like this, it merely restates and redescribes our problem, although it is also true that Douglas, and Floud and Halsey[16] show that procedures like the use of teachers' reports produces a class bias additional to that already involved with tests of measured intelligence in much the same way that the use of financial criteria would have done.

However, while teachers' reports and financial criteria may have the same results in class terms, it would be somewhat surprising if exactly the same members of each class were selected for grammar and technical schools under the two kinds of system. Thus we might expect the post-war system to favour less affluent but more educated sections of the middle class. In Bourdieu's terms we would expect an increase in the reproduction of cultural capital, and we shall look at this in Chapter 5.

LEGISLATIVE DECLARATION AND SOCIAL FACT

These are all at best partial explanations of the stubborn persistence of links between class origins and educational destinations and of the absence of any dramatic impact from the Education Act of 1944. We should therefore perhaps end this chapter with the suggestion that after all there was not so very much to explain. Acts of Parliament are as often legislative confirmation of socially accomplished fact as they are innovations in social practice. The 1944 Act seems to be an example. The secondary-school 'revolution' was a slow one, with origins in the nineteenth century and a steady expansion of grammar- and other selective-school opportunities in the state system from at least the 1902 Act. As we saw in Chapter 2, both the number of places in these schools and the proportion of them in relation to the child population, had already grown to a point where able boys of working-class origin were competing for them success-fully in large numbers. The aftermath of 1944 was not so much a further expansion of opportunity. Admittedly, fees were abolished, but service- and intermediate-class competition for *free* places was bound to become more severe and, as we have seen, from increasing numbers of children with relative advantages of home background.

When grammar-school education became free it presumably became more attractive to parents who would otherwise have chosen the private schools. The point can most easily be made with indifference curve analysis,[17] but a simple verbal argument would be this: before the war a proportion of parents must have believed the educational (and social) advantages of the most prestigious private schools to outweigh the financial advantages of a subsidized place at a grammar school. But since the post-war reforms increased the financial advantages by making grammar-school education completely free, and probably did so without affecting their educational standing, this would alter the cost and benefits facing that minority of parents in a position to make a choice (namely the affluent parents of able children) and some of them might thus choose differently. By increasing the subsidy, therefore, the state may have tempted some parents of able children to forsake the private sector of education for the state one, and the extra competition from these children may thus have nullified any gains which the working class would otherwise have obtained from the reforms. The point is an important and paradoxical one for social policy. A service is made free in order to enable the poor to take advantage of it, but this also makes the service more attractive to the rich.

CONCLUSION

The transition from primary to secondary education evolved in our period towards transfer from one stage of education to another on meritocratic principles. Or at least that was the intention even though a private sector remained alongside wide local variations in the terms of competition for the more selective and academic forms of secondary schooling. The 1944 Act put a legislative stamp on forty years of progress towards separate, competitive and free secondary education for all and declared that every child should have an education fashioned according to his or her 'age, aptitude and ability'. We have therefore looked at this important phase in the expansion of educational opportunity from four points of view. First, how was access to secondary schooling affected by the existence of a private sector? Second, what was the effect on the pattern of class chances for secondary education? Third, how homogeneous were classes of origin in their experience of the variety of secondary schools? Fourth, and finally, what was the outcome as measured in terms of meritocratic criteria?

The continuing existence of the private schools, albeit for a small minority, structured class chances and built class bias into the meritocratic development of the state system from the outset. Over one-half of those who started along the private educational road stayed on it. These children had thirty-six times the chance of their state contemporaries of going on to one of the private Headmasters' Conference or 'public schools'. It was not, of course, a caste system of upbringing. A majority of those who entered the highly prestigious Direct Grant schools and a one-third minority even of entrants to HMC schools began in the state primary schools. Nevertheless, despite considerable traffic both ways across the divide between state and private schools, the two systems remained divided fundamentally along lines of social class. This has been and remains the essential function of the private sector; and within it there is further social differentiation between, at the top the famous 'public' schools and, at the bottom, the more obscure proprietary schools outside the HMC.

To arrange the types of school, whether public or private, in a widely acknowledged hierarchy of academic prestige is also to arrange them in the same order of probability of access for boys of different class origins. Three-quarters of working-class boys went to elementary, secondary modern, or comprehensive schools, whereas nearly three-quarters of the sons of the service class went to some kind of selective secondary school. Looking from inside the schools back towards the social origins of their pupils, it appears that two-thirds of the secondary-modern boys were working class, while two-thirds of the 'public school' boys were from the service class.

None the less, while stressing the class character both of the social distribution of opportunity and the social composition of schools, it must also be pointed out, with a paradox more apparent than real, that educational scattering from social origins has been a continuing feature of the English and Welsh secondary schools. We even showed on one view (involving a threefold division of schools into non-selective, state selective, and private) that the class of higher-grade professionals, managers, and proprietors is the one with the greatest educational scatter. Classes, we must always remind ourselves, are not castes.

The main thrust of the chapter, however, is towards assessing whether educational development and its legislative confirmation and completion in 1944 brought the country nearer to meritocracy. Our verdict has to be that it did not. Making the contentious assumptions that measured intelligence indicates meritocracy and is an attribute of individuals independent of their class origins, it still turns out that meritocracy has been modified by class bias throughout the expansion of secondary-school opportunity.

These depressing findings for the potency of liberal-egalitarian policies to change the pattern of class chances in the past leave us recognizing the remarkably powerful explanatory power of the demographic forces which have shaped the supply of children in a period of sustained attempts at class abatement through education.

NOTES

1. The Common Examination for entrance to the Public Schools is set by a Board of Managers consisting of three representatives from the Headmasters' Conference, and three from the Incorporated Association of Preparatory Schools. For details see T. Burgess, *A Guide to English Schools* (Penguin, 1969).

2. See W. Z. Billewicz, 'Some remarks on the measurement of social mobility', *Population Studies* 9 (1955), 96–100.

3. The reason for this is as follows. The formula for the Index of Association is $Nf_{ij}/n_{i.} n_{.j}$. The maximum value of the index must therefore depend on the size of the cell frequency, f_{ij}. This will be n_j when $n_{.j}$ is smaller than $n_{i.}$ and the index accordingly takes the value $N/n_{i.}$. This is the case with the HMC schools – *all* the places at the schools can be taken up by boys from private primary schools. But where $n_{.j}$ is larger than $n_{i.}$ the maximum number in the cell becomes $n_{i.}$ and the maximum value of the index becomes $N/n_{.j}$. (This is the case with the grammar schools – there are so many places at grammar schools that they could not all be filled by boys from private primary schools.)

4. It is a feature of Christopher Jencks's analysis of the effects of family and schooling in America (op. cit. 1972) that within-category differences are always the focus of his attention. This is misleading but we woud not, on the other hand, want to follow his critics in assigning paramount importance to 'between category' differences.

5. In his survey of public schools Kalton, op. cit. (1966), p.28, found that whereas only 6 per cent of boarders at HMC schools were recruited directly from state schools, this was true for as many as 46 per cent of the day boys.

6. For the definition, see above, p.38.

7. A very similar picture of the class differentials in access to the different types of secondary school is given in Table 9 of *15 - 18* (The Crowther Report), Central Advisory Council for Education, Ministry of Education, (HMSO, 1960).

8. Evidence on the relation between social class and measured intelligence is given in J. Floud and A. H. Halsey, 'Intelligence tests, social class and selection for secondary schools', *British Journal of Sociology* 8 (1957), 33, 39, and J. W. B. Douglas, *The Home and the School* (MacGibbon & Kee, 1964). These sources suggest that the measured intelligence of children whose fathers had professional and managerial occupations is considerably higher than that which we have attributed to our respondents from service-class social origins. What we have tried to do is compensate for the fact that our service class is considerably larger than the professional and managerial classes

used by our sources. It is, of course, quite straightforward for the reader to recalculate our predictions using different assumptions. Burt also gives some estimates (C. Burt, 'Class differences in general intelligence: III', *British Journal of Statistical Psychology*, 12 (1959), 15–23) but recent criticisms suggest that little reliance can be placed on this source: see D. D. Dorfman, 'The Cyril Burt question: New Findings', *Science*, 201 (1978), 1177–86.

9. We would wish to stress that we do not necessarily endorse these ideals ourselves. Moreover, we are aware of the controversial character of the assumption that ability can be measured by IQ or other predictive tests independently of the social-class situation in which they are used. The point we wish to make is that 'equality of opportunity for children of equal ability irrespective of their social origins' has been a major goal of the English educational system, particularly in the post-war period. What we are doing is judging how far this goal has been achieved.

10. Peaker in his study of *The Plowden Children Four Years On* gives some evidence on the mean IQ of children at different secondary schools. That of children at Direct Grant and independent Schools (HMC and non-HMC combined) was 1.15 standard deviations above the grand mean. The figure for grammar schools was 1.01 standard deviations, and for technical schools 0.37 above the grand mean, while for comprehensive schools it was 0.03 standard deviations below.

11. A deviation from meritocracy may occur because the candidates presenting themselves for an examination are an unrepresentative sample of the population. We are including this as a 'non-meritocratic factor' in addition to actual biases in the selection procedure itself.

12. An alternative possible notion of maximal dissimilarity would be when the members of a class flow out to polarized destinations, i.e. in this case to independent schools and non-selective state schools. Even this approach would still give the largest dissimilarities to Classes I and II but the level of polarization is low for all classes.

13. A Little and J. Westergaard, 'Trends of Class Differentials in Educational Opportunity in England and Wales', *British Journal of Sociology*, 15 (1964), 301–15.

14. Boudon, op. cit. (1973), p.50.

15. The reader may be worried that, while the *trend* is now the same, the *absolute* figures still differ markedly from those of Little and Westergaard. However, the differences are largely due to the differing classifications of social class used. If we attempt to reclassify our data in broadly the same way as Little and Westergaard, our results become quite closely in line with theirs.

16. J. E. Floud and A. H. Halsey, 'Intelligence Tests, Social Class and Selection for Secondary Schools', *British Journal of Sociology*, 3 (1957), 33–39.

17. See Heath, op. cit., for a discussion of the application of indifference curves to the study of social behaviour.

CHAPTER 5

Reproduction of Cultural Capital?

We have now traced the social history of selection for secondary education in Britain from an early point in the development of a national system of secondary schools. The familiar relationship between social class and secondary schooling has been reconfirmed, admittedly with some modification of the previously received narrative and arithmetic, but most pointedly with little encouragement for the hopes for equality of opportunity which were enshrined in the 1944 Education Act. All the more reason, then, that so stubborn a correlation should be an object of our attempts at explanation, and it is to this task that we give renewed attention in this chapter. Monitoring this correlation has been a preoccupation of the sociology of education, and rightly so because the facility with which the more fortunate social classes turn the advantages of the parental into the opportunities of the filial generation is one of the main ways, if by no means a certain one, in which members of these classes pass on their positions to their children.

Explanation will require us to take up the work of those writers we reviewed in Chapter 1 who have advanced theories about the cultural obstacles to equality of opportunity. We shall concern ourselves particularly in this chapter with the theories of cultural capital of which Bourdieu's is a well-known version.[1] The idea of cultural capital denoted here comes from recent attempts, notably by Bernstein, to analyse the process of cultural transmission. Bernstein is well known for his pioneering work in associating linguistic codes with classes as an element in the explanation of class differences in educational achievement. In his parallel studies Bernstein, like Bourdieu, has proceeded to an analysis of education as an agency of social control and has emphasized its subtlety in modern forms of infant education, which he links to an empirical distinction within the middle class between the traditional bourgeoisie and the new middle class which has been created by the expansion of new professions concerned with personal services.[2] For both writers cultural capital is an increasingly important component of the perpetuation of classes through generations. We shall also refer to another version of the transmission of cultures through families as portrayed in the study by Jackson and Marsden.[3]

It is, of course, part of the liberal tradition of optimism which can be traced from John Stuart Mill and Alfred Marshall, to conceive of modernization as entailing 'investment in man'. Among later writers like Daniel Bell, investment in man is the mark of 'post-industrial society' and has given rise to what Dahrendorf calls 'the education class'. But the concept of capital employed by such writers also distinguishes between material and cultural forms, where the former is marketable and legally alienable while the latter is neither, being transmitted through pedagogical relations (formal or familial) and legally attached to persons only where it takes the form of public credentials. Obviously there is room for argument as to the epistemological usefulness of the distinction: it is, to be sure, an analogy; and no clear and agreed definition of cultural capital is to be found in standard use among the writers we have cited.

However, following Marshall, there has been an identifiable line of economists of education who explain the distribution of education and its outcomes within the framework of a process of economic development in which an essential if not the fundamental element is the accumulation of cultural capital in the sense of technological and administrative organizational skill. Marshall saw this process as a combination of accumulation and democratization of cultural capital in what has been termed the 'educational-embourgeoisement thesis'.[4] A policy of educational expansion (in association with economic policies aimed at high wages, high productivity, and short hours) would make the occupations and culture of the gentleman universal. But Bourdieu, an egalitarian pessimist rather than a liberal optimist, sees the same process as a mechanism not so much for accumulating and equalizing cultural capital as for reproducing social strata through family transmission both directly and through the passing on of skills and 'socially conditioned attitudes' which enable children to profit from or successfully manipulate publicly provided resources such as schools, theatres, information networks, bureaucracies, and the like. As Bernstein has put it, 'historically and now, only a tiny percentage of the population has been socialized into knowledge at the level of the meta-languages of control and innovation, whereas the mass of the population has been socialized into knowledge at the level of context-tied operations.'[5] Unequally divided cultural capital in this sense is seen as the foundation of new classes. It is held to have grown in importance in a modernized society with a growing public sector of the economy and an increasing proportion of resources allocated through political and bureaucratic mechanisms.

Parents then may be thought of as investing in cultural capital for their children's future. However, the question also arises as to whether those *educated* parents who themselves already have cultural capital are disproportionately successful in making this investment as compared with their middle-class or working-class peers. One argument here is that children secure more from their schooling if they already have acquired from their parents the linguistic and cultural competence needed to comprehend what school has to offer. As Bourdieu puts it,

The education system reproduces all the more perfectly the structure of the distribution of cultural capital among classes (and sections of a class) in that the culture which it transmits is closer to the dominant culture and that the mode of inculcation to which it has recourse is less removed from the mode of inculcation practised by the family . . . An educational system which puts into practice an implicit pedagogic action, requiring initial familiarity with the dominant culture, and which proceeds by imperceptible familiarization, offers information and training which can be received and acquired only by subjects endowed with the system of predispositions that is the condition for the success of the transmission and of the inculcation of the culture.[6]

Thus where Alfred Marshall forecast both a burgeoning economy of affluence and reduced inequality, as well as an increasingly democratic 'national heritage and culture', through educational embourgeoisement, Bourdieu and Bernstein see the same underlying transformation of the division of labour as leading to more subtle forms of social control and class inequality through the passing on of cultural capital.

CULTURAL CAPITAL AND EDUCATION CLASSES

To test Bourdieu's argument on cultural capital we must assume that parents who have passed through the academic institutions of grammar school, public school, or university will have a greater understanding of the educational system and its culture and will be better equipped to help their children cope with the demands of that system. Their children will be more likely to acquire 'that system of predispositions' necessary for success in the competitive selection tests that have been prevalent in the English educational system throughout our period. We would therefore expect the children of these 'educated' parents to have substantial advantages in the competition for selective school places. In addition, as we suggested in Chapter 4, we might expect the reforms of the 1944 Act to have shifted the balance of power further towards those with cultural capital, and away from those with financial capital only. We shall test these two expectations in this chapter; but the most rigorous test of Bourdieu's theory we must postpone to Chapter 8. There we shall consider whether children from educated backgrounds profit more from school in the form of examination successes than do those from less educated backgrounds. Bourdieu could reasonably argue that it is not mere *attendance* at a selective school which is important, but the acquisition of those academic credentials which our educational system offers to all but dispenses unequally. In the meantime, however, the question of attendance at selective schools is not uninteresting, and the results are given in Table 5.1.

Table 5.1 in effect takes the outflow form of a conventional mobility table with parents and sons categorized as members of 'education classes'. Looked at in this way, it appears that the diagonal cells are dominant, i.e. there is considerable self-recruitment between generations of the education classes. Sons tend to follow the secondary-school example of their parents. It should be noticed, however, that the highest degree of self-recruitment is in the lowest education class (72 per cent). This feature parallels the findings of Goldthorpe and Llewellyn[7] with respect to intergenerational mobility among occupational classes. They have emphasized, by contrast with the findings of the earlier LSE (1949) study, that it is the working class and not the service class that tends towards closure or integenerational continuity. In fact a parallel change in the structure of opportunities occurred in education as in the occupational sphere, giving increased opportunities 'at the top' for sons compared with fathers. Goldthorpe and Llewellyn demonstrate this in their occupational mobility analysis. Table 5.1 does the same in the case of the education classes: the off-diagonal cells are not empty, those to the left and below the diagonal representing upward mobility, while downward mobility is represented by those to the right and above.

The extent of upward and downward mobility is best seen through the bracketed figures in Table 5.1 which are percentages of the total sample. As much as one-fifth of our respondents came from 'uneducated' parents and went

Table 5.1

Parents' and Respondents' Secondary Schooling

Parental Schooling	Private schools	State Selective	Non-selective	All
One or both parents attended private secondary schools[1] (N = 383)	47.7 (2.2)*	31.1 (1.4)	21.1 (0.9)	99.9 (4.5)
One or both attended state selective schools (N = 1204)	11.7 (1.7)	44.7 (6.3)	43.6 (6.2)	100.0 (14.2)
Both parents attended non-selective schools (N = 6923)	3.1 (2.5)	25.2 (20.5)	71.7 (58.3)	100.0 (81.3)
All (N = 8510)	(6.4)	(28.2)	(65.4)	(100.0)

[1] Where one parent attended a private secondary school and the other attended a state selective school, the parental schooling has been coded as private.

* Figures in brackets give the cell or marginal frequency as a percentage of the total.

to state selective schools. These figures also show more generally that over two-thirds were intergenerationally stable (the diagonal cells) between education classes, nearly a quarter were upwardly mobile (lower left cells) and only 8 per cent were downwardly mobile. Educational expansion in our period therefore produced marked net upward mobility, the bulk of it being short-range from the 'uneducated home' to the state selective school class. This is largely a consequence of the shapes of the distributions and of their rate of change. The private sector is so small that even if all its members were recruited from the intermediate educational class only 45 per cent of the members of that class would be upwardly mobile. And since there is in any event a high degree of self-recruitment in the private sector, it is not surprising that only 12 per cent of the intermediate educational class were upwardly mobile. In contrast, 28 per cent of the lowest educational class were upwardly mobile, the great majority of these 'mobile' individuals moving into the grammar and technical schools. These respondents can be regarded as 'first generation' grammar-school boys and technical-school boys, and Table 5.2 shows that they constituted a huge majority

Table 5.2

'First Generation' Pupils at Selective Schools[1]
(percentages)

Technical	80.0
Grammar	67.5
Direct Grant	47.4
Independent non-HMC	47.6
Independent HMC	27.1

[1] 'First generation' pupils are defined as pupils at selective schools both of whose parents had attended only non-selective schools.

of those at grammar and technical schools. Eighty per cent of those at technical schools came from what may crudely be termed 'uneducated' backgrounds, and two-thirds of those at grammar schools. This is a striking result. It means that the state selective schools (much more than the private schools) were doing far more than merely 'reproducing' cultural capital; they were creating it, too. They were bringing an academic or technical training to a very substantial number of boys from homes that were not in any formal sense educated. They were not the preserve of an educated middle class in the same way, and to the extent that the independent HMC schools were, and accordingly they were not merely maintaining a 'cycle of privilege' in which cultural capital is acquired by those from educated homes. They were at least offering an opportunity to acquire cultural capital to those homes which had not secured it in the past. True, as we have already noted, mere *attendance* at a grammar or technical school does not ensure the acquisition of educational skills and credentials. The question of whether cultural capital in the family determines success within selective schools remains an open one. For the moment, however, it is clear that at least *formal*, if not *effective*, opportunity is offered to many boys from 'unschooled' backgrounds.

We should also note that the extent of net upward mobility is not a product only of the shape, and rate of change of this 'educational class structure'. The expansion of the state selective schools does indeed mean that some net upward mobility was inevitable but this alone would not necessarily have generated the observed pattern. Following Boudon, we can compare the actual pattern of mobility with the one that would have occurred, if all places had been allocated on a strictly hierarchical basis. By a strictly hierarchical allocation we mean that all boys from privately educated backgrounds are allocated to private schools themselves and the remaining surplus of places (due to expansion, differential fertility, and so on) are then given to boys from intermediate backgrounds (that is, from homes in which one or both parents was educated at a state selective school), all the remaining boys from intermediate backgrounds are then allocated to state selective schools, the remaining surplus of places being finally given to boys from the lowest educational class. Table 5.3 gives the results, and it shows

Table 5.3

The Hierarchical Model[1]
(percentages)

Parental Education	Respondent's Education			
	Private	State Selective	Non-Selective	
Private	100.0	0	0	100
State Selective	13.0	87.0	0	100
Non-Selective	0	19.5	80.5	100

[1]   For explanation, see text.

that the expansion of the selective schools in this hierarchical model would necessarily have led to upward mobility for 19.5 per cent of the members of the lowest educational class. This contrasts with the actual figure of 28 per cent, one that is considerably nearer to the 34.5 per cent that would be expected on the basis of random allocation than to the figure from the hierarchical model. Clearly then, something was going on in addition to the growth of the 'education' classes and their tendency to reproduce themselves. The proneness towards self-recruitment within each class is consistent with substantial mobility both upwards and downwards, the actual movement being considerably in excess of that forced by changes in the educational structure.

TRENDS TOWARDS MERITOCRATIC SECONDARY EDUCATION?

Is this unforced surplus of educational mobility a reflection of a trend towards meritocratic selection for secondary education? We shall pursue this question with the aid of cohort analysis, emphasizing first the parallels and departures of our findings on educational mobility compared with those in Chapter 4 on class chances. The pattern of outflow in successive cohorts to selective secondary schooling is shown in Table 5.4. As in the social-class pattern of secondary schooling, there is both self-recruitment and mobility. But there is also a crucial difference. The pattern of the log distances is quite different from the ones we

Table 5.4

Attendance at Selective Schools by Birth Cohort and Parental Schooling

Parental Schooling	Birth Cohort				All
	1913–22	1923–32	1933–42	1943–52	
One or both at private secondary schools	71.6 *101**	82.4 *98*	89.2 *101*	75.7 *108*	78.8 *102*
One or both at state selective schools	58.0 *80*	71.6 *84*	57.7 *57*	49.4 *65*	56.4 *69*
Both at non-selective schools	26.1 *0*	30.8 *0*	32.5 *0*	25.8 *0*	28.3 *0*
All	29.6	37.0	38.8	34.8	34.6

* The figures in italic give the log distances (see Chapter 3, p.37).

saw in Chapter 4. First of all, the distances between the 'highest' (private parental education) class and the 'lowest' (non-selective parental education) show no significant narrowing throughout the whole period. Indeed, there is a slight widening at the end of the period. On the other hand, there is a marked drop in the post-war period in the distance between the 'middle' (state selective parental education) and the 'lowest' education class. Here at last we have found an interesting, and sustained, drop in differentials. It is a drop, too, that we had not predicted. Our earlier remarks in Chapter 4 had suggested that the 1944 Act might rather have *increased* the differential by making it easier for educated but less affluent parents to secure a selective education for their offspring. However, we now see that the 1944 Act did not make it easier for educated parents to get their children into selective schools. On the contrary, the advantage which these parents had over those with no selective schooling actually declined.

Following the line of argument which we used in Chapter 4, two possible explanations for this drop immediately suggest themselves. First, as we showed in Chapter 4, an expansion of selective school places relative to both the service class and the population as a whole would enable higher proportions of all classes to attend; in terms of our Figure 4.1 this meant that the line E moved to the left, leading to more equal class chances. The same argument could apply in the case of our 'education classes'. Alternatively, if selection procedures became more meritocratic, this would also lead to a decline in differentials. In terms of Figure 4.1 again, this would mean that the lines come closer to the vertical. We can test these rival explanations as we did in Chapter 4 by seeing what pattern of differentials our meritocratic model predicts over time, starting from the following assumptions:

(i) the number of vacancies at selective schools, and the number of children from the different 'education classes', that is, supply and demand, changed in the way they actually did;

(ii) procedures remained throughout perfectly meritocratic, with selective schools as a group having first choice of pupils, and choosing solely on the basis of measured intelligence.

(iii)   the average IQ of the different 'education classes' remained fixed over time.

From our social-class analysis in Chapter 4 we have IQ assumptions and we know the social-class composition of the education classes. Hence, if we assume that the child's IQ is determined solely by social class and not by parents' education, we can immediately calculate a new set of IQ assumptions. These are that children whose parents attended private secondary schools will have an average IQ of 106, those whose parents attended state selective secondary schools will average 103, and those whose parents attended non-selective schools will average 100. In fact parents' education almost certainly does affect children's IQ somewhat, and the effect of this would be to spread out the IQs rather more. For the analysis we have in mind, however, this problem does not embarrass us since we are concerned with trends, not with judging how meritocratic or unmeritocratic the selection system was.[8]

Table 5.5

Attendance at Selective Schools:
Predictions of the Meritocratic Model over Time
(percentages)

Parental Schooling	Birth Cohort			
	1913–22	1923–32	1933–42	1943–52
One or both parents attended private secondary schools	44.3 *44*	52.2 *39*	53.7 *38*	48.3 *41*
One or both parents attended state selective schools	36.0 *24*	43.8 *21*	45.2 *21*	39.9 *22*
Both parents attended non-selective schools	28.4 *0*	35.5 *0*	36.8 *0*	31.9 *0*

*   Figures in italic give the log distances (see Chapter 3, p.37).

Table 5.5 gives the predictions of the meritocratic model for these different education classes over time. The predicted pattern is the same as the one generated in the equivalent social-class analysis in the previous chapter: a substantial rise in attendance at selective schools is predicted at all levels in the 1923–32 cohort; there is a further slight increase predicted in the 1933–42 cohort, and then a fall-back in the final cohort. The log distances, on the other hand, are predicted to remain fairly stable, with a very slight equalisation in the middle two cohorts. This pattern approximates that of the real world with respect to increased attendance at all levels in the 1923–32 cohort, and a general fall-back in the 1943–52 cohort. But the narrowing in the post-war period in the distance between the 'middle' (selective parental education) and the 'lowest' (non-selective parental education) class is certainly not predicted. Supply and demand factors, therefore, do not seem able to explain the narrowing of the differential. Does this mean, then, that selection actually did become more meritocratic? It could plausibly be argued that, before the war, educated parents could choose to pay the fees needed to secure a place at a grammar school, whereas after the war this option was not open to them. Our earlier guess about the trends in differentials was mistaken, therefore, because we had not realized that most educated parents were in fact able to pay the fees. After the war, however, parental choice was reduced, and those who valued education for their children were less able to secure it if their children did not have the requisite ability. This would manifest itself as a trend toward meritocracy.

Further support for this argument may be found by calculating the IQ handicaps (for entry to selective secondary schools) between our 'middle' and 'lowest' education classes. These were (on our assumptions about IQ) 9 IQ points in the 1913–22 cohort, rising to 12 points in the next cohort, and then falling to 6 points in the final two cohorts. Against this, however, the relative sizes of the education classes were changing, and hence our assumption (iii), of constant IQ, must be unsound. In the first cohort only 6 per cent of our respondents had selectively educated parents, while a further 4 per cent had privately educated parents. In the final cohort these figures had increased to 25 per cent and 6 per cent respectively. It is clear that the average IQ of our 'middle' education class will be considerably closer to that of the 'lowest' in the final cohort, and we need a change of only 3 IQ points to wipe out the hypothesized movement towards meritocracy. Clearly, when we know the answer we seek, it is easy to make the appropriate assumptions. To keep a check on our imagination, however, we can compare the mean IQ of different-sized occupational classes, using data from Floud, Halsey, and Martin's study of South-West Hertfordshire in 1952.[9] Their top occupational group comprises 7.4 per cent of their sample. Let us equate this with our 'top' education class. Their next occupational group contains 7.9 per cent, the third 18.5 per cent. If we equate the second group with our 'middle' education class in the earliest cohort, and the second and third combined with the 'middle' education class in the most recent cohort, we find that the mean IQ falls by 3.8 IQ points. There will also, of course, have been a fall in the mean IQ of the remaining categories (Floud's third, fourth, and fifth occupational groups being equated with our 'lowest' education class in the first cohort, and the fourth and fifth class in the case of the most recent cohort). The drop here works out at exactly 1 IQ point, the gap between the two lower education classes thus closing by 2.8 IQ points. This method of calculation is necessarily somewhat rough and ready, but it does suggest very strongly that the most firmly grounded conclusion is that there was no movement towards meritocracy. The onus must be on those who claim a movement to demonstrate it. It would therefore appear that there is no need to postulate a trend towards meritocracy in order to account for the observed changes in differentials. The 'supply and demand' explanation was not sufficient on its own, but once we recognise that as the 'middle' education class expanded, the average IQ of its members must necessarily have dropped, we can provide a parsimonious explanation. As it has expanded, the 'middle' education class has become less 'select' in its composition, and its ability to win places at selective secondary schools has thus declined relative to the 'lowest' education class.

The expansion of selective schooling among the parental generation has had another consequence for the schools. If we again define a 'first generation' grammar- or technical-school boy as one whose parents *both* went to non-selective schools, it follows (other things being equal) that as the number of parents with selective schooling increases, the number of first-generation school-boys will decrease. Thus, while for the sample as a whole, as we saw earlier, the grammar and technical schools were not merely 'reproducing cultural capital', they would have been doing so to a much greater extent by the end of our period. Table 5.6 shows that there was indeed a considerable decline in the number of 'first generation' boys in the selective schools over the course of our period. The fall, however, was largest in the case of the private and Direct Grant schools, where the proportion halved. It was smallest in the case of the technical schools; even in our most recent cohort over one half of our respondents at these schools (and at the grammar schools) were still 'first generation' pupils. Recruits to the post-war state selective schools were still, more often than not, new to their academic tradition.

Table 5.6

'First Generation' Pupils at Selective Schools by Birth Cohort
(percentages)

Respondent's Secondary Schooling	Year of birth			
	1913–22	1923–32	1933–42	1943–52
Technical	86.1	78.6	75.9	63.6
Grammar	80.2	67.1	69.9	54.5
Direct Grant	66.7	55.2	39.3	31.7
Independent non-HMC	54.8	53.1	51.2	27.8
Independent HMC	36.0	27.6	22.9	15.8
All selective	78.1	69.2	65.1	49.9

CLASS, CULTURE, AND ACCESS TO SECONDARY EDUCATION

So far we have made two separate analyses of educational chances: one for those from different social-class backgrounds, and another for those from different 'cultural' backgrounds. But by putting the two together a number of important further questions can be tackled. First, we saw in the case of private primary education that the 'effect' of parental education was much greater in the service than in the working class, and we argued that this was largely a result of less stringent financial constraints. Privately educated parents in the working class could not obtain a similar education for their children simply because they could not afford it, whereas service-class parents could and hence the kind of education which they had had themselves became an important factor in the choices they implemented for their children. If this argument is correct we would expect to find a similar interaction effect in the case of *private* secondary education but none in the case of *state* selective education where financial constraints have been much less. Indeed, the extent to which there is an inter-action effect may be a good indicator of the extent to which the working class have experienced financial constraints, and it will be interesting to see whether or not there was an interaction effect before the War in the state sector. This analysis may add to the evidence we cited in Chapter 2 on the extent to which able working-class children were unable to take up places in the pre-war grammar schools.[10]

Cross-tabulating social class and parental education will also enable us to look at some of the claims made by Jackson and Marsden about their sunken middle class. In their study of eighty-eight working-class boys who went to grammar school, Jackson and Marsden found that a large proportion (in fact over one-third) came from the sunken middle class: They wrote:

we have to record that right at the beginning of this 'working class' survey we find ourselves dealing with a large number of homes that reveal themselves to be submerged wings of middle class families thrusting their way upwards through free education. The actual proportion comes to over one-third of our sample. It suggests that one of the consequences of throwing open grammar school education has been that middle class families who have collapsed through ill-health, bankruptcy, foolishness or any of the stray chances of life, have been able to educate their children out of their fallen condition and reclaim the social position of their parents and grandparents.[11]

Jackson and Marsden did not have a control group, so they could not in fact show that the proportion of sunken-middle-class people they found in their sample was any greater than could have been expected purely on the basis of chance. But their implication is certainly that it was greater, and they explicitly advance the hypothesis that the proportion of sunken-middle-class families getting their children to grammar school will have increased after the 1944 Education Act. Both of these claims we can, after a fashion, test.

Unfortunately, our test cannot be very precise. Jackson and Marsden had defined the sunken middle class as working-class families (that is, ones where the male head of household had a manual occupation) with at least one middle-class grandparent, or with middle-class aunts and uncles, or (curiously) ones in which the head had formerly owned a small business.[12] Because our own survey did not include questions on the occupations of aunts, uncles, or grandparents, we are unable to test Jackson and Marsden's thesis in the precise terms in which they formulated it. Instead we have to take as our definition of the sunken middle class those families in which the head of household had a working-class occupation but he or his wife had a selective secondary education. This definition will certainly include many cases covered by Jackson and Marsden's definition. Indeed, Jackson and Marsden say that 'by and large those with grammar school experience themselves were also of the submerged middle class, cherishing the tone and polish for their children' (p.74). But we should not exaggerate the overlap between the two definitions. As we saw earlier, many grammar-school boys come from working-class backgrounds, and always have done, and we would be very reluctant to hold that a grammar-school education on its own is sufficient to make someone middle class. Nevertheless, although we should be careful how we describe them, evidence on those from working-class but educated backgrounds is important and interesting in its own right.

Table 5.7

*Attendance at Private Secondary School by Father's Class
and Parental Education*[1]
(percentages)

Father's Class	Parental education		
	Private	State Selective	Non-Selective
I, II	62.9	23.3	14.5
III, IV, V	36.2	9.8	4.8
VI, VII, VIII	10.2	2.8	1.0

[1]   Parental education is defined as in Table 5.1.

Table 5.8

*Attendance at Grammar and Technical Schools by Father's Class
and Parental Education*[1]
(percentages)

Father's Class	Parental education		
	Private	State Selective	Non-Selective
I, II	26.8	52.6	47.4
III, IV, V	37.9	43.3	29.8
VI, VII, VIII	36.7	38.5	20.8

[1]   Parental education is defined as in Table 5.1.

Tables 5.7 and 5.8 give the data for our sample as a whole. They show that the expected interaction effect does occur with private secondary education and a quite different, and unexpected, interaction effect within the state sector. Within the service class the chances of going to a private secondary school *increase* very dramatically if one or both parents had been to a private school themselves. In the intermediate class, where financial constraints may be expected to be somewhat greater, the increase is smaller. In the working class, the increase is negligible. By contrast, we find almost the opposite in the case of the state sector (Table 5.8). In the service class the chance of going to a grammar or technical school *falls* dramatically if one or both parents had been to a private school, and it is in the working class that having selectively educated parents increases one's chances of going to a selective school oneself by the largest amount. These results, then, confirm our expectation that financial constraints operated against educated members of the working class in their search for private schooling for their children. At the same time it appears that educated working-class parents were much better able than their less educated peers to secure free places at grammar and technical schools for their offspring. But we should be cautious in our interpretation of this interaction effect in the case of state selective schools. Our meritocratic model of educational selection suggests that so few service-class respondents with privately educated parents went to grammar and technical schools simply because so many were already attending private schools. It is not, as a casual glance at Table 5.8 might have suggested, that the state system discriminates against these children. Rather the reverse. Of those who were left, once the private sector had had its pick, 72 per cent went to grammar and technical schools. This suggests that we should recalculate the table in a somewhat different way, looking at the percentages of those *not* chosen for private schools who managed to secure places at grammar and technical schools.

Table 5.9

Percentage of respondents remaining within the state sector who attended grammar and technical schools

		Parental education	
Father's Class	Private	State Selective	Non-Selective
I, II	72.4	68.6	55.5
III, IV, V	59.5	47.9	31.3
VI, VII, VIII	40.9	39.6	20.9

[1] Parental education is defined as in Table 5.1.

The results from this alternative analysis are given in Table 5.9. This time they are much closer to the linear additive ones that we had anticipated. One's chances of getting to a grammar or technical school were improved at *all* social-class levels if one had formally educated parents, and the advantage was not substantially greater in the working class than in the service class. To have an educated background was useful, but there is little sign that the educated working class were any more advantaged compared with their peers than were the educated service class compared with theirs. The idea of a sunken middle class put forward by Jackson and Marsden does not in the end turn out to be useful on the evidence of our study.

Turning to trends over time, we face the problem of small numbers in more elaborate cross-tabulations. Our solution is to divide the sample into those educated before the War (the 1913–22 and 1923–32 cohorts), and those educated after the War (the 1933–42 and 1943–52 cohorts), and to combine our 'top' two education classes, producing a single category of respondents one or both of whose parents attended any kind (private or state) of selective school. The results in Table 5.10 show that there is no sign of the educated working-class families increasing their advantage after the 1944 Act. Quite the reverse. We see again that the advantage of an educated background is generally lower, at all social-class levels, in the post-war period, but also that the decline has been most dramatic in the case of the educated working class. Within the working class the selective/non-selective parental education log distance falls from 98 to 43. To the extent, then, that these families can be regarded as the sunken middle class, our findings cast grave doubt on Jackson and Marsden's claim that the 1944 Act was particularly efficacious in allowing them to 'thrust their way upwards through free education'. The truth, on our findings, is in the opposite direction. These authors, we must note, have fallen into the common

Table 5.10

Percentage of Respondents remaining within the State Sector who attended Grammar and Technical Schools

Father's Class	Parental Education			
	1913–32 cohorts		1933–52 cohorts	
	Selective[1]	Non-selective	Selective[1]	Non-selective
I, II	75.0 *24**	59.0 *0*	67.7 *26**	52.4 *0*
II, IV, V	58.9 *62*	31.7 *0*	46.2 *40*	30.9 *0*
VI, VII, VIII	54.4 *98*	20.5 *0*	32.9 *43*	21.4 *0*

[1] This includes both private and state selective parental education.
* Figures in italic give the selective/non-selective log distance within each social class.

academic trap of ignoring the technical schools. But in any case, even if we accept the problem in their terms and confine our attention to chances of grammar-school attendance, the data available to us refute their interpretation. Within the working class, the selective/non-selective parental education log distance falls from 89 in the pre-war period to 45 in the post-war, a larger drop than in the case of either the service class (55 falling to·24) or the intermediate class (86 falling to 53). Again, then, we find that the relative advantage of the educated parent has declined.

MATERNAL AND PATERNAL INFLUENCE

In Chapter 3 we discussed the importance of paternal and maternal educational background on the choice of private schooling for children.[13] It may, therefore, be useful to examine another of Jackson and Marsden's findings concerning the relative importance of mother and father in the child's education. Jackson and Marsden had written:

It is useful to indicate again a crucial difference between the middle-class and the working-class home. Such pointers as could be gleaned from the slender middle-class sample drew attention to the father as the dominant parent in matters of education. But behind the (working-class) schooldays that we are now to examine, it is clear that the centres of power usually lay with the mother. In two-thirds of the families there was either an equality of interest, or else the child could not or would not attest the major influences of one parent. In the 29 families where the child made distinctions about his parents' influence 23 claimed that the mother was the important and pressing parent, and 6 claimed this for the father.[14]

Our own data, however, give a very different picture. Table 5.11 shows that a child's chances of a selective education are substantially improved by having a parent who went to a selective school, but it makes very little difference whether it was the mother or the father. This holds true even when we control for social class. There is no sign that fathers are more important in the middle class and mothers in the working class, rather the reverse, though the differences (and numbers) are so small that we would not wish to assert the primacy of one parent over the other in either social class.

Table 5.11

Attendance at Selective Schools by Father's Class and Parental Education[1]
(percentages)

		Parental Education		
Father's Class	Neither parent attended selective secondary school	Mother (but not father) attended selective school	Father (but not mother) attended selective school	Both parents attended selective secondary schools
I, II	61.9	80.5	77.1	84.4
III, IV, V	34.6	53.0	51.5	69.8
VI, VII, VIII	21.7	34.8	38.9	54.7
All	28.6	51.5	57.6	73.1
(N − 8029)	6479	398	399	553

[1] Parental education is defined as in Table 5.1.

On most issues, then, our results seem to be signally at variance with Jackson and Marsden's. Why is this? One possibility is simply that our definitions are different. We have already mentioned that we do not have data on the sunken middle class as Jackson and Marsden have defined it, and there are other discrepancies too. Jackson and Marsden were interested in grammar schools in particular, and their respondents were boys who had stayed on into the sixth form; our interests are more in selective schooling as a whole. Jackson and Marsden included foremen in their definition of the working class; we have included them in the intermediate classes. However, we doubt if these discrepancies can account for the differences. We cannot correct for the difference in measurement of the sunken middle class, but we can redefine our classes and school categories, and when we do so our results remain essentially as before.

Perhaps a more important difference between the two studies is that Jackson and Marsden's main interest lies in the processes that take place within the family, ours in the biographies of our respondents and their parents. Thus Jackson and Marsden, after describing the importance of the working-class mother in the child's education, say: 'This could not altogether be accounted for by the mother s education or her superior station before marriage, though both these mattered. Its roots seemed to push much deeper into the basic rhythms and expectations of working-class life, belonging to that whole pattern of social living in which the mother rather than the father was the organic centre.'[15] Now a large-scale national survey such as ours could not hope to capture the basic rhythms and expectations of working-class life, whereas this is precisely the strength of a more qualitative study like Jackson and Marsden's which engages in intensive interviewing and something approaching participant observation. Unfortunately, however, we cannot dispose of the differences quite so easily. Jackson and Marsden do venture more demographic statements of the same kind which we offer. Thus they say: 'Over the whole sample there were 20 families in which one of the parents had actually had a grammar school education themselves. There were twice as many instances in which this was the mother rather than the father.'[16] Our demographic statements and correlations must also imply some processes within the family. If a working-class boy's chance of getting to selective school is improved as much by having an educated father as by having an educated mother, there must be some processes which lie behind this, processes which Jackson and Marsden apparently failed to pick up. Perhaps educated husbands marry educationally ambitious wives who focus their energies on their children's advancement; this could reconcile our findings; but it is surprising that, if it is true, Jackson and Marsden found no sign of it.

We are led, therefore, to the conclusion that our results differ because of the different scale and scope of our studies. Jackson and Marsden had eighty-eight working-class grammar-school boys who were contemporaries of theirs in Huddersfield; we had 495 working-class grammar-school boys drawn in a national random sample of adult males. We do not doubt that Jackson and Marsden's results are valid for their own particular time and place, and they themselves do not attempt to generalize them further. But the disparity between the two sets of results should warn us of the dangers of generalizing from the results of small and possibly atypical groups, a warning which applies as much to ourselves when we attempt elaborate cross-tabulations as it does to readers of Jackson and Marsden.

CONCLUSION

Three main conclusions deserve recapitulation. First, our evidence does not dispose us to accept any exaggerated claim for the concept of cultural capital as an exclusive means of cultural reproduction of the social classes. The concept is useful as an umbrella term for a set of mechanisms through which families influence the formal educational experience of their children. But the twentieth-century history of secondary-school expansion, at least in Britain, draws attention to the accumulation and dissemination of cultural capital as much as to its preservation and concentration. Our figures show the large volume of upward intergenerational educational mobility and the overwhelming feature of the state selective schools throughout our period was the presence in them of a dominant element of first generation novitiates into the 'national cultural heritage'.

Second it has emerged that the relative chances of those from educated backgrounds for selective secondary schooling have fallen, not risen. This again is evidence unfavourable to undue reliance on Bourdieu's cultural capital theory. And since this trend towards diminished advantage is especially marked for working-class boys it leads us to doubt, if not reject, the sunken-middle-class theory advanced by Jackson and Marsden.

Third we have looked at the much emphasized matrilineal element in the received picture of the working-class family as a transmitter of attitudes and aspirations towards education. The classic source here is, of course, Richard Hoggart's[17] autobiographical sketch of a Leeds childhood in the period of our first cohort (but one about which it must be remarked that the author was orphaned and brought up by women. His men are somewhat shadowy figures). We have ourselves directly compared our survey evidence with that of Jackson and Marsden who present a Hoggartian interpretation of the key role of the mother. But our data lent no support to this view. Either or both parents play their part in forming the educational fate of children.

NOTES

1. See Pierre Bourdieu, 'Cultural reproduction and social reproduction', in J. Karabel and A. H. Halsey (eds.), *Power and Ideology in Education*, (Oxford University Press, New York, 1977), pp.487–511.
2. B. Bernstein, 'Class and pedagogies: visible and invisible', in J. Karabel and A. H. Halsey (eds.), op.cit., pp.511–34.
3. B. Jackson and D. Marsden, *Education and the Working Class* (Routledge & Kegan Paul, 1963).
4. Cf. A. H. Halsey, 'Sociologists and the Equality Debate', *Oxford Review of Education*, 1. 1 (1975), pp.9–23.
5. Bernstein, 'Social class, language and socialization', in Karabel and Halsey, op.cit., p.477.
6. Bourdieu, op.cit., p.493.
7. J. H. Goldthorpe and C. Llewellyn, op.cit.
8. We must expect, however, that the discrepancy between the real world and the predictions of our model will be greater in the present case than in that of the social class analysis, if parents' education does, as we would suppose, affect children's IQ.
9. Floud, Halsey, and Martin, op.cit., p.59.
10. See Chapter 2 above, p.26.
11. Jackson and Marsden, op.cit., p.70.
12. It is hard to see why other heads of households who had held other middle-class jobs earlier in their careers were not included.
13. See above, Chapter 3, p.39.
14. Jackson and Marsden, op.cit., p.97.
15. Jackson and Marsden, op.cit., p.97.
16. Jackson and Marsden, op.cit., p.73.
17. R. Hoggart, *The Uses of Literacy* (Chatto & Windus, 1957).

CHAPTER 6

The Influence of Family and Primary Schooling on Entry to Secondary Education

We have discussed the transfer of boys from their primary to their secondary education in two ways. In Chapter 4 we traced the development of patterns of transfer from private and state primary schools and from the different social-class backgrounds to the places made available in secondary schools, selective and non-selective, state and private. A secondary stage evolved from the separate elementary and secondary systems of the beginning of the century until, after the 1944 Act, the vast majority moved at age 11 from a primary to a secondary school. But the evolution of an end-on relation of primary to secondary schools was not accompanied by transformation of either the relative chances of selective secondary schooling for boys from different social origins or any steady trend towards selection for such schooling solely on the principle of merit as measured by intelligence test. Though measured intelligence was an important factor in the allocation of boys to selective schools, both state and private, its power did not increase after the 1944 Act. There remained an element of non-meritocratic selection and the traditional educational disadvantage of a working-class family origin persisted. Indeed educational chances were shown in Chapter 4 to be the outcome essentially of shifts in the supply of children from the different classes and the provision of places in the different kinds of secondary schools.

We then went on in Chapter 5 to a second approach, exploring the developing links between primary and secondary schools from the point of view of the accumulation and distribution of cultural capital - a concept which we judged to be of limited utility in portraying the informal mechanisms through which families influence the educational fate of their children. From this point of view the outstanding feature of the expansion of secondary schools by the state was the creation of new cultural capital in each generation and every class.

BACKGROUND FACTORS AND TYPE OF SECONDARY SCHOOL

We are now in a position to try to put together these two approaches and to describe the varying influence of some of the 'material' and 'cultural' factors which have been at work to allocate children to secondary schools. Then, more particularly, we can carry forward the analysis of entry to primary schools which occupied us in Chapter 3 by asking how much the early and crucial decision whether to use the state or the private sector also predetermines choice at the point of entry to secondary schools. Still more particularly, we can ask how far the experience of private primary schooling is itself an independent influence on whether a boy passes into the private sector of secondary education.

The essential question we are asking, then, is what is the relative importance of these different factors in determining the path of individuals through the changing map of secondary schools that we have described. To begin our answers we return initially to Chapter 3 where we discussed the social influences behind the choice of private or state primary schooling. We shall repeat this analysis with respect to entry to secondary schooling, asking how these background factors are similar or different in their association with the paths chosen or imposed at these two major transition points in the educational journey.

The meaning of the results crucially depends on the technical definitions and analytical procedures through which they are obtained. We must, therefore, as we did in Chapter 3, explain precisely what we are doing. Type of secondary education is the *dependent* variable and this we measure in two ways: first according to whether the school is private or state; second according to whether the school is selective or non-selective. The first version of this variable is labelled RPS – Respondent's Private Secondary education – each case being scored 1 if the respondent attended an HMC, a non-HMC, or a Direct Grant School, and 0 otherwise. The second version of the dependent variable is labelled RSS – Respondent's Selective Secondary schooling – each case being scored 1 if he attended a technical, grammar, Direct Grant, HMC, or non-HMC school, and 0 otherwise.

Table 6.1 shows the correlations between our dependent and independent variables. If this table is compared with the correlations given in Table 3.6 it appears that the correlation of the background factors with respondents' private secondary schooling are of very similar magnitude to those we found with respondents' private primary schooling. By contrast, however, many of these independent or background factors have a substantially lower correlation with respondents' *selective* secondary schooling. More specifically, the correlations of FPP, MPP, FPS, MPS, and FHE with RSS are much lower than they were with RPP or RPS. But this is not at all surprising given the very different distributions of the variables. The private sector at both primary and secondary level is small by comparison with the division between selective and non-selective schools at the secondary level. Consequently relatively low correlations are inevitable.[1]

There are, however, more things at work in this table than the distributions of the variables. RPS has an extremely skewed distribution of scores, RSS is considerably less skewed, and FC (father's class), for example, is less skewed again. This means that the maximum possible correlation between FC and RSS is a great deal higher than the maximum possible between FC and RPS (both, of course, are negative). The two maxima are −.861 and −.567 respectively. We might therefore have expected the observed correlation between FC and RSS to be higher than that between FC and RPS, but Table 6.1 shows that the two are in fact remarkably similar. The explanation is that the 'effect' of social class on selective schooling (as measured, for example, by the size of the class differentials given in Table 4.8) is much smaller than its 'effect' on private schooling. The observed correspondence of the correlations, therefore, is the result of two opposing tendencies which cancel each other out.

However, in order to explore further the different pattern of correlates with private secondary and selective secondary entry we can, as we did in Chapter 3,

Table 6.1

Correlation of Background Factors with Respondents' Secondary Schooling

	RPP	FPP	MPP	FPS	MPS	FSS	MSS	FHE	FC	DA	OO	CH	NS
RPS	.511	.336	.275	.350	.295	.285	.229	.295	−.329	.288	.230	−.127	−.132
RSS	.251	.170	.143	.176	.156	.260	.224	.183	−.332	.257	.263	−.136	−.204

Note: The definitions and scoring of the variables appears in the text (Chapter 3, p.41, and Chapter 6, p.91).

group the background variables together and compute the multiple correlation coefficients. Doing this first for the education group of variables (FPP, MPP, FPS, MPS, and FHE)[2] we obtain coefficients of .471 and .318 with private and selective secondary education, compared with the coefficient of .491 in the case of private primary education. The 'material' group of variables (FC, DA, OO, CH, NS) yield coefficients of .388 (in the case of RPS) and .399 (in the case of RSS) compared with the coefficient of .377 reported in Chapter 3.

A pattern seems to be emerging, therefore. The association with the 'cultural' group of factors is strongest at the primary level and weakest at the selective secondary level. And the reverse happens with the material group of factors, the strongest association being with RSS and the weakest with RPP. This clearly suggests the hypothesis that cultural factors are relatively more important than material factors in the case of primary education, but that the balance between the two shifts as we move to private secondary and then selective secondary education.

INFLUENCE OF TYPE OF PRIMARY ON TYPE OF SECONDARY SCHOOL

We examine this hypothesis more effectively later in the chapter. Meanwhile we consider the role of primary education itself with respect to secondary education. Table 6.1 shows that RPP correlates with private secondary schooling more highly than any of the variables we have so far mentioned, and its association with RPS persists even if we control for the background factors that we have already considered. This can be seen most easily if we compare the amount of variance explained when we regress RPS on the full set of material and cultural background factors with the amount explained when we add RPP to the equation. Thus in the former case we explain 27 per cent of the variance; in the latter the inclusion of RPP increases the explained variance by nearly one-third to 35 per cent. In the case of selective secondary education the increase is much less substantial, explained variance barely increasing from 18 per cent to 19 per cent, and so there is little further explanation to be sought in this direction. The increase in the case of private secondary education, on the other hand, warrants further investigation.

The result we have just obtained can be put in the form of the assertion that knowledge of the primary school background of a boy permits much more accurate prediction of whether or not he will go on to a private secondary school. The sociological problem, however, is to discover what processes lie behind this gain in predictability. The simplest interpretation is that private primary schooling is not merely a channel through which privileged children pass on their way to the so-called public schools, but is an experience which gives children advantage in the competition for entry to the private sector of secondary schooling *irrespective of their social origins*. On this interpretation private primary schooling is not only a transmitter of prior class and family advantages; the fact that it increases the predictive power of our equation over and above that given by our home-background factors means that it confers benefits of its own and can thus break into the 'cycle of privilege' as well as reinforce it. Few children from poor backgrounds attend private primary schools but those who do so increase their chances of getting into the prestigious HMC schools, as do boys from the higher reaches of the service class who have trodden the path of traditional privilege through one of the preparatory schools.

This particular interpretation infers causal processes in a direct and straightforward way from the regression equation. If going to a private primary school is associated with a higher probability of going on to a private secondary school, then the former is held to cause the latter, and we can therefore speak of preparatory schooling conferring benefits in the competition for secondary-school places. However, just as we must hesitate to infer causes from correlations, so we must be careful in inferring causes from regression equations or path models. The equations, we must constantly remember, are simply descriptive of the patterns of association: it is the sociologist who attributes causes. Thus a diametrically opposed interpretation is also possible on the basis of the same results. It could be that parents who send their children to private primary schools differ from those who use the state sector not only in ways which we have already captured with our measures of parental class, education, and material circumstances, but also in their attitudes to private and state education. Our measure of a child's primary education may thus be highly correlated with this unmeasured attitudinal variable and may stand as a proxy for it. In short, what we had supposed to be an effect of primary schooling may in reality be a consequence of parental attitudes. In other words, we are dealing again with the problem of spurious correlation: variable A may be correlated with variable B, but when we control for variable C the correlation disappears since the observed correlation was due to the fact that C influenced both A and B. Thus, if parental attitudes to state and private education determine their choice both of primary and secondary education, failure to control for parental attitudes could lead to an observed, but spurious, correlation between primary and secondary schooling. Since our data do not provide us with a direct measure of the parental attitudes in question, we run the risk of falling into this trap.

FAMILY CLIMATE AND TYPE OF SECONDARY SCHOOL

However, there are ways of avoiding this particular error, and two of them, both borrowed from the work of Blau and Duncan, are open to us. In their analysis of educational and occupational attainment, Blau and Duncan, like us, wanted to obtain a measure of family climate but were unable to do so directly from their survey data. They wrote:

It is of interest to ascertain whether differences in the families' 'intellectual climate', as well as the structural characteristics investigated, affect the achievement of sons. Does an achievement motivation that induces sons to pursue their education and strive for success prevail in some families but not in others? Attitude surveys and psychological tests administered to all members of families combined with information on the later attainments of sons would yield data adequate to answer this question. Unfortunately no such data are available in this study. As a matter of fact these data could not even be collected for a sample like ours, since many members of the respondents' families are no longer living.[3]

We face the same problem to the extent that the 1972 British study followed the design of Blau and Duncan's American study. But the American authors went on to suggest the following alternative:

An admittedly second-best alternative to such data is to use the education of a man's eldest brother as a crude indication of the extent to which a family promotes achievement. Other conditions being equal, the education of a man's eldest brother can be assumed to reflect the extent to which learning and achievement are valued and encouraged in his family. To be sure, so does the respondent's own education, but it cannot be used as the independent measure of family climate, because it is to serve as the major dependent variable. Other conditions, of course, are not equal, because the education of the eldest son, just as that of other children, is known to be affected by the educational and occupational level of the father as well as by other background factors, notably color. The correlation between eldest brother's and own education primarily reflects the influence of these background factors on both and not simply the effect of one on the other. If background factors are controlled, however, brother's education does provide a rough indication of the degree to which the family climate furthers education and achievement.[4]

Our objective in the present case is not to measure the extent to which the family promotes achievement but, more narrowly, to obtain a measure of the extent to which the parents value private secondary education. Accordingly we use as our proxy for parental values not brother's educational attainment but whether or not he attended a private secondary school (BPS).[5] If we add this measure to our independent background factors in the equation, but exclude the respondent's primary education, then R^2 rises to 0.445 from the figure of 0.270 which resulted when RPS was regressed on the original set of background variables. Then, if respondent's primary education (RPP) is added to the expanded equation, there is a small further increment in R^2: its value rises to 0.472. In this way it becomes clear that much of the work done in the original regression by RPP is now done by the proxy variable for family values. Admittedly the parental values variable does not eliminate RPP: primary schooling still has an effect even when we control for parental values, and it is therefore still possible to attribute some causal significance to attendance at a private primary school. Nevertheless the causal role of private primary school attendance is now much smaller than we might have been led to suppose before we introduced a measure of family climate or parental attitude.[6]

This same important point can be made in another way by looking at the regression coefficients in the different equations. This is done in Table 6.2. In the first row of the table (Equation 1) we give the regression coefficients obtained when RPS is regressed on the usual set of background factors together with RPP (but excluding BPS), and in the *third* row (Equation 3) we give the regression coefficients obtained when BPS is added to the set of independent variables. Now we cannot compare these two sets of coefficients directly since they are based on different samples. Whereas Equation 1 can be estimated from a sample of 8529, only 5558 respondents reported the details of a brother's education, and the coefficients of Equation 3 are thus estimated from this reduced sample. Some of the changes in the coefficients, therefore, could conceivably be due to this change in sample size. To check this we need to re-estimate the coefficients of Equation 1 from the reduced sample. This is done in the second row of the table.

Comparing the second and third rows we see that the introduction of the

Table 6.2

*Regression Coefficients obtained when Respondent's Private Secondary Schooling (RPS)
is regressed on different sets of independent variables*

	BPS	RPP	FPP	MPP	FPS	MPS	FHE	FC	DA	OO	CH	NS	R²
							Independent Variables						
1	—	.351	.076	(.026)	.148	.118	.165	−.009	.017	(.010)	−.021	(−.002)	.351
2	—	.354	.081	(.023)	.104	.172	.141	−.009	.016	(.010)	−.021	(−.002)	.357
3	.436	.219	.044	(−.030)	.041	.096	.101	−.005	.010	(.010)	−.011	(−.001)	.472

Note: ·Coefficients are bracketed when they are less than twice their standard error.

additional variable of brother's attendance at a private secondary school does indeed have a marked effect on the size of the other coefficients. If we exclude the bracketed figures, we find that in all eight cases there is a substantial drop, the figures in Equation 3 being around 60 per cent of those in Equation 2. RPP is no exception to this rule. Once we introduce our proxy variable for parental values, then, primary schooling loses much of its original importance. This is a salutary reminder that what we get out of regression equations depends very much on what we put in. In particular, it will be seen that the coefficients for respondent's primary schooling are much reduced and so, from this vantage point also, it appears that the effect which might have been attributed to primary schooling in the absence of a measure of parental attitudes is much exaggerated. Nevertheless, in order to maintain an accurate perspective, it must be pointed out that the effect of primary schooling is still substantial. From comparisons of coefficients with the second row it emerges that parental values, as measured by brother's private secondary schooling, is by far the most important determinant, that respondent's primary schooling is fairly important, and that most of the others are relatively insignificant. More strictly, the different sizes of the coefficients mean that, controlling for the other variables, those whose brothers attended private secondary schools were much more likely to attend such schools themselves than were those whose brothers did not; that those who had attended private primary schools themselves were somewhat more likely to attend private secondary schools than those who had not; and that, again controlling for the other variables, there was little difference in the probability of attending private secondary schools between those, for example, whose father had attended such schools and those whose fathers had not.

A PATH MODEL OF THE DETERMINANTS OF TYPE OF SECONDARY SCHOOL

The upshot of this analysis, then, is to give some, albeit substantially reduced, support to the simple interpretation with which we began, namely that the experience of attending a private primary school in itself gives a child an advantage in the competition for a private secondary school place. Our confidence, however, in this interpretation will still depend on our appraisal of the validity of our 'brother's schooling' variable as a measure of family values. It is not unassailable: but, as we intimated, a second method is available to us from the work of Blau and Duncan which is more realistic sociologically, although it involves a greater number of numerical assumptions.

In order to use this second method we begin with a simple causal model. We assume that the major determinants of whether or not respondents and their brothers attend private primary schools are the material circumstances of the family and parental attitudes. In turn we assume that the major determinants of whether or not the respondent will attend private *secondary school* are also these same two factors, and in addition whether or not he attended a private primary school. These assumptions can be represented in conventional path diagram form as follows:

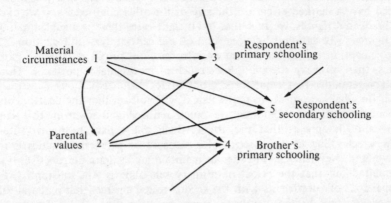

Material circumstances 1

3 Respondent's primary schooling

5 Respondent's secondary schooling

Parental values 2

4 Brother's primary schooling

Note: An assumption implicit in this path diagram, and essential to the solution offered, is that the residuals to Variables 3, 4, and 5 are uncorrelated with one another and with prior variables in the model.

Note also that here we are using brother's primary schooling, not, as in Table 6.2, his secondary schooling.

Following conventional notation, a line with a single arrow indicates a postulated causal relationship. Thus, in this model, no causal effect is postulated between brother's schooling and the respondent's primary or secondary schooling in either direction. This assumption would not be so reasonable if we were concerned with school attainment: we could not, for example, ignore the possibility that sibling rivalry might be an ingredient of academic success. It can be argued, however, that with respect to the decision to send a child to a private school, the assumption is more reasonable. Whatever the degree of sibling rivalry, the decision itself is presumably in the hands of the parents. Even so, we cannot be absolutely confident, since, especially in the case of an elder brother, a previous decision to use the private sector might in effect foreclose the decision in question on grounds of fairness within the family. In this way the experience of the brother might have an indirect effect on the decision about the respondent's schooling and this kind of effect is not allowed for in the path diagram.

We cannot compute the coefficients in the path model directly from our data because 'parental values' is a hypothetical variable which we have not measured directly.[7] However, the basic theorem of path analysis does enable us to do so from knowledge or assumption of the correlation coefficients. The theorem itself states:

$$r_{ij} = \sum_q p_{iq} r_{qj} \qquad\qquad \text{Equation 6.1}$$

where i and j denote the variables in the system and the index q runs over all variables from which there are paths leading directly to x_i. It follows from this that

$$r_{34} = p_{31} r_{14} + p_{32} r_{24} \qquad\qquad \text{Equation 6.2}$$

$$r_{13} = p_{31} + p_{32}r_{21} \qquad\qquad \text{Equation 6.3}$$

$$r_{24} = p_{42} + p_{41}r_{12} \qquad\qquad \text{Equation 6.4}$$

Now we already know from our data that $r_{34} = 0.731$. Let us also assume that $r_{13} = r_{14} = 0.377$. This is the value of the multiple correlation between respondent's primary schooling and what we have termed the material group of background factors. The correlations derived from our data between the components of this group of factors and brother's primary schooling are very similar to those between the same components and respondent's primary schooling. Finally, let us assume that $r_{12} = 0.3$. This is the most contentious of our assumptions. But it is the one that Blau and Duncan make in a comparable analysis, and it is worth noting that father's class (the major component of the material group of background factors) also has correlations of around 0.3 with most of the parental education variables which we have measured and these variables can be assumed to correlate quite highly with parental values. We cannot, however, pretend that this last assumption is as firmly based as are the others. We can only invite the reader to experiment for himself in order to see what difference is made if a different value for the correlation is assumed.

With these assumptions it is a matter of straightforward algebra to solve for the path coefficients and the remaining correlations. Moving, then, to the right-hand side of the path diagram we know from the basic theorem that:

$$r_{51} = p_{51} + p_{52}r_{21} + p_{53}r_{31} \qquad\qquad \text{Equation 6.5}$$

$$r_{53} = p_{51}r_{13} + p_{52}r_{23} + p_{53} \qquad\qquad \text{Equation 6.6}$$

$$r_{54} = p_{51}r_{14} + p_{52}r_{24} + p_{53}r_{34} \qquad\qquad \text{Equation 6.7}$$

We also know from our data that $r_{35} = 0.511$, $r_{45} = 0.506$, and we assume that $r_{15} = 0.389$ (the multiple correlation between respondent's private secondary schooling and the material group of factors). We thus have three equations with three unknowns, and it is again a matter of elementary algebra to solve for the path coefficients. We can also calculate the size of the residual paths.

We now enter these values in our path diagram as follows:

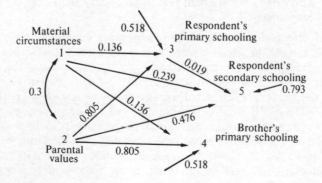

There are a number of notable features in this diagram, but before we discuss them we must repeat our warning that what comes out of a path analysis is dependent on what goes in. Thus altering the assumed correlation between 'material circumstances' and 'parental values' will necessarily alter the size of the path coefficients derived from our equations.[8] If the correlation is set at zero, p_{31} and p_{41} reach their maximum value of .377, while p_{32} and p_{42} fall to .697. Conversely increasing the size of the correlation will increase the estimated effect of parental values and reduce that of material circumstances.

It is also important not to pay too much attention to the labels attached to the variables but instead to concentrate on their construction. This is particularly important with hypothetical variables such as parental values. The equations given earlier reveal that 'parental values' represents (numerically) the observed similarity of experience between brothers with regard to private primary schooling except for the part allotted to material circumstances. Thus we begin with the (very high) observed similarity between brothers. The (relatively low) correlation which we have assumed between material circumstances and private primary schooling means that material circumstances (as we have defined them) can account only for a part of the similarity between brothers' primary schooling, and 'parental values' consists of all those other sources of similarity between brothers which were not captured via the variable 'material circumstances'. Variables such as family income, therefore, which are not adequately represented in the group of indicators of 'material circumstances' will operate instead through the only available channel, 'parental values'.

With these caveats in mind we can turn to the path diagram itself. The main features are as follows:

1. The effect of respondent's private primary schooling on his secondary schooling is very small compared with the effect of the other variables in the model.
2. The importance of parental values is much greater than that of material circumstances, but
3. The relative importance of parental values declines at the secondary-school level while that of material circumstances increases.
4. The size of the residual paths increases at the secondary-school level. This amounts to saying that the amount of variance explained in respondent's primary schooling is greater than that in secondary schooling, R^2 being .732 and .371 respectively.

The lack of effect of respondent's private primary schooling on his secondary schooling is a result in which we can have considerable confidence. It is not sensitive to changes in assumptions about r_{12} or r_{13}. To increase the size of p_{53} substantially it would be necessary either to increase r_{53} or reduce r_{54}, but r_{53} and r_{54} in the model are calculated directly from our data and are thus firmly grounded. The essential point here is that r_{53} and r_{54} are of very similar magnitudes; since we have assumed that brother's primary schooling will have no direct effect on respondent's secondary schooling, the similarity between the two being mediated by family background, it follows that respondent's own primary schooling will have no direct effect on his secondary schooling. The symmetry of the correlation coefficients imposes a symmetry on the path coefficients.

This can be shown as follows. From the basic theorem of path analysis, Equation 6.1, we know that

$$p_{53} = r_{53} - p_{54}r_{43} - p_{52}r_{23} - p_{51}r_{13}$$ Equation 6.8

$$p_{54} = r_{54} - p_{53}r_{34} - p_{52}r_{24} - p_{51}r_{14}$$ Equation 6.9

We have already assumed that $r_{14} = r_{13}$ and that $r_{24} = r_{23}$. We have just noted that $r_{54} = r_{53}$. Substituting in Equation 6.9, we obtain

$$p_{54} = r_{53} - p_{53}r_{34} - p_{52}r_{23} - p_{51}r_{13}$$ Equation 6.10

Subtracting Equation 6.10 from Equation 6.8, we find that

$$p_{53} - p_{54} = p_{53}r_{34} - p_{54}r_{34},$$

therefore

$$p_{53}(1 - r_{34}) = p_{54}(1 - r_{34})$$

therefore

$$p_{53} = p_{54}$$

Given the model we have been using, therefore, it followed that, once we found that r_{53} has approximately the same value as r_{54}, so p_{53} also had to be approximately equal to p_{54}.

Put slightly differently, the background factors postulated to account for the similarity of brother's primary and respondent's secondary schooling can also account for the similarity between respondent's primary and secondary schooling without any need to introduce extra causal factors. We thus have little hesitation in rejecting the hypothesis with which we began this chapter, that private primary schooling can 'break into the cycle of privilege' and confer benefits in the competition for secondary school places.

However, the second inference from our model is not so well grounded. The greater importance of parental values than material circumstances is, as we have already explained, a consequence of the assumptions we have made about r_{12} and r_{13}, as well as of the empirically derived r_{34}. More serious is the point we have already made, namely that variables such as family income which are not adequately captured by the material circumstances variable, will operate instead through 'parental values'. This means that p_{32} provides an upper limit of the effect that values, if directly measured, might have. The true figure might be considerably smaller.

Turning to the third inference, however, we need not be so negative. While the absolute sizes of the relevant path coefficients may be in doubt, the differences at primary and secondary level are reliable. This can be seen clearly by asking what changes in the correlations would have been needed for p_{51} to be the same as p_{31}, and for p_{52} to be the same as p_{32}. To obtain this 'no change' result it would be necessary to increase both r_{35} and r_{45} to .731, the same value as r_{34}. But these two correlations are directly based on our data and can therefore be taken as given. Given further that r_{45} is actually considerably less than .731, p_{52} must be less than p_{32}: there is a lower degree of similarity between brothers for the hypothetical variable of parental values to account for, and the path coefficient falls, as will the correlation coefficient r_{52}. With respect to material circumstances on the other side of the path diagram, however, there is no symmetry. The correlation coefficient r_{51} is slightly larger than r_{31}, whereas r_{52} is estimated to be much smaller than r_{32}. Given that the other correlations are falling (as compared with the 'no change' assumptions) this means that the *relative* importance of the direct link between material circumstances and secondary schooling must rise. Again, then, this seems a firmly based result. True, there are questions about the measurement of material circumstances, but the crucial point is that correlations r_{31} and r_{51} are based on the *same* method of measuring it and hence we can be confident in our result.

Finally, the conclusion that there is decline in the amount of variance explained at the secondary stage compard with the primary stage is convincing. The absolute size of R^2 will depend on the assumptions made about r_{12}, r_{13}, and r_{51}, but the differences in R^2 will depend on the observed correlations.

We have given a statistical account of the various inferences from a path diagram designed to assess the relative effect of material circumstances and parental values on the choice of private secondary schooling: but how are we to account for them sociologically? The answers, we think, are straightforward. First, as we suggested earlier in this chapter, the high correlation but low path coefficient between private primary and secondary education simply reflects parental preferences between private and state education. Next, the increased importance of material circumstances at the secondary level can reasonably be ascribed to the greater importance of fees at this level. Parents who value private education could normally find a primary school with fees to suit their pocket, but when it comes to secondary education a good number must surely find themselves excluded by the size of the fees. Finally, the decline in R^2 could well be due to the control which the private secondary schools exercise over the selection procedure. This, of course, will be particularly true of the HMC and Direct Grant schools which typically imposed rigorous academic standards on their entry. It is true that the non-HMC schools were there to mop up those who could not meet these standards, but against this some parents had the choice of a grammar school rather than a non-HMC school, and it is not obvious that a belief in the value of private education always outweighed the superior education offered by many grammar schools.

CONCLUSION

To sum up and translate a somewhat technical analysis we have, in this chapter, explored the question of what determines whether a boy finds his way into the private sector of secondary education and whether he attends a selective secondary school, state or private.

It is clear that an excellent basis for predicting a destination in the private or state sector of secondary education is whether or not the boy started in a private primary school. If he did, his chances of staying out of the state system are much higher than if he did not. But this correlation or continuity leaves open the question as to whether it is the experience of private primary schooling itself or some other factor in his family and class background which is decisive.

Our conclusions from various statistical analyses are, first, that it is not primary schooling in itself which determines use of private secondary schooling. Rather, it is the material and cultural background of the family which largely determines both the choice of private primary schooling and, to a lesser but still crucial extent, private secondary schooling.

Second, the answer to the question of exactly what it is about a family – its material position or its cultural attitudes – that determines the choice, remains unclear. Both money and preferences are involved and if we are to avoid triv-ialising the concept of class, we must recognize that circumstance and con-sciousness are not randomly related but more or less closely tied together. We have, nevertheless, tried to distinguish them by imperfect indicators, and our analyses lead us to put greater emphasis on cultural than on material determinants.

Third, we are, on the other hand, more sure that the weight of material circumstances increases when secondary schools, with their more substantial fees, are chosen and, moreover, that the choice is in any case less exclusively in the hands of the family at this point than it was when the boy started at his primary school.

NOTES

1. On the same argument, the correlations of RSS with FSS and MSS should be higher than those of RPS. In fact they are not. The distribution of selective schooling in the parents' 'generation' is closer to that of private then selective schooling among their sons.
2. Note that when we compute the multiple correlation between RSS and the education group of variables FPS and MPS are replaced by FSS and MSS.
3. Blau and Duncan, op.cit., p.316.
4. Ibid., pp.316–17.
5. For a number of reasons, we designed our survey to obtain information on any brother, and not simply the eldest brother. This naturally increased the size of the 'respondent with brother' sample, and it also rules out the possibility referred to by Blau and Duncan in the quotation above, that the sibling correlation is the result of a one-way direct influence rather than the product of a shared family background. The interview procedure was to list all brothers (including half-brothers or step-brothers) who had reached the age of 16, and if there were two or more to select one of them for detailed investigation, using a simple randomizing procedure. This meant that older or younger brothers had equal chances of selection, while at the same time the choice was not left to the respondent (in case respondents tended to select in some systematic, but un-known way, e.g. the brother most similar to themselves).
6. It is interesting to speculate that Douglas's finding (*The Home and The School*, ch. XIII, esp. p.110) that attending a state primary school with a good record of securing grammar-school places improved one's chances of passing the 11-plus, might also be demonstrated to be a spurious correlation if data on brothers were available. The point is essentially the same as the one we have made already. Parents who send their children to 'good' primary schools may differ from other parents in ways which Douglas fails to control but which are causally connected with success at the 11-plus. Attendance at a 'good' school thus acts as a proxy for these unmeasured parental variables.
7. See Appendix IV for a more general discussion of issues related to hypothetical variables.
8. See Appendix IV.

CHAPTER 7

The Experience of Secondary Schooling

Having followed our respondents from their primary to their secondary schools we may now ask what is their fate once they are there. Is their type of secondary education finally determined at the age of eleven, or is it, as the 1943 White Paper on *Educational Reconstruction* hoped, 'subject to review as the child's special gifts and capacities develop' (para. 27)? How long do the children stay in their secondary schools, and what certificates and credentials do they get for their pains? Is the inequality of opportunity at eleven followed by a like inequality of opportunity for entry into the sixth form – the traditional gateway to the universities and the professions? We shall begin by describing the experience of secondary schooling from the point of view of the extent of transfer between different types of secondary school, the length of the school career, and the passing of examinations. Then we shall go on to try to explain the patterns of development of these aspects of secondary-school experience. The expansion of secondary education since the Second World War and its reconstruction along comprehensive lines, especially in the 'sixties and 'seventies, has given rise to much debate about allegedly declining standards, promoted particularly by 'Black Paper' writers. It is against this background that we put forward our description and explanation of the course of development in secondary education as experienced by our four birth cohorts.

MOVEMENT BETWEEN TYPES OF SECONDARY SCHOOL

The extent of transfer between different types of secondary school can be briefly described. Our data were coded according to the respondent's highest[1] school and also according to whether he had changed his type of school. Cross-tabulating the two we find that 16.9 per cent of those whose highest school was a technical school had changed school type, 7.4 per cent of those at grammar schools, 3.4 per cent of those at non-HMC schools, 7.4 per cent of those at Direct Grant, and 0.5 per cent of those at HMC schools. For the sample as a whole the percentage was 3.4. By definition no one whose highest school was a secondary modern or comprehensive had changed from one type of school to another, but it is reasonable to assume that the traffic was largely out of the non-selective schools into the others. Of course, there could also have been some switching between the other types of school, for example from technical to grammar schools, but this was probably much less common.

More interestingly, there was a marked increase in the number of transfers in the post-war period. Before the War less than 2 per cent of our respondents reported transfers between types of school; after the War the rate of transfer went up to 4.8 per cent. But while the proportion may have doubled, from the point of view of the individual boy, particularly one at a secondary modern school, the chances of a transfer must still have seemed fairly remote. Even after the 1944 reforms the secondary-school destination of the vast majority of boys had been finally decided at the age of 11, and if this meant a secondary modern school, there was little hope of reprieve. True, there was still the possibility of the 'alternative route' of further education at a later age,[2] but schooling at least was settled by the age of 11. It is also interesting, although not perhaps surprising, to note that middle-class boys were somewhat more likely to transfer than were working-class boys: 2.5 per cent of our working-class respondents transferred; 4.1 per cent of the intermediate class, and 5.9 per cent of the service class. Are the middle classes, then, more likely to develop special gifts and capacities? We doubt it. Bearing in mind the fact that those who transferred were also likely to stay on beyond the minimum school-leaving age, we may guess that this particular class differential is simply another example of the well-known association between school leaving and social class. In other words, we would guess that many of the transfers were simply children at secondary modern schools who wanted to stay on beyond the minimum leaving age and who transferred to schools which had sixth forms or courses for older pupils.

SCHOOLS, LEAVING AGES, AND EXAMINATIONS

Let us now turn to the general relationship between type of school, length of school career, and examination success. As we might expect, there is a close association between the place of a child's school in the academic-cum-social hierarchy which we have described and his chances of staying on and of securing academic certificates. Elementary- or secondary-modern-school boys typically left at the earliest possible moment without passing School Certificate or its modern equivalent of GCE O-Level. At the other extreme, virtually all those who went to the HMC or Direct Grant schools stayed on and the great majority of them obtained School Certificate. Table 7.1 gives an overview. Column 1 shows the percentage who stayed on beyond the minimum school-leaving age to age 16 or later; column 2 shows the percentage obtaining School Certificate or one or more O-Level passes; and column 3 shows what we have called the school's success rate, namely the ratio of column 2 to column 1. This is not to be understood as the proportion of boys staying on who obtained School Certificate. Many boys had already obtained School Certificate by the time they reached the age of 16 and are therefore included in column 2. They must clearly be included in any measure of the success rate even though this makes it theoretically possible for the rate to exceed 1.0. But equally clearly, column 2 on its own is not a fair indication of the success rate since most boys who left at the minimum age had no effective chance of obtaining School Certificate or O-Level. In the absence of detailed information about the number of candidates actually entered by the schools for the examinations, this ratio seems the best measure of success.

In general, the school's success rate is in accordance with its place in the academic hierarchy, and this is, of course, what is required by the meritocratic model which we developed in Chapter 4. There are, however, some striking features of the table to notice. In the first place, the HMC and Direct Grant schools have been better at retaining their pupils in school, have steered more of their pupils through School Certificate and O-Level, but have no better a success rate than the grammar schools. This conflicts with our assumption that these

Table 7.1

School Attendance and School Examinations

| | Percentage staying on until 16 or later | Percentage obtaining School Certificate or one or more O-Levels | Success Rate (Column 2 as a proportion of Column 1) |
	(1)	(2)	
Independent HMC (N = 199)	94.5	82.9	.88
Direct Grant (N = 135)	93.3	78.5	.84
Grammar (N = 1411)	83.3	70.8	.85
Independent non-HMC (N = 206)	75.8	53.4	.70
Technical (N = 988)	27.6	15.6	.57
Comprehensive (N = 121)	43.0	24.8	.58
Secondary Modern (N = 5450)	7.8	4.7	.60
All (N = 8510)	28.1	21.4	.76

schools were creaming off the ablest pupils, but if instead the numbers obtaining School Certificate or *five* or more O-Levels are examined, it appears that the success rates of the HMC and Direct Grant schools are, as our model would predict, superior to the grammar schools. Of course, it is also possible to account for the superior success rate of the HMC schools with respect to five or more O-Levels in other terms. Thus it is certainly possible that they provide more effective teaching than their rivals, and Kalton's study of HMC schools offers some evidence consistent with this contention. He looked at boys at the HMC schools who had 'failed' the 11-plus and found that no less than 72 per cent of them went on to obtain four or more O-Level passes compared with 67 per cent of grammar-school boys who achieved the same standard. Against this, however, must be set the point that Kalton does not control in this analysis for length of school career:[3] the success of the 11 plus 'failures' at HMC schools is undeniable, but it may be due more to the schools' ability to retain their pupils beyond the minimum statutory leaving age than to anything else.[4] This is a point to which we shall return in Chapter 9.

The next feature to notice in Table 7.1 is that the non-HMC schools were almost as good as the major private schools and grammar schools in holding their pupils but that they had a much inferior success rate. This can be most parsimoniously explained in terms of their lower place in the academic hierarchy and their lesser power to attract able pupils. If, as we have assumed, they were a refuge for the ambitious middle-class parents of less able children, their high rates of attendance beyond the minimum leaving age, but lower success rates, become easily explicable.

The position of the technical schools, however, would seem to run counter to our theory. Their success rate is indistinguishable from that of the comprehensive and secondary modern schools, whereas it should be markedly higher. But this anomaly is more apparent than real. The number of children attending technical schools declined sharply over the period covered by our four cohorts, while those attending comprehensives almost all came from the youngest cohort. At the same time, as we shall see, rates of school attendance beyond the minimum leaving age and levels of educational attainment (as measured by O- and A-Levels) rose rapidly. This means that the comparisons in Table 7.1 between technical schools and comprehensive schools could be misleading. The performance of the technical schools is heavily weighted by that of the older age-groups; that of the comprehensives by the younger. What we must therefore do, if we are to make sensible comparisons, is to look at the results of the youngest (i.e. 1943–52 cohort) which contains the bulk of those who attended comprehensives. These results are given in Table 7.2. Here the anomalous position of the Technical schools is removed and they regain the position our theory would

Table 7.2

School Attendance and Examination Success for Those Born 1943–52

	Percentage staying on until 16 or later (1)	Percentage gaining one or more O-Levels (2)	Success rate (Column 2 as a proportion of Column 1)
Independent HMC (N = 67)	97.0	88.1	.91
Direct Grant (N = 44)	97.7	90.9	.93
Grammar (N = 515)	90.5	81.5	.90
Independent non-HMC (N = 68)	82.4	69.2	.84
Technical (N = 149)	69.1	51.6	.75
Comprehensive (N = 108)	46.3	27.8	.60
Secondary Modern (N = 1498)	20.4	10.7	.52
All (N = 2449)	44.5	34.0	.76

predict for them above the comprehensive schools, which are in turn clearly ahead of the secondary modern schools.

Table 7.2 does, however, contain another interesting feature. It shows that the comprehensive schools were somewhat better than the overall average in holding children beyond 16 and that they were markedly inferior in their rate of O-Level success. Could this be interpreted, following 'Black Paper' belief, to indicate that the net result of a system of comprehensive secondary schools will be to reduce rates of school attendance and examination success below those which obtained under the old tripartite system? Thus Iris Murdoch enjoins us to be 'alarmed at the lowering of academic standards which seems to be envisaged and accepted by those who advocate non-selective schooling and even speak calmly of non-selective universities'.[5] 'The children', she asserts, 'who will be lost for ever are the poor clever children with an illiterate background who on the "chance" system are being denied the *right* to a strict academic education which can only be achieved on the basis of some sort of selection.'

Such a conclusion would be premature in the extreme. The results in Table 7.2 are based on only 108 respondents who attended comprehensive schools, and they were, of course, doing so in the very early stages of comprehensive reorganization. Our data cannot provide a firm basis for conclusions about comprehensive schools: another generation, as we argued in Chapter 2, will have to pass before firm judgement can be made. We cannot properly gauge the effect of comprehensive reorganization from the experience of a tiny minority of comprehensive-school pupils within an essentially selective system. For example, many of the comprehensive schools which our respondents attended would have been in areas where able pupils were still being creamed off by grammar schools, and the 'success rates' of these schools thus tell us little about the character of a system where selection has been genuinely abolished. To examine the effects of changing a system, therefore, we must compare systems, not patterns within a system. We shall take up this point in Chapter 9, where we will attempt such a comparison between systems, and we must therefore resist the temptation to draw conclusions about comprehensive reorganization from the data of Table 7.2 (or from any other data similarly based on the early stages of reorganization within the tripartite, selective system).

TRENDS IN LENGTH OF SECONDARY SCHOOLING AND EXAMINATION SUCCESS

From this necessarily inconclusive discussion, we move on to something more firmly based, namely the trends in school attendance and examination success over our period, looking first (Table 7.3) at the successive cohorts without regard to their distribution between different types of secondary school. During the period covered by our study there was an enormous increase in the numbers staying on to 15, mainly because of the raising of the school-leaving age in 1947. More interesting is the fact that a high rate of growth in school attendance at 16, 17, and 18 years of age appears throughout the post-war period. The apparent stagnation of the pre-war years has been followed by a continuing boom in school attendance since the War. True, the highest increases occurred among the 1933–42 cohort who were entering secondary education in 1944 and were thus having to make decisions about school leaving from 1948 onwards. But substantial increases were also recorded by the 1943–52 cohort who were making their decisions in the late 'fifties and early 'sixties.

Table 7.3

Trends in School Attendance and School Examinations

		1913–22	1923–32	1933–42	1943–52
Percentage staying on at school until	15	22.8	27.5	94.8	100.0
	16	15.6	18.1	31.0	44.4
	17	8.3	7.8	14.5	23.7
	18	3.4	4.0	7.7	14.2
Percentage obtaining	O-Level	11.9	14.0	23.2	34.0
	A-Level	2.1	3.6	7.1	15.1
Success rates	O : 16	.76	.77	.75	.77
	A : 18	.62	.90	.92	1.06

Note: The first four rows indicate the percentage of boys staying at their secondary schools until the age indicated or a higher one. To obtain the percentage *leaving* at a given age we have to subtract from the percentage given for that age the percentage for the next higher age. For example, in the 1943–52 cohort the percentage leaving at fifteen was 100 − 44.4 = 55.6.

We have computed the A-Level success rate for the proportion of those staying on until 18 because relatively few people who left at 17 obtained A-Levels before doing so. 4.8 per cent of those who obtained an A-Level pass (or Higher School Certificate) left school at 16 or earlier; 15.8 per cent left at 17; 63.7 per cent at 18; and 15.7 per cent left at 19 or later.

The general increase in school attendance at all levels is, moreover, highly impressive. Over the period as a whole the percentage of each cohort staying on until 16 or later increased by 185 per cent. Remembering that the size of the cohorts themselves also increased, this means that the actual *numbers* who stayed on increased by 242 per cent. This figure can be put in perspective by noting that Britain's gross national product over the comparable thirty years increased by only 52 per cent,[6] that the intake into the private schools increased by only 75 per cent and that even the intake into the grammar schools increased only by 138 per cent. Thus there were general increases in provision, but the increases were greater among the more selective and prestigious forms of secondary education. Grammar-school places doubled, but the numbers entering the sixth forms more than trebled, and the numbers staying on to complete a sixth-form course rose fourfold.[7] We have here an example of a general characteristic of educational expansion in advanced industrial countries since the Second World War; the higher the educational level the faster the rate of growth.

This is a phenomenon which we can also observe when we turn from school attendance to examination successes. Table 7.3 shows that the percentage of the cohort obtaining O-Levels (or School Certificate before the war) increased by 186 per cent while that obtaining A-Levels (or Higher School Certificate before the war) increased by a massive 619 per cent. This means, of course, that the 'success rate' of the secondary-school system as a whole has stayed remarkably constant at O-Level but has increased quite dramatically at A-Level. The O-Level success rate has remained constant at around 0.76 while the A-Level figure has risen from 0.62 to 1.06.

However, there is a serious problem of comparability here. The measure we have used equates a single A-Level with Higher School Certificate and a single O-Level with School Certificate. This will not do. We have tried to devise a more accurate comparison, for example by equating five or more passes at O-Level with a pass at School Certificate, but even this is unsatisfactory. The fact is that the old School Certificate was a different type of examination from the General Certificate of Education, requiring passes in certain specified subjects. It is therefore mistaken to suppose that any given number of O-Level passes can be equated with School Certificate and, since we did not have data on the actual subjects in which passes were obtained, no other way of assimilating the two types of examination was open to us. Instead we have to recognize that there was a change in the examination system. This means that we must be particularly careful in our comparisons. We can reasonably look at trends *within* the pre-war period and *within* the post-war period since in each case the system was effectively unchanged, the change-over from School Certificate to GCE being introduced in 1950. Comparison between the two periods must, however, be undertaken only with caution. With these warnings in mind we may note that in the case of School Certificate there was a small increase in the pre-war period, a much larger increase in the post-war period after the introduction of GCE 'O' Level, and a very large jump between the two periods. At the same time, we can see that these increases mirrored the increases in attendance until 16, and so the 'success rate' remains virtually constant throughout the whole of our period. On the other hand, Higher School Certificate and A-Level present a different picture. There was a large increase (of 71 per cent) in the numbers obtaining Higher School Certificate before the war; there was an even bigger increase (of 97 per cent) with the change-over to A-Levels; but the biggest increase of all (113 per cent) came in the post-war period. The 'success rate' also shows a marked increase over the period but the largest rise occurred in the pre-war period and there was virtually no change in the success rate with the change-over to A-Levels.

How, then, are we to account for these trends? We shall consider four different explanations or theories: first, declining standards; second, the theory of response to technological need; third, a version of conflict theory; and fourth, a version of the 'pool of ability' theory.

Explanation I. Declining Standards

One possibility is that there has been a general decline in the standards required by examining authorities. As more pupils have presented themselves for examination, so the authorities have lowered their standards, thus allowing the success rate to remain constant despite the falling quality of the candidates or indeed, in the case of A-Level, actually allowing the success rate to rise. Some explanation of the growth of school attendance could follow the same lines. Declining standards make it worth while for less able pupils to stay on in the expectation of better chances of examination success.

This is an argument which would appeal to, or come from, a writer of the Black Papers. It is not, however, one which we find persuasive. In the first place, the argument has difficulty with the contrasting trends in the case of O- and A-Level. The rapidly increasing numbers, and the constant success rate in the case of O-Level, is certainly consistent with the view that the examiners pass the same proportion of candidates each year irrespective of the actual standards attained. The pass mark could thus be argued to decline as the size of the field of candidates increases. But this argument fails to deal with the situation at A-Level where the success rate has actually increased.[8] True, it could be argued that standards declined even faster at A-Level than they did at O-Level, thus stimulating an even faster rate of growth in entries. This could 'explain' both the rise in numbers and the rise in the success rate, but it leaves us the problem of explaining why standards should have declined more rapidly at the higher level. We may have solved one problem by this line of argument, but only by creating another one.

Second, we should be clear that the argument that standards have declined is almost impossible to test in any sensible way. It is not enough to show that the average IQ of the children obtaining O-Level passes has fallen. This has almost certainly happened, given the increase in numbers, but to advance this in evidence is precisely to miss the point. What we want to know is whether slightly less able children than before could attain the same standards by harder work and better teaching. It is possible that they did not but this we cannot assume without evidence. We must consider, therefore, what a proper test of the claim that standards have fallen would entail. We would ideally like a selection of scripts from different periods which could then be given to a panel of judges. But would even this suffice? Would there not be changes over time in what counts as relevant knowledge? The story of the Oxford don who remarked that 'the questions are the same every year – we only change the answers' is apocryphal: but there is an important element of truth in it. Certainly the knowledge that students are required to master at university level has changed enormously over the past forty years, and it would be remarkable if there had not been similar changes at O-Level and A-Level. Certainly the syllabuses and text-books have changed. If this argument is sound, it becomes difficult and perhaps impossible to devise a test of standards which is fair between generations. What a given cohort of pupils is expected to know will be specific, at least to some extent, to its own time and the notion that standards have declined *in general* becomes an incoherent one. True, specific standards may have declined: pupils may know less Latin grammar than they used to, but they may also know more about, say, Latin literature. To claim that standards have declined, therefore, may instead be a plea that certain kinds of traditional knowledge ought to be valued. The notion that general standards have fallen is accordingly not likely to be a helpful one in exploration of the trends in our data.

Explanation II. Technological Need

What, then, are the alternative explanations that might be advanced? One which was popular in the 1950s and 1960s but has since lost favour, is what has been called the theory of technological needs. This accounts for educational expansion in terms of the demands of an advanced industrial economy, and in particular the growth of higher-level occupations for the exploitation of new scientific and social functions which require highly educated personnel. Thus Trow argues that:

The immediate force behind the [expansion of] both secondary and higher education are changes in public sentiment – in people's ideas of what they want and expect for their children in the way of formal education . . . Behind these changes in sentiment are other social forces, not least among which is another change in our occupational structure, parallel to the massive growth in the white-collar population which underlay the growth of the public secondary school system. The current change is the immense growth of demand for more highly-trained and educated people of all kinds . . . between 1950 and 1960 the total labor force increased by only 8 per cent – but the number of professional, technical, and kindred workers grew by 68 per cent – and these, of course, are the occupations that call for at least some part of a college education.[9]

There is undoubtedly some truth in this approach to the explanation of educational expansion, but it can be objected that the growth in education outstrips the growth in the relevant occupations. This can be tested from our own data. If we consider the jobs available to our respondents on entry into the labour market we find that for our oldest cohort (those born 1913–22) 6 per cent of the jobs were in Classes I and II, whereas for our youngest cohort (1943–52) the coresponding figure was 15 per cent,[10] giving an overall increase of 150 per cent.

Service-class jobs are the ones that typically require educated people, and on the technological need theory we would accordingly expect this growth of 'need' to be matched by a corresponding increase in 'supply'. This is true at O-Level where as we have seen the increase was 186 per cent, but the 619 per cent increase at A-Level far exceeds the amount required on this simple definition of occupational need.

The evidence, therefore, lends a degree of plausibility to the 'technological need' theory, but it does not seem able to explain the whole of the growth in educational qualifications. True, the difference in the growth rates at O- and A-Level could be explained in theory by an increase in the educational requirements of existing jobs. The advance of technology, it could be argued, requires that there should not only be more engineers, technicians, and managers, but that they should also be more highly trained than before. It is impossible for us to test this version of the theory from our own data, but the claim has come under considerable attack, and writers such as Berg[11] have plausibly argued that the educational level of the US labour force has changed in excess of that which is necessary to keep up with the skill requirements of jobs and that over-education for available jobs is becoming increasingly apparent.

Explanation III. Conflict Theory

While we cannot, then, discount the claims of either of the first two theories, it is clear that they are not so powerful as to exclude other alternatives. The most popular of these is the conflict theory advanced by Randall Collins. This sees the growth in education as the result of a demand by families and status groups for 'mobility opportunity'. It shifts the focus from the factors influencing the demand for educated personnel to those that influence the supply. Collins argues that:

Education has been associated with high economic and status position from the [American] colonial period on through the twentieth century. The result was a popular demand for education as mobility opportunity . . . Higher educational requirements, and the higher level of educational credentials offered by individuals competing for position in organizations, have in turn increased the demand for education by the populace. The interaction between formal job requirements and informal status culture has resulted in a spiral in which educational requirements and educational attainments become ever higher.[12]

Collins's argument, although superficially attractive, is exceedingly vague and gives no precise account of the mechanisms underlying the 'spiral in which educational requirements and educational attainments become ever higher'. As it stands, it is almost impossible to test Collins's claims, but what we can do is reformulate his argument in more precise terms that do allow some empirical investigation. If we think of education as a demand for mobility opportunity, then we are simply saying that people stay on at school and obtain qualifications in order to improve their job prospects. Using a rational-choice approach[13] we can put this rather more formally. The benefits from obtaining a qualification depend on the difference it makes to one's job prospects, and this decomposes into two parts. On the one hand there is the difference which the qualification make to one's chances of getting a job, and on the other there is the utility of the job itself. We can summarize this in the following equation:

$$\Delta U_q = \Delta P_{qj} \, \Delta U_j \qquad \qquad \text{Equation 7.1}$$

where ΔU_q represents the additional utility one obtains by securing the qualification,

ΔP_{qj} represents the difference which obtaining the qualification makes to the probability that one will obtain the job, and

ΔU_j represents the difference in utility from the job itself.[14]

Equation 7.1 contains two important principles. First, it brings out one of the fundamentals of rational choice theory, namely that one compares the benefits of a given course of action with those of the alternative courses. It is worth obtaining a qualification only if it *improves* one's chances of getting a good job, and it is the extent of the improvement that is the relevant consideration. Second, it contains the important principle of 'expected utility maximization', the principle that is usually held to be the rational one for making decisions in situations of risk. This states that the benefits of a risky course of action have to be weighted by the probabilities of securing them.

If we now assume that the demand for education depends on the size of the benefits it brings, that is on ΔU_q, we obtain some leverage on the problem of the rate of growth in school attendance. A simple model indicates the argument. Assume that there are 100 jobs and 200 school leavers competing for them. Assume, too, that employers select all the qualified candidates first and then make up any remaining vacancies with unqualified applicants. (This kind of model will be familiar to readers of Boudon.) Now if there are, say, ten qualified candidates, their chance of securing the job will be 1.0, and there will be ninety places left for the other 190 applicants, giving them a probability of .47 of securing a job. The *difference* which having the qualification makes to one's chances of getting the job is thus .53. As the number of qualified applicants increases, however, we can see that the difference will increase. Thus if there are fifty qualified applicants, all with a chance of 1.0, the chances of the unqualified will be .33, and the difference has widened to .67. We thus reach the proposition that the more people have achieved a given level of qualification, the more important it is for the remainder to achieve that qualification too. This is a process that could easily generate a more rapid growth in education than in the number of jobs, one of the major problems that any theory of educational expansion must deal with.

There would seem to be one flaw in this proposition, however, namely that once the number of qualified exceeds the number of vacancies, the difference in chances starts to *decline*. On the face of it, this suggests that the incentive to acquire the qualification will also decline and hence that, other things being equal, the numbers staying on should decline too. There is an element of truth in this, the point being that the incentive to *leave* after securing the qualification will decline. However, we can overcome this difficulty by a further and useful elaboration of the theory. Following the job competition model of writers like Thurow[15] we can assume that, once the number of qualified exceeds the vacancies, employers will start to use *higher*-level qualifications to select applicants. There will then be a further incentive to stay on for the extra year: pupils will stay on for an extra year not just to obtain, say, O-Levels and then leave, but as a stepping-stone to A-Levels. In other words, the reason for staying on for the extra year will include the increment to one's chances of gaining higher qualification. We thus obtain the new equation:

$$\Delta U_{q_1} = \Delta P_{q_1 i} \, \Delta U_j + \Delta P_{q_1 q_2} \, \Delta U_{q_2} \qquad\qquad \text{Equation 7.2}$$

where we have used the subscripts 1 and 2 to indicate the lower and higher qualifications respectively. $\Delta P_{q_1 q_2}$ indicates the difference which the lower qualification makes to one's chances of obtaining the higher one. And ΔU_{q_2} represents the additional utility derived from the higher qualification. It will also be possible to write an expression for ΔU_{q_2} on the same lines as Equation 7.1, and so we can see that this will generate further increases in school attendance as pupils now begin to set their sights on the higher qualification.

We can also see that processes of the kind postulated here could generate more rapid rates of increase at the higher educational levels once substantial numbers have reached the lower levels. In the model described above we see that there will be no incentive to obtain higher-level qualifications so long as there are more vacancies than there are applicants with the lower-level qualifications. But once the number of vacancies is less than the number of applicants with lower-level qualifications there will be an incentive to obtain the higher ones, and this incentive will now be increasing at a faster rate than the incentive to obtain the lower ones. A model of the kind given above indicates that $\Delta P_{q_2 j}$ will be increasing, and $\Delta P_{q_1 j}$ will be declining. If we also assume that ΔU_j and $\Delta P_{q_1 q_2}$ remain constant over time,[16] it follows that U_{q_2} must be increasing more rapidly than U_{q_1}.

Equations 7.1 and 7.2, then, provide a mechanism for Collins's postulated 'interaction between formal job requirements and informal status cultures [that results] in a spiral in which educational requirements and educational attainments become ever higher.' Unlike the 'declining standards' and 'technological need' theories they suggest cogent explanations for the fact that educational expansion has outstripped occupational expansion, and the fact that expansion at A-Level has been more rapid than that at O-Level.

These are important achievements for the model, but it does not seem able to account as it stands for one further empirical finding, namely that the *rate* of expansion at A-Level has been increasing. Table 7.3 shows that the growth in numbers obtaining A-Level or its equivalent has been accelerating. Now we have assumed that the rate of growth at A-Level will be a function of $\Delta P_{q_2 j}$ and Table 7.4 shows that this has remained remarkably constant over time, if anything declining in the most recent period. To calculate $\Delta P_{q_2 j}$ we have assumed that service-class jobs are the ones to which educational qualifications lead and that A-Levels and O-Levels represent the higher and lower qualifications respectively.

Table 7.4

Educational Qualifications and Job Opportunities

Respondents' Qualifications	Percentage Obtaining Service-Class Occupations on First Entry into the Labour Market, by Birth Cohort			
	1913–22	1923–32	1933–42	1943–52
A-Levels or Higher School Certificate	69.0	68.5	76.1	64.5 (74.2)
O-Levels or Ordinary School Certificate	24.0	30.4	29.1	27.3
None	2.4	3.8	4.0	4.2
All	6.0	9.0	13.1	14.9

Note: Figure in brackets is the percentage assuming that all those for whom data are missing, because they were still in full-time education in 1972, went on to obtain service-class jobs.

Thus in the 1913–22 cohort 69 per cent of those with A-Levels and 24 per cent of those with O-Levels obtained service-class jobs on first entry into the labour market, giving an estimate of .45 for $\Delta P_{q_2 j}$. In the youngest cohort this estimate becomes something between .47 and .37, depending on what assumptions we make about missing data.

The most notable feature of Table 7.4, then, is the constancy of $\Delta P_{q_2 j}$ and $\Delta P_{q_1 j}$ over time, and we cannot therefore look to these to explain the changes over time in the growth rates at O- and A-Level. One possibility, of course, would be to look at changes in wage differentials, but there is another, more sociological, complication to the model which may suffice to explain the trends. We shall examine this in the next section.

Explanation IV. The Pool of Ability

The final argument which we shall look at is a variant on the 'Pool of Ability' theme. The essentials of the argument can again be put in rational choice terms. Thus:

$$P_y = f(U_y) \qquad\qquad\qquad \text{Equation 7.3}$$

$$U_y = P_{yq}\,\Delta U_q - C_y \qquad\qquad\qquad \text{Equation 7.4}[17]$$

where P_y is the probability of staying on for a given year beyond the mini-
          mum leaving age;
      U_y is the utility of that year;
      P_{yq} is the probability of obtaining a qualification at the end of it;
      ΔU_q is the additional utility which that qualification yields; and
      C_y is the cost of that year, i.e. utility foregone.

It can be seen that Equation 7.4 is another example of the principle of expected utility maximization. In simple language what it means is that the value of an extra year at school depends on the benefits of that year less the costs, the benefits being the qualification attained at the end of it, and the increased job prospects thereby secured. The model used here is thus an extension of the one used in the previous section. There, we concentrated on the utility of a given qualification. We are now extending this to include the probability and the costs of obtaining that qualification. The two models are thus complementary.

Among the different terms in Equation 7.4, therefore, we have already dealt with ΔU_q. The evidence from the previous section suggests that this has remained more or less constant over time, and attention thus shifts to the other two terms. First, costs consist of the income forgone by staying at school rather than taking a job, and in addition the direct costs of maintenance for that year – the costs of food, clothing, and accommodation. We would expect these costs to be less of a burden in a more affluent family (hence the class differences in school attendance which we shall see in Chapter 8), and we would expect them to be less of a burden as general standards of living rise. Thus it would have been much more difficult for a working-class family to keep a boy at school in the 1920s or 1930s than it would today.

Second, consider P_{yq} – the probability of obtaining qualifications as a result of the extra year at school. The more able the child is, the higher will be this probability. Or rather, the more able the child is believed to be by himself and other relevant decision-makers, the higher this probability will be, for it is not the 'objective' truth but what people believe to be true that guides their action.

It follows, therefore, that, other things (notably social class) being equal, the ablest boys will be the first to stay on. Then, as costs fall over time, boys of lesser ability will find it worth their while to stay on. We can visualize this process in terms of Figure 4.1. Line A starts well to the right of the diagram and slopes diagonally from left to right. The diagonal slope indicates the differential impact of costs on the members of the different classes. The working-class boy has to have a much higher probability of success for $P_{yq} \Delta U_q$ to exceed C_y. As C_y falls, so boys for whom P_{yq} is lower will come to find that $P_{yq} \Delta U_q$ exceeds C_y, and the diagonal line will thus move gradually across to the left. At lower levels of P_{yq} there will be more and more boys with the requisite ability and for whom $P_{yq} \Delta U_q$ thus exceeds C_y. This means that the numbers staying on will not merely grow: the *rate* of growth will actually accelerate. There will, however, be an eventual decline in the rate of growth, and finally a limit to the leftwards movement of the diagonal line A. This limit will come when the 'pool of ability' of all those who are believed to have the capacity to achieve the given qualification is exhausted. When P_{yq} finally equals zero, further reductions in the costs of staying on at school have no effect and school attendance will have reached its ceiling or saturation level.

Equations 7.3 and 7.4, therefore, when coupled with some empirical assumptions about the distribution of 'ability' and the decline in costs, give some clear predictions about the pattern of growth in school attendance. They predict that the numbers staying on will start off from a low base, will then increase more and more rapidly before finally levelling off as the 'saturation level' is reached. This will give a curve shaped like an elongated 'S'. If we draw separate curves for each social class, the service-class curve will reach saturation first and the working-class last. We shall be able to test this theory in Chapter 8.

Before testing whether this is so, we should say rather more about the meaning of this 'pool of ability'. As we have already explained, it is not some 'objective' measure of the 'true' reserves of ability such as measured IQ that we have in mind. What we are looking at is the end-product of a set of social processes, involving culturally generated abilities to secure O- and A-Levels, and culturally determined beliefs about the distribution of these abilities.

THE GROWTH IN SCHOOL ATTENDANCE: FURTHER INVESTIGATION

To test the existence of these S-shaped curves we must use more detailed evidence than the data on the four cohorts given in Table 7.3. Annual data will give us a much better guide to the character of the trends. We can obtain these from our own survey, but there are also official data[18] that will give us a useful check on our data and that will, as we shall see, enable us to undertake a more detailed study. Figure 7.1 gives the two sets of data. It shows, for each year, the proportion staying on at school until the age of 16 or later. Similar diagrams could be constructed to give the proportion staying on until 17 or 18, but they would present essentially the same picture. From the point of view of the theory we are advancing, the reassuring feature is the similarity of the trends derived from the two sources. In both cases the picture is one of little or no growth in the pre-war years, a temporary increase immediately after the War, and then a period of steadily increasing school attendance with the fastest rates of growth being achieved in the mid 1960s. Finally, after the end of our period, the minimum school-leaving age was raised to 16, and both curves would therefore rise abruptly to 100 per cent if we were to continue them. The picture up to 1971 is not, however, without interest.

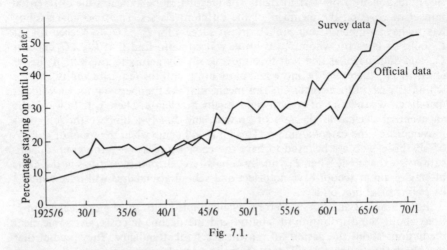

Fig. 7.1.

But before investigating the trends in detail, we must attend to the discrepancies between the two sets of data. The most marked discrepancy is that our sample-survey data consistently give higher estimates of the proportion staying on than do the official statistics. This can be accounted for, we believe, in a number of ways. First, the official data exclude the independent schools (although they include the Direct Grant schools). This would tend to inflate our figures, although it would not bridge the whole gap. Second, and more important, we suspect that our respondents may have exaggerated their age on leaving school if they had a birthday in the holiday immediately after they left school. A boy who left school at the end of the summer term and reached the age of 16 shortly afterwards would have been recorded in the official statistics as leaving at 15 (as indeed he did in a strict sense), and yet he may well have thought of himself as a 16-year-old school leaver and have so reported to us. After all (in the post-war period) he would have stayed on at school for a year after the age at which he could legally have left, and he would have spent the whole of his sixteenth year at school. We suspect that exaggeration of this kind is the most likely explanation for the higher estimates that we obtained from our questionnaire.[19]

So much, then, for the discrepancies between the two sets of data. The absolute estimates derived from our data are suspect, but the overall patterns would seem to be sound. What, then, are we to make of these overall patterns with their various kinks and bulges? Why is there recurrent stop–go? Does it really support the hypothesis of an S-shaped curve? The minor fluctuations in our own data can be attributed to sampling error. The average number of our respondents born in any one year is only 200 or thereabouts, and year-to-year fluctuations are therefore to be expected. But serious attention must be paid to the various kinks in the official trends.

It turns out, however, that a simple demographic explanation, of the kind we used earlier in analysing the history of class chances of access to secondary schools, also suffices to account for the irregularities in the curves that record length of secondary-school attendance. The total size of the cohort (or more precisely, the total number of school leavers as given in the official statistics) has a marked inverse correlation with the proportion of leavers staying on to the higher ages. The total number of leavers is plotted in Figure 7.2, and the 'peaks' in Figure 7.1 in 1946 and 1955 are exactly matched by corresponding 'valleys' in Figure 7.2, while the 1961 valley in Figure 7.1 is matched by a peak in Figure 7.2.

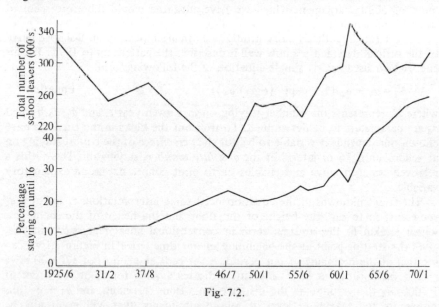

Fig. 7.2.

The sociological processes underlying this inverse correlation are easy to suggest. On the one hand a sudden increase in the size of the cohort, as in 1961, will stretch the physical capacities of the schools, and teachers or headmasters who wish to avoid the worst problems of overcrowding are likely to make harder-than-usual efforts to deter marginal candidates from continuing their education. A shortage of physical capacity will, therefore, squeeze out a number of pupils who would otherwise have continued their education. Thus in 1961 we can guess (by simply smoothing out the curve) that if the size of the cohort had stayed constant at 300 000 boys, an extra 5 per cent of them would have stayed on until 16 or later.

Conversely, when, as in 1946 or 1955, the size of the cohort falls, there will be the threat of surplus capacity in the schools, and teachers may be correspondingly *more* encouraging to marginal pupils. The pupil lucky enough to be born in a year of low fertility will accordingly have a better chance than he might otherwise (all other things being equal) of a long school career.

These processes of deterrence and encouragement will doubtless not be the only ones at work. There may be similar processes influencing the pupils themselves. Pupils will tend to judge themselves relative to their contemporaries, and if the cohort is bigger (or smaller) a boy of given ability will have more (or fewer) contemporaries above him. His judgement of his own abilities will thus vary according to the size of the cohort and his academic aspirations may be expected to vary too.

Processes of this kind may suffice to account for the various kinks in the trend, but they cannot account for the underlying trend itself, and it is to this we must now turn. The underlying picture seems to be one of little or no growth before the War, followed by a gradual acceleration after it, reaching a maximum in the mid-sixties, and then a gradual deceleration for the rest of the period. The 'pool of ability' argument which we have advanced would therefore seem to receive some support.[20]

To test this hypothesis more strictly, we can attempt to fit an S-shaped curve to the official data and see how well it describes the pattern up to 1971. To this end we have used a fairly simple equation of the following form:

$$N_t = a_1 + a_2/(1 + \exp(-(t-a_3)/a_4)) \qquad \text{Equation 7.5}$$

where N_t represents the number staying on in a given year t, and a_1, a_2, a_3, and a_4 are parameters to be determined. To iron out the kinks in the curve we have chosen our dependent variable to be not the *percentage* of the cohort staying on at school until 16 or later, but the *absolute numbers* staying on. This yields a relatively smooth curve and enables us to omit cohort size as an explanatory variable.

The four unknowns in the equation need some interpretation. a_1 and $a_1 + a_2$ represent, so to say, the height of the floor and the height of the ceiling. a_1, which is akin to the constant term in conventional linear regression analysis, gives the starting-point at the beginning of our time series. In Figure 7.1 we can see that at the beginning of our period, 8 per cent of a cohort of 320 000 boys stayed on until 16 or later, and this indicates a value for a_1 of the order of 25 000. a_2 then represents the distance from floor to ceiling, and $a_1 + a_2$ thus represents the maximum level of school attendance that will eventually be reached. a_3 stands for the date at which the mid-point between floor and ceiling is reached; this will also be the date at which the rate of increase starts to decelerate. We shall call this the inflexion point of the curve, and it can be seen from Figure 7.1 that this will be around 1963. Finally, a_4 is inversely proportional to the slope at the inflexion point.

What the equation generates, then, is a symmetrical curve starting from the value given to a_1, climbing slowly at first, and then more and more rapidly until the inflexion point is reached. The second half of the curve is then the mirror image of the first half. The rate of climb is initially very rapid, and it then becomes slower and slower until it reaches a plateau at the value given to $a_1 + a_2$.

We can now fit this equation to the official data on those staying on until 16, 17, and 18. (See Appendix III for the method employed.) The results are given in Table 7.5.

Table 7.5

Estimates Derived from the Logistic Curve

Dependent Variable		Parameter				
		a_1	a_2	a_3	a_4	R^2
Number staying on until	16 or later	32 800	156 800	1962.5	5.0	.989
	17 or later	13 990	66 600	1961.4	3.8	.994
	18 or later	6100	48 900	1962.0	4.4	.993

The most striking feature of this exercise is clearly the astonishing proportion of variance explained. We shall not obtain results like this anywhere else in the present volume, and they show that the model employed is about as good as one could possibly apply to the data available to us. Further tinkering with the model can yield only negligible improvements.

We must now consider rather more precisely just what this impressive R^2 means and what inferences we can draw. In the first place, we should not be over-impressed by a high R^2. It is far from being the only test of a good model. Thus we have relatively few observations to which the curve may be fitted, only twenty-six to be precise, and with enough unknowns in the equation it would be quite easy to obtain a value of 1.0 for R^2. Indeed, even the following simple linear equation

$$P_t = -6.0 + 1.1t \qquad \text{Equation 7.6}$$

where P_t represents the *percentage* of the cohort staying on yields a value of 0.68 for R^2. Moreover, extremely high R^2 of the order of .99 could easily be obtained from a cubic equation of the form:

$$P_t = a_1 + a_2 t + a_3 t^2 + a_4 t^3. \qquad \text{Equation 7.7}$$

It is not the size of R^2 that is crucial. R^2 has to be used as a test of the goodness of fit of *alternative* models, but we are not absolved from using other, more sociological, considerations in evaluating alternatives. Thus we may conclude from the values of R^2 that the logistic curve gives a better description of the past trends from 1925 to 1971 than does the linear equation, and it can also be preferred to the cubic equation on the quite different grounds that the cubic equation predicts that there will eventually be a massive *downswing* in school attendance. There are no good sociological grounds for expecting this, and therefore we have no hesitation in rejecting the cubic alternative.

We prefer our logistic curve, then, to the linear and cubic alternatives. It is far superior to these, the most obvious competing models, and we conclude that this test gives considerable support to the 'pool of ability' argument. It is the only one of the four arguments we have looked at that accounts convincingly for the trends in school attendance over time. It is not, of course, incompatible with the other arguments, and indeed it is natural to combine it with our formulation of the conflict theory. Thus Equation 7.2, which provides the kernel of our formulation of the conflict theory, can be substituted in Equation 7.4, the kernel of our formulation of the 'pool of ability' argument. What this yields is a single rational choice model which accounts for all three of the major findings of this chapter: the findings that educational expansion has outstripped occupational expansion, that the growth in A-Levels has outstripped the growth in O-Levels, and that the rates of growth were accelerating until the early 'sixties, although thereafter tending to decline.

INFERENCES FROM THE MODEL

We can now go on to use these S-shaped or logistic curves to make further inferences about the 'pool of ability'. Do our equations mean, then, that we can make confident predictions about the height of the eventual ceiling? The answer is clearly No. The raising of the school-leaving age to 16 in 1972 brings out starkly a point that is always present in any attempt to predict, namely that attempts to extrapolate into the future always depend on the assumption that variables not in the model, most notably in this case the institutional arrangements, remain unchanged. At best our equation would have allowed us to predict that, had the institutional arrangements remained unchanged, a maximum of 189 000 boys would eventually stay on at school until 16 plus.

Even this kind of qualified prediction must be taken cautiously. As we have explained, our logistic equation entails that the second half of the curve will be the mirror image of the first. Everything depends, therefore, on the accurate identification of the inflexion point. If we have not actually reached the inflexion point, it becomes impossible to make any sensible predictions about the eventual ceiling at all. We could obtain excellent and equally good fits with a number of widely different postulated ceilings. In the present case, of course, Figure 7.1 shows clearly that we have passed the inflexion point, but equally clearly that we are not far beyond it, and we have not really had time to see how the curve settles down. This could be a problem if there were, for example, particular features operating in the mid-sixties that we have not included in our model. Thus the economic downturn then might have encouraged more teenagers than usual to stay on at school, since they were unable to secure employment in the labour market, and the increases in school attendance might thus have been abnormally high. The 'true' inflexion point might thus be somewhat later than our model postulates, and the ceiling would be correspondingly higher. The further along the curve we have already travelled, therefore, the more confident we will be able to be about its general shape, although equally the less surprising will be any predictions we make. By making predictions at the moment, when we are not long past the postulated inflexion point, we run the risk of being badly wrong, although there is also the possibility of advancing more interesting hypotheses about future developments.

One useful exercise we can carry out using these logistic curves is to look at the changing level of inequality in schooling and to suggest what the eventual outcome might be in the absence of government intervention. Now if we had assumed that school attendance was growing in a linear fashion extending into the indefinite future, our prediction would be that schooling would become more and more equal. A model based on logistic curves like ours, however, predicts that, in the absence of outside intervention, there will be a limit to this trend towards equality. Once the ceilings of the different curves have been reached, there will be no further move towards equality.

To estimate the degree of inequality of schooling we can use the techniques developed by economists to measure the inequality of wealth or income. The simplest technique is to look at the total stock of wealth and to see what proportion of it is owned by the richest, say, 10 per cent, the next-richest 10 per cent, and so on. In the case of schooling we can look at the total number of years of schooling received by a given cohort, and we can then estimate the proportion of the total received by the 10 per cent who stay on at school longest. The calculations are very straightforward. Once we know the number of children leaving at each age, it is easy to calculate the total number of years of schooling received. We can then take those leaving at each age and see what proportion of the total they received. Thus among the 1925–6 school leavers 1.3 per cent left at the age of 18, and they received 1.8 per cent of the total years of schooling received by the cohort. 2.0 per cent of the leavers left at 17, and they received 2.8 per cent of the total years. We can continue this exercise for those leaving at the earlier ages, and by interpolation we can calculate what the 'top' 10 per cent received, and so on.

The most convenient percentile group for us to take is in fact the top 20 per cent. In 1925–6 this group received 22.2 per cent of the total years of schooling. By 1946 their share had increased to 24.2 per cent. The raising of the school-leaving age then reduced it to 22.8 per cent in 1950, but it again increased to 23.4 per cent in 1970. Thus up to this point there was a small, although definite, underlying trend towards inequality which was interrupted by the raising of the school-leaving age. Continuing along our logistic curves to 1990, by which time the ceilings would effectively have been reached, we find that the share of the top 20 per cent would have been reduced slightly to 23.0 per cent if the school-leaving age had not been increased, or rather more to 22.5 per cent if the school-leaving age had been increased to 16 and remained there.

The underlying trend towards inequality is thus reversed and a very slight tendency towards greater equality takes its place. However, by the time the 'saturation levels' are reached, this tendency has not progressed very far. Even with the two increments in the minimum school-leaving age, the degree of inequality at the end is still marginally larger than it was in the beginning. The lesson is clear, then. We cannot rely on 'natural forces' to produce a more equal society. Direct government intervention is essential as well.

The critic may reasonably object that, on the figures just presented, the level of inequality is at no point very great. By the figures we have become used to in economics, where the top 20 per cent receive something like 40 per cent of the total income (and even more extreme figures in the case of wealth), the striking feature of the distribution of schooling is its equality, not its inequality. There is certainly some truth in this, income is distributed more equally than wealth, and schooling is distributed more equally than either. On the other hand, measuring schooling in years will grossly underestimate the degree of inequality since a year of primary-school education is a great deal cheaper and makes much less claim on the nation's educational resources than a year in the sixth form. If we could weight each year by its cost, we would obtain a considerably more unequal result. The trends over time may not be very marked, but if we look at the distribution of educational resources in this way, taking account of the cost of schooling at different levels and institutions, we cannot so readily dismiss the problem of 'unequal schooling'.

CONCLUSION

Our period, which covers the rise of the tripartite system of secondary education and the beginnings of comprehensive reform, is one in which a boy's *type* of secondary schooling was largely fixed at the age of 11. But it was also a period of remarkable growth in *length* of secondary schooling - especially in the more selective and prestigious schools - and in *examination* success.

We have documented the development of the elongation of secondary schooling and the growth of secondary school certification. We have then tried to explain the patterns described. Some contribution to that explanation is to be had from the theory that secondary schools and secondary-school examinations expanded to meet the demand for more qualified manpower in a society making technological progress. Part of the explanation, too, might be had from a theory of status competition. Nor is the evidence sufficient to refute, though it does not support, the view that expanding numbers have involved declining examination standards. Yet the main outcome has been that we have been able to develop a version of the idea of 'a pool of ability' into a rational choice theory with realistic sociological and psychological assumptions which fits well with the fundamentally S-shaped curve of expansion that we have described.

NOTES

1. Highest, that is, in terms of the rough educational-cum-social hierarchy implied, for example, in Table 7.1. For this purpose, however, non-HMC schools were ranked above grammar schools. See Chapter 2, p.23.
2. For a detailed analysis see D. Raffe, 'The "Alternative Route" Reconsidered', *Sociology* 13 (1), 1979.
3. The details appear in G. Kalton, op.cit., p.102, Table 6.22. Kalton adds: 'In part these data reflect the later age of leaving of the public school boys, which results for example in more of them taking A-Level. But a similar picture emerges when the analysis is restricted to leavers who have taken A-Level. The proportions obtaining two or more passes among those who have taken A-Level are: public school leavers known to have passed the 11+ - 86%, and failed the 11+ - 63%; grammar school boys - 77%; and boys leaving maintained secondary schools other than grammar, technical and comprehensive schools - 42% (no figures are published on this subject for secondary modern schools on their own).'
4. We should also note that Douglas found that, controlling for social class and measured ability, there was no difference in the success rates of independent and grammar schools. Douglas, however, combines both HMC and non-HMC schools and it would thus be quite reasonable to argue that the HMC schools provided better, and the non-HMC schools worse, teaching than the grammar schools.
5. *Black Papers 1975*, edited by C. B. Cox and Rhodes Boyson (J. M. Dent & Sons Ltd., 1975), p.8.
6. Deane and Cole, op.cit., p.331.
7. We have defined the number entering the sixth form as those who stayed on until 17 or later and those completing the sixth form as those staying on until 18 or later.

8. We should remember that our data do not relate to entries. It is therefore possible that the A-Level examiners passed a constant proportion of entries and that the increase in success rate is due to a greater proportion of those staying on to 18 deciding to take the examination.
9. J. Karabel and A. H. Halsey, (eds.), *Power and Ideology in Education*, (Oxford University Press, New York, 1977), p.111.
10. This is almost certainly an underestimate. In the youngest cohort, 5 per cent reported that they had not had a job by 1972. Almost all this group were still engaged in full-time higher education, and were thus likely to enter jobs in Classes I and II with far greater frequency than the average for the age-group as a whole. Assuming all did so, the maximum figure is 20 per cent, giving an overall increase of 233 per cent.
11. I. Berg, *Education and Jobs: The Great Training Robbery* (Praeger, 1970).
12. J. Karabel and A. H. Halsey, op.cit., pp.130 and 132.
13. A. F. Heath, *Rational Choice and Social Exchange* (Cambridge University Press, 1976).
14. We have stated the argument throughout for a two-job model. If we use j_1 and j_0 to indicate the higher and lower jobs, and q_1 and q_0 to indicate the presence and absence of the qualification, we can write:

$$U_{q_1} = P_{q_1 j_1} U_{j_1} + (1 - P_{q_1 j_1}) U_{j_0}$$

$$U_{q_0} = P_{q_0 j_1} U_{j_1} + (1 - P_{q_0 j_1}) U_{j_0}$$

$$U_{q_1} - U_{q_0} = P_{q_1 j_1} U_{j_1} + (1 - P_{q_1 j_1}) U_{j_0} - P_{q_0 j_1} U_{j_1} - (1 - P_{q_0 j_1}) U_{j_0}$$

$$= (P_{q_1 j_1} - P_{q_0 j_1})(U_{j_1} - U_{j_0}).$$

This can, of course, be generalized to the n-job case.
15. L. C. Thurow, 'Education and Economic Equality', *The Public Interest*, 28 (Summer 1972), 66–81.
16. A more sophisticated model could be developed to include changes over time in ΔU_j, that is in relative wage rates. It is harder to know what to do about $P_{q_1 q_2}$. The evidence shows clearly that the actual proportion of people with, say, O-Level who go on to obtain A Level have been changing quite considerably over time. But the proportion who do so may be expected to vary with, among other things, $\Delta P_{q_2 j} U_j$. The proportion of those with the lower qualification who go on to obtain the higher qualification cannot therefore be taken as a direct measure of $\Delta P_{q_1 q_2}$. $\Delta P_{q_1 q_2}$ is better taken to depend on the relative difficulty of the two examinations, and in the absence of good evidence to the contrary, we shall assume that this has remained constant.
17. Strictly we should give ΔP_{yq} here rather than P_{yq}, but for the sake of simplicity we shall assume that no-one who left at the minimum leaving age obtained O-Levels or Ordinary School Certificate. This is not far from the truth. There is no need to write ΔU_y or ΔC_y since we are concerned with things that are by definition *increments*, that is with the utility and cost of an *extra* year at school.
18. Published in *Statistics of Education*, 1971, vol. 2 (HMSO, 1973), pp.2–3.
19. There is a third discrepancy between the two sets of data, although we doubt if it systematically affects the relation between them. This is the fact that our data give the percentage of the cohort, that is, the percentage of those *born* in any given year, who stayed on until the specified age, whereas the official statistics classify pupils by the year in which they left school. Thus the 'official' percentages presented here give the percentage of *leavers* in any given year who stayed on until the specified age.
20. We should note, however, that alternative explanations for the occurrence of an S-shaped curve can be advanced. Contagion theories have been used to account for the spread of diseases, which often follow a similar curve, and the same idea has been applied to growth in the demand for education. For an account, see J. Vaizey, *The Political Economy of Education* (Duckworth, London, 1972).

CHAPTER 8

Selection and Survival in Secondary School

In Chapter 7 we examined the overall patterns of attendance and attainment in the secondary-school system, and we now turn our attention to class differences in attendance and attainment. Social selection through education is a familiar feature of modern society. It has been documented throughout the twentieth century by sociologists of education, with characteristic emphasis in Europe on the implications for working-class children as secondary schools have been reformed to lie 'end-on' to the primary stage rather than, as previously, forming a separate system largely confined to the middle classes. In the context of the 1944 Act in Britain the earliest formulation of the problem, by Floud, Halsey, and Martin, aimed first to dissect the forces between and within social classes which resulted in differing rates of entry into selective secondary schools, and second to analyse the operation of these forces within the secondary-school career to reproduce further patterns of class inequalities of survival.

Survival, according to these authors, was the crucial problem for the future, the test of the effectiveness of the 1944 Act, and especially of whether this legislative step towards meritocracy would be rendered ineffective by the continuance of the tripartite structure of secondary education. Writing in 1953 they remarked that

any attempt to increase still further the social equity of current selection procedure is of course to be welcomed. But it would be naive to expect that any way of by-passing the individual's life history is likely to be discovered, or to suppose that such a discovery would necessarily be of more than theoretical interest to educators; existing selection procedures after all, perhaps just because they draw to some extent upon the individual's past experience, give a fairly efficient prediction of success in the grammar school. From the point of view of social mobility, it may be more relevant to enquire whether the present structure of secondary education provides the best possible means of fostering all grades and types of ability at all social levels. We have seen, for example, that the educational and social changes discussed above have made virtually no impact on the unskilled section of the working class . . . If, moreover, we consider those of their children who in fact succeed in reaching the grammar school, we see that what differentiates them most sharply from other children is the shortness of their school careers and that their subsequent occupations are not, on the average, superior to those of children of similar social origins who have attended the technical schools, with their practical bias and substantially lower prestige . . . this is perhaps the most important field of work for those concerned with the social aspects of education.[1]

The wastage of talent caused by drop-out of able working-class children from the grammar schools continued as one of the main foci of research and policy in British education. Thus James Douglas found that the social class inequalities in opportunity observed in the primary schools have increased in the secondary and extend, in a way which was not in evidence at the time of secondary selection, even to the highest levels of ability. It seems that the able boys and girls from working class families, although encountering no obstacles at entry to the selective secondary schools, have been heavily handicapped in their later secondary school careers through relatively early leaving and poor examination results.[2]

Douglas added that the social class differences were even greater among the children at the borderline level of ability for grammar-school entry.

BOUDON'S PRIMARY AND SECONDARY EFFECTS

Thus there seems to have been a double handicap suffered by the working class. Not only was the working-class child likely to have lower measured intelligence than the middle-class child, thus reducing his chances of a grammar-school place; but also, even if he scored highly in these tests, he would tend to leave school earlier and with less examination success. More recently Raymond Boudon in a novel treatment of these issues, has called these the primary and secondary effects of stratification. He sees the primary effects of stratification as the differences in school achievement resulting from the cultural differences between the social classes. Thus the differences which British researchers had found in the test scores of children from different social classes, which they attribute, *inter alia*, to the different levels of parental interest in the middle and working classes, constitute primary effects of stratification in Boudon's terminology. The secondary effects are those which are generated by other means than cultural inequalities. Thus Boudon writes 'one circumstance typical of the secondary effects of stratification is that two youngsters exactly comparable in other respects and particularly with respect to school achievement, but different with respect to social background, will have different probabilities of surviving [in school beyond the given age].'[3]

The terms used by Boudon are confusing in that they presuppose a 'cultural' explanation for the primary effects of stratification. We prefer to leave open the explanation of the class differences in question but to use Boudon's distinction so as to compare class differences in allocation between types of school at age 11 with class differences in length of secondary schooling.

The interest of Boudon's work lies mainly in his claim that 'the secondary effects of stratification on inequality of educational opportunity are, other things being equal, probably much more important than their primary (cultural) effects'.[4] Boudon believes that there has been a general tendency to overestimate the importance of the primary (cultural) effects of stratification and to ignore the secondary. In the British context this is tantamount to saying that we have allowed the problem of achieving equality of opportunity at '11-plus' to overshadow the even more serious problem of achieving equality of opportunity at '16-plus'. Indeed it might be argued that the introduction of comprehensive schools and the dismantling of the tripartite system was primarily designed to eliminate the former inequalities but does nothing to tackle the letter. Certainly it renders the former invisible, so that Floud, Halsey, and Martin's definition of the emerging problem as one of a shift of the crucial point of selection from entry to grammar schools to entry to the sixth form has become a definition of the problem of class differences in educational opportunity in comprehensive schools.

The strength of Boudon's claim with respect to 'primary' and 'secondary' effects rests largely on the validity of the exponential, or multiplicative, model which he develops. The idea is a simple one, although perhaps novel to those sociologists who are used to dealing with linear regression models. Suppose, says Boudon, that a boy of high school achievement and high social class has a probability of 0.85 of staying on for an extra year at school while a boy of high achievement but low social class has a probability of 0.60. Suppose, moreover, that these probabilities of survival stay constant at each 'branching point', as Boudon calls it; that is to say, suppose that boys of high achievement and high social class not only have a probability of 0.85 of staying on for one extra year beyond the minimum leaving age but also, if they survive for that year, again have a probability of 0.85 of surviving for a second year. Obviously this generates an exponential model: the probability of surviving for two years is 0.85^2, for three years is 0.85^3, and so on. Table 8.1 shows the pattern of class differentials that results from these hypothetical figures. The log distance between the upper and lower classes increases from 35 at 15 to 139 at 18, and if the same probabilities of survival from one year to the next continued into and through university, the distance would continue to grow. In this way, then, the secondary effects of stratification reassert themselves again and again throughout the life of a cohort, and even if we were to eliminate the primary effects of stratification, these secondary effects would still produce massive inequalities between the social classes.

Table 8.1

An Exponential Model of School Attendance
(Percentage of children of high achievement
attending school at different ages:
Hypothetical data)

| | AGE | | | |
	15	16	17	18
High social class	85.0	72.2	61.4	52.2
	*35**	*70*	*105*	*139*
Medium social class	70.0	49.0	34.3	24.0
	15	*31*	*46*	*61*
Lower social class	60.0	36.0	21.6	13.0
	0	*0*	*0*	*0*

* Figures in italic give log distances: see Chapter 3, p.37.

This result, that the log distance between the social classes will widen as we move upwards through the educational system, holds true whatever values we choose for the initial survival rates. Notice, however, that the *difference* between the percentages as distinct from the log distance may follow a variety of paths depending upon the precise value of the survival rates. Thus we see in Table 8.1 that the difference between the high and low social classes reaches a maximum of 40 percentage points at 17, and then begins to narrow slightly. Had we continued that table through to university we would have found that the difference would narrow further, and more rapidly. Moreover, had we chosen different initial values we might have obtained a quite different pattern. Thus with a very wide initial disparity, say 0.85 and 0.10, the gap would have been at its widest, in difference terms, at 15, and thereafter would have narrowed.

Table 8.2

Percentage Attending School at Different Ages

Father's social class	AGE			
	15	16	17	18
I, II	88.2	70.0	48.1	28.8
(N = 1072)	*46**	*143*	*210*	*226*
III, IV, V	67.3	32.6	15.1	7.7
(N = 2475)	*19*	*66*	*94*	*94*
VI, VII, VIII	55.9	16.8	5.9	3.0
(N = 4482)	*0*	*0*	*0*	*0*

* Figures in italic give log distances; see Chapter 3, p.37.

Let us turn now to our own data. Table 8.2 shows the pattern for the sample as a whole. It shows that working-class children were much more likely to leave early and that, in accordance with an exponential model of the kind just outlined, the log distance widens as our sample moved up though the schools. Over four times as many service class as working-class boys were still at school at 16, but nearly ten times as many stay on until 18. However, we also see that the gap, in difference rather than distance terms, first widens and then narrows. This has a simple and useful interpretation. It means, in this case, that it was the typical experience for a service-class boy to be at school at 16 but a quite atypical experience for the working-class boy. But by 18 it was the typical experience for both groups to have left school and to be in the labour market. Less than one-third of our service class respondents stayed on until 18, and these were thus the exceptional ones. For most people, service class and working class alike, full-time education has been completed a year or more before that.

Admittedly Table 8.2 gives a somewhat misleading picture since it includes both those who left at 14 and those who had to stay on until 15 after the minimum school-leaving age was raised in 1947. To correct the picture therefore we must look separately at our successive birth cohorts and this we do below: but first let us compare our actual figures for the whole sample (Table 8.2) with those of an exponential model of school attendance (Table 8.3). As we have said, the pattern we get with an exponential model will depend on the starting figure. If we set the figures at 0.7, 0.3, and 0.2 the pattern so generated is similar to that which occurred. The congruence with the actual pattern is, indeed, quite

Table 8.3

An Exponential Model of School Attendance
(Percentage of children staying on until a
given age or beyond: Hypothetical data)

Father's social class	AGE		
	16	17	18
I, II	70.0	49.0	34.3
	125*	*251*	*376*
III, IV, V	30.0	9.0	2.7
	41	*81*	*122*
VI, VII, VIII	20.0	4.0	0.8
	0	*0*	*0*

* Figures in italics give log distances; see Chapter 3, p.37.

striking and certainly lends support to our use of an exponential model. But there are also some discrepancies. In reality the gap is even wider than that predicted by the exponential model at age 16 but is subsequently smaller than that which is predicted. This means that the survival rates as pupils move up the school do not remain constant as Boudon assumed. Instead they tend to converge (Table 8.4). The table shows an enormous drop-out of working-class

Table 8.4

Survival Rates at Different Ages
(proportions)

Father's social class	AGE			
	15	16	17	18
I, II	0.88	0.79	0.69	0.60
III, IV, V	0.67	0.48	0.46	0.51
VI, VII, VIII	0.56	0.30	0.35	0.50

Note: 15 = survival from 14 to 15. 16 = survival from 15 to 16, and so on.

boys at the minimum school-leaving age, but the longer a working-class pupil survives within the school system the more closely do his chances of surviving yet further approximate to the service and intermediate class pupils' chances. By the time the children have reached the sixth form the differences have become very small indeed: assimilation is virtually complete.

This is a striking and important result. It suggests that the secondary effects of stratification, although reasserting themselves at each stage, may do so with less and less vigour. It suggests that the able boys from working-class homes, although heavily handicapped at 15 and 16 may, if they survive these hurdles, compete on more equal terms at 17 and 18. To test this hypothesis we must attempt to isolate the secondary from the primary effects. We do not have

Table 8.5

*Percentage of Children Attending School until Different Ages or beyond.
1933–52 Cohorts*

Father's social class		Non-selective Schools AGE		
		16	17	18
I, II	N = 196	38.8 *117*	14.3 *174*	5.1 *163*
III, IV, V	N = 801	18.1 *41*	4.7 *63*	1.6 *47*
VI, VII, VIII	N = 1692	12.0 *0*	2.5 *0*	1.0 *0*

Father's social class		Technical Schools AGE		
		16	17	18
I, II	N = 43	79.1 *54*	34.9 *82*	18.6 *118*
III, IV, V	N = 131	51.9 *11*	13.7 *−12*	7.6 *29*
VI, VII, VIII	N = 175	46.3 *0*	15.4 *0*	5.7 *0*

Father's social class		Grammar Schools AGE		
		16	17	18
I, II	N = 258	96.1 *17*	74.0 *67*	50.8 *80*
III, IV, V	N = 301	89.0 *9*	48.2 *24*	29.6 *26*
VI, VII, VIII	N = 328	81.1 *0*	37.8 *0*	22.9 *0*

Father's social class		Private Schools AGE		
		16	17	18
I, II	N = 180	95.0 *13*	83.9 *34*	52.8 *41*
III, IV, V	N = 99	83.8 *0*	58.6 *−2*	30.3 *−15*
VI, VII, VIII	N = 37	83.8 *0*	59.5 *0*	35.1 *0*

Figures in italics give log distances; see Chapter 3, p.37.

measures of what Boudon refers to as school achievement and we would refer to as ability. But what we can do is examine the pattern of school leaving in the different types of secondary school on the argument that class differences *within* a school can be ascribed to the secondary effects of stratification while those *between* schools may be held to come from the primary effects. The division we use in this analysis is fourfold: non-selective, technical, grammar, and private schools are distinguished, and in order to deal with the raising of the school leaving age we shall restrict ourselves to the 1933–52 cohorts. The results appear in Table 8.5 and 8.6.

Table 8.6

Survival Rates, 1933–52 Cohorts

Father's social class	Non-selective Schools AGE		
	16	17	18
I, II	0.41	0.37	0.36
III, IV, V	0.19	0.26	0.34
VI, VII, VIII	0.13	0.21	0.40

Father's social class	Technical Schools AGE		
	16	17	18
I, II	0.81	0.44	0.53
III, IV, V	0.56	0.26	0.56
VI, VII, VIII	0.50	0.33	0.37

Father's social class	Grammar Schools AGE		
	16	17	18
I, II	0.96	0.77	0.69
III, IV, V	0.89	0.54	0.61
VI, VII, VIII	0.81	0.47	0.60

Father's social class	Private Schools AGE		
	16	17	18
I, II	0.96	0.88	0.63
III, IV, V	0.84	0.70	0.52
VI, VII, VIII	0.89	0.71	0.59

Table 8.5 shows, first, that there is a general tendency for the log distances to increase as boys move into the higher age ranges. In all four types of school the distance between the service and working classes is greater at 18 than at 16. There are no exceptions to this pattern, and we can therefore infer that the

secondary effects of stratification are at work in all types of school. Secondly, however, we can see from Table 8.6 that there is an equally general tendency for the survival rates to converge. In all four types of school that we have distinguished, the difference between the service-class and the working-class survival rates is substantially smaller at 18 than it was at 16. Again there are no exceptions.

The survival rates do not always, however, exhibit a straightforward linear convergence. In the non-selective and technical schools there is indeed a linear movement, the difference between the service- and working-class survival rates being smaller at each successive age. In the grammar (and to a lesser extent the private schools), on the other hand, the survival rates start relatively close together at 16, then widen dramatically at 17 before closing again at 18. What this means is that working-class boys have a not dissimilar chance from their service-class contemporaries of staying on for an extra year and, as we shall see, obtaining O-Levels. A big working-class drop-out then occurs at entry into the sixth form, although once into the sixth form the working-class boy again has almost as good a chance of completing the course as the boy from the service class. It is at entry into the sixth form, then, that the serious inequality of opportunity persists. It is here that the secondary effects of stratification operate most strongly.

This working-class drop-out in the grammar schools should not, on the other hand, blind us to the considerable assimilative capacity of the grammar schools. The working-class boy at grammar school still has a superior chance to the service-class boy at a technical school or non-selective school of an extended school career. This is a reminder of the importance of the primary effects of stratification.

SPONSORSHIP, CONTEST, AND SURVIVAL

All this throws doubt on Boudon's claim that 'the secondary effects of stratification on inequality of educational opportunity are, other things being equal, probably much more important than their primary (cultural) effects.' The secondary effects of stratification will clearly become larger the more often they reassert themselves and the wider the class differential in survival rates at each stage. Boudon is able to obtain very dramatic effects by keeping the differential constant and by allowing a large number of branching points. But the British educational system, particularly since the school-leaving age was raised, has relatively few branching points, and, as we have just seen, the class differential itself eventually disappears. Further doubt was cast on Boudon's claim when we noted how fateful is the allocation of children to different types of secondary school at the age of 11. As we have seen, the working-class child at a selective school is much more likely to stay on beyond the minimum school-leaving age than the service class child at a non-selective school. There are class differentials in school attendance *within* each type of school, but Tables 8.5 and 8.6 suggest that there are even wider differentials *between* the schools. This, of course, reflects the well-known distinction between 'sponsored' and 'contest' modes of ascent through education,[5] and one would tend to expect the secondary effects of stratification to have greater play in a 'contest' system. The 'sponsored' system, one might imagine, would tend to depress the prospects of the service class at non-selective schools and raise those of the working class at selective ones, and we might thus speculate that the introduction of comprehensive schools will lead to an increase in the magnitude of the secondary effects.

To be fair to Boudon we should point out that he was concerned with education systems of a 'contest' character, but even so it may be instructive to estimate more precisely what the relative importance of the secondary effects were in the British educational system. We may have cast doubt on Boudon's claim, but we have not yet refuted it. One way in which we can attempt to assess the relative importance of primary and secondary effects is to compare what would have happened had primary effects been removed completely with the results that would have occurred had the secondary effects been eliminated. To eliminate the primary but preserve the secondary effects we can construct a model where children from each class have identical chances of winning places at selective secondary schools but where their survival rates after the minimum school-leaving age are those which occurred in the real world (the 'secondary effects model'); and to eliminate secondary but preserve primary effects we can construct a model where the children from different classes in a given type of school have identical survival rates but where their chances of winning places at selective schools are those which actually occurred in the real world (the 'primary effects model').[6] These two models will now give us hypothetical figures for class differentials in school attendance beyond the minimum school-leaving age at selective and non-selective schools respectively, and we can of course combine the results for these two types of school to give us the overall class differentials.

The next stage is to compare the results generated by our two models, that is, to compare what happens when primary effects are eliminated with the consequences of eliminating secondary effects. The analysis was carried out for the post-war period, that is, for 1933–52 cohorts. The results from the 'primary effects' model appear in Table 8.7 and from the 'secondary effects' model in Table 8.8. Comparing these with each other and with the 'real world' (Table 8.9), it is clear that Boudon's thesis has to be rejected in the case of England and Wales. The primary-effects model is closer to reality. At 16, 17, and 18 the predictions of the primary-effects model are closer to the real world than those of the secondary-effects model. The reasons have already been adumbrated and are four: the British system of secondary education is 'sponsored' rather than

Table 8.7

Predictions of the 'Primary Effects' Model

Father's social class	AGE			
	15	16	17	18
I, II	97.9	67.9	42.9	26.3
III, IV, V	95.9	42.3	19.4	10.7
VI, VII, VIII	94.8	32.2	12.7	6.7

Table 8.8

Predictions of the 'Secondary Effects' Model

Father's social class	AGE			
	15	16	17	18
I, II	96.9	58.6	33.8	19.4
III, IV, V	97.6	42.1	19.4	10.6
VI, VII, VIII	95.8	34.8	15.3	8.5

Table 8.9

The Real World: 1933–52 cohorts

Father's social class	AGE			
	15	16	17	18
I, II	98.4	78.1	56.9	36.0
III, IV, V	95.9	42.3	19.4	10.7
VI, VII, VIII	95.6	26.0	9.6	5.2

'contest' in the terminology coined by R. H. Turner; it has a small number of branching points in Boudon's phrase; the survival rates tend to converge rather than to stabilize, and the different types of secondary school have different patterns of attendance and survival.

It may be objected however that the sponsored system of tripartite schools is now fast disappearing. As it does so will not the result be that secondary effects will come to dominate selection in a comprehensive secondary system? Our first response to this question must be to point out the need to be careful in interpreting these models. They do not claim to show what would *actually* have happened if, for example, primary effects really had been eliminated. Rather, they are a way of *isolating* the effects which the primary and secondary sources of stratification had in the past. The reason for this is simple. If primary effects really were eliminated, perhaps by having quotas for children from each social class at the different types of school, it would be highly implausible to suppose that the secondary effects would remain the same as before. Rather, class differentials in survival rates would almost certainly widen and thus the secondary effects would take up a lot of the inequalities removed by eliminating the primary effect. Hence, while it is tempting to suppose that the secondary-effects model, which eliminates primary effects, shows what might happen when comprehensive schooling replaces the tripartite arrangements we must resist the temptation. We can, moreover, be sure that the abolition of the grammar schools and of the earlier system of 11-plus selection has not meant and will not mean the abolition of primary effects. Far from it. Social class will still affect children's measured intelligence, and this is what Boudon meant by primary effects. The main question therefore is whether the able working-class children who would have gone to grammar schools under the old arrangements will now be more likely to drop out of school under the new. Within the limitations of our data we can only make further progress on this question by using the multiple regression analysis which we employed in Chapter 6, controlling 'family climate' and looking for 'school effects'. This we shall do in Chapter 9.

TRENDS IN SCHOOL ATTENDANCE

We saw in Chapter 7 that there have been impressive increases in school attendance beyond the minimum leaving age over the course of our period. How have these increases been shared by the different social classes? Table 8.10 gives the picture cohort by cohort for attendance till 16 or later.

The most striking features of this table are, first, the very different rates of increase at different social class levels and, second, the consequential decline in class differentials. Thus the proportion of boys from service-class homes who stayed on to 16 or later increased by 50 per cent, the proportion from the intermediate class increased by 200 per cent, and that from the working class by 240 per cent. The distance between the classes shrank accordingly, the service-class/working-class log distance shrinking from 174 to 91, and the intermediate-/working-class log distance shrinking from 56 to 43. As we have found before, therefore (as in our examination of selective schooling in Chapter 4) expansion has been associated with increased equality. But whereas the pre-war expansion of selective school places and consequent equalization of class chances was followed by a post-war contraction, the expansion and equalization in staying on has been sustained.

Table 8.10

Trends in School Attendance
Percentage staying on until 16 or later

Father's social class	Birth Cohort			
	1913–22	1923–32	1933–42	1943–52
I, II	52.4 *174**	61.0 *185*	77.3 *136*	78.6 *91*
III, IV, V	16.1 *56*	23.9 *91*	34.6 *56*	48.5 *43*
VI, VII, VIII	9.2 *0*	9.6 *0*	19.8 *0*	31.6 *0*

* Figures in italic give log distances; see Chapter 3, p.37.

The picture given by Table 8.10 is not, however, a simple one of a linear trend towards equality of class chances. The distances between classes first rise and then fall. The maximum inequality, as measured by the log distance, occurs not in the earliest cohort but in the 1923–32 cohort. And we must also note that the *difference* (measured in straightforward percentage terms) between the service and working class is actually greater at the end of the period than at the beginning. The difference starts at 43 percentage points, widens to 51 points, and falls back marginally to 47 points in the final cohort.

It is easy to make sense of these somewhat complicated patterns, however, if we visualize the three social classes as moving along three separate logistic curves which start to rise, inflect, and saturate at different dates from each other.

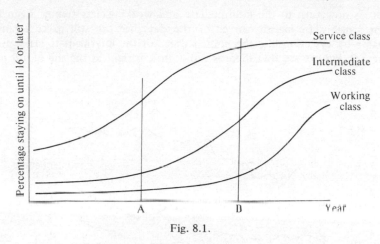

Fig. 8.1.

Figure 8.1 gives three such curves. We can imagine that Table 8.10 covers the segment from A to B in the diagram, during which the service class curve approaches saturation, the intermediate class curve approaches its inflexion point, and the working-class curve starts its journey from the 'floor'. Three logistic curves arranged in this way could generate exactly the pattern of changing percentages and distances revealed by Table 8.10. Such a pattern is also one predicted by the 'pool of ability' argument described in Chapter 7. Both the distribution of ability and the distribution of material advantages between the social classes predict, given our model, that the service class will saturate first and the working class last.

It would be useful at this point if we could fit logistic curves to the data as we did in Chapter 7, and thus derive estimates of the future ceilings for each of the three social classes. True, we must remember that the school-leaving age was raised to 16 after the end of our period; the percentages staying on until 16 or later will thus have risen abruptly to 100 per cent for all three classes. Nevertheless, it is of some interest to estimate what the 'natural' course of events and the 'natural' trend in class inequalities might have been.

In practice we can sensibly fit a logistic curve only to the service class data. As we remarked in Chapter 7, 'everything depends on the accurate identification of the inflexion point. If we have not actually reached the inflexion point, it becomes impossible to make any sensible predictions about the eventual ceiling at all.' In the service-class case, of course, the inflexion point has been passed and we can obtain a sensible estimate of the ceiling. Fitting the logistic curve to our data (and taking the *percentage*, not the absolute number staying on as our dependent variable) we obtain estimates of 24.1 for a_1, 62.0 for a_2, 1934 for a_3, and 12.2 for a_4. This thus predicts an eventual saturation level of 86 per cent. R^2 comes to .904, a considerably lower value than those obtained in Chapter 7. This should not, however, surprise us when we remember that we are now unable to control for cohort size and that we are dealing with annual estimates based on relatively small samples and hence involving considerable year-to-year fluctuations.

Let us now turn to the intermediate and working-class trends. Even if we cannot sensibly fit logistic curves to the data, we can still make a range of estimates by eye. Consider the annual data for the intermediate class given in Figure 8.2. We can see that there is rapid growth right at the end of our period

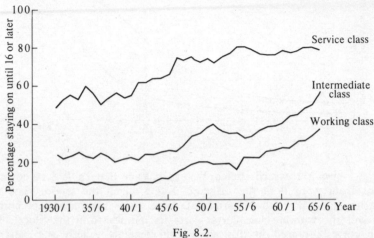

Fig. 8.2.

with the biggest increase in the very last year. One possible assumption, therefore, would be that the inflexion point is about to be reached. On this assumption, the curve has already risen from a 'floor' of 20 per cent to an inflexion point at 57 per cent, that is, by 37 per cent. If we assume further that attendance would have continued along a symmetrical logistic curve, we can predict that the ceiling will be a further 37 percentage points above the inflexion point, giving a saturation level of 94 per cent.

It might reasonably be argued that this puts undue weight on the final figure of our time series. If this figure of 57 per cent is regarded as sampling fluctuation, it could be that the 'true' inflexion point had already occurred somewhat earlier. The earliest it could plausibly have occurred is in 1961, when the percentage attending was 44. This would give a lower estimate of 68 per cent for the saturation level.

Finally, consider the working-class time series. We can be fairly confident that the inflexion point had not been reached. If we set it at the end of our time series, this will give us a very conservative estimate of the eventual saturation level. Since the working-class floor was 8 per cent and the final figure was 37 per cent, our estimate of the saturation level becomes 66 per cent.

These estimates clearly contain a considerable margin of error, but they do suggest that there would eventually have been a striking narrowing of class differentials. The most conservative estimates suggest that in another twenty or thirty years class differences would have narrowed to 20 percentage points, giving a log distance of 26 between the service and working classes. Less conservative estimates suggest that the gap between the social classes might have been eliminated altogether.

A useful check which we can carry out on these estimates is to look at the IQ thresholds which they imply. Thus, if the top 86 per cent of service-class boys were to stay on till 16 or later, this would imply (on the assumptions given in Chapter 4) that all service-class boys with measured ability of 94 points and over were staying on. Similarly, if the top 66 per cent of working-class boys were to stay on, this would imply that all those with measured ability of 92 points and over were doing so. These estimates of 94 and 92 points are encouragingly close together (particularly when we remember that the expansion of the service class probably means that our estimate of their average IQ is too high). This, then, again provides some support for the 'pool of ability' model described in Chapter 7. The argument there outlined stated that the limit to the growth in school attendance occurs when the 'pool of ability' of all those who are believed to have the capacity to achieve the given qualification is exhausted. When the probability of achieving the qualification finally equals zero, further reductions in the costs of staying on at school have no effect and school attendance will have reached its ceiling or saturation level. Another way of putting this is to say that if 86 per cent of service-class boys stay on, then some of those doing so must have IQs no higher than 94 points (and, of course, they may be lower if the strict queuing assumption does not hold); 94 points can, therefore, be taken to be roughly the minimum-ability level at which it is worth while to attempt O-Level and CSE examinations and accordingly if all working-class boys with that level of ability were to stay on and attempt these examinations, approximately two-thirds of the working class would in fact stay on.

This analysis has important implications for the raising of the school leaving age. To suggest that our logistic curves trace the 'natural' progress in school attendance might be taken to imply that the raising of the minimum leaving age was an 'unnatural' and mistaken social policy. But this would be a misleading inference. What our model does, if it is sound, is to indicate what *might* have happened if institutional arrangements such as the pattern of examination at 16-plus had remained unchanged and if parents' capacity to support their children had continued to grow in the same way that it had done over the previous forty years. If no change is made in the examination structure and no provision made for, say, maintenance grants, then the raising of the school-leaving age means that there will be many 'reluctant' pupils who would not voluntarily have chosen to stay on. What our analysis does, therefore, is indicate the need for changes in institutional arrangements if the problem of reluctant pupils is to be avoided. Our model indicates the discrepancy between what pupils are now required to do and what they would voluntarily have done if the situation had remained unchanged, but this does not provide an argument against change: it can equally provide an argument in favour of further changes in order to take account of the (educational and economic) interests of those now required to stay on.

The same kind of analysis can also be carried out for school attendance at 17-plus and 18-plus. Table 8.11 gives an overview of the 18+ trends. We see that the service-class curve has passed through its period of rapid growth and is now flattening out, while the intermediate and working-class curves look as though they had not reached their inflexion points by the end of our period. As before,

Table 8.11

Trends in School Attendance
Percentage staying on until 18 or later

Father's social class	Birth Cohort			
	1913–22	1923–32	1933–42	1943–52
I, II	15.7 *162**	20.0 *216*	32.2 *214*	38.2 *179*
III, IV, V	6.1 *68*	6.2 *99*	5.9 *44*	14.4 *81*
VI, VII, VIII	3.1 *0*	2.3 *0*	3.8 *0*	6.4 *0*

* Figures in italic give log distances; see Chapter 3, p.37.

then, it is sensible to fit a logistic curve only to the service class data. When we do so, we obtain estimates of 13.6 for a_1, 24.7 for a_2, 1950 for a_3, and 5.5 for a_4. R^2 comes to .908.[7] We thus obtain a service-class saturation level of 38.3 per cent, and this gives us an IQ threshold of 113. If we assume that intermediate- and working-class attendance will continue to grow until the same threshold is reached, we obtain saturation levels of 21.2 per cent and 13.9 per cent, respectively. This suggests that the distances between the classes will decline quite sharply from their present levels, the service-/working-class log distance of 179 points that we found for our 1943–52 cohort eventually declining to 101 points. It is interesting to note, however, that this is still considerably larger than the 26 point log distance that we earlier suggested was the one that the 'natural' trends in attendance at 16+ would ultimately have generated. While the trend may be towards greater equality, therefore, the higher the educational level the greater will be the eventual inequality. The point is essentially the same as the one made in Chapter 4 in our discussion of social class and secondary schooling. Class differentials are lowest at the bottom of the educational hierarchy, both in the real world and in our meritocratic model. If public schools head the queue, then, even a meritocratic selection procedure will give them the greatest class differentials. Similarly, a meritocratic selection procedure that creams off smaller and smaller numbers of pupils for higher levels of education will be yielding larger class differentials at succeeding levels.

Furthermore, we can see that if a process of 'credentialization' is occurring in which higher levels of educational attainment are required as more pupils attain the lower levels, the trends towards equality that our logistic curves revealed may be fundamentally misleading. While differentials may be closing at one level, they may be widening at a higher one, and the 'overall' situation may remain relatively static. Consider once again the meritocratic queuing model developed in Chapter 4. We can visualize the growth in school attendance at different ages as a series of vertical lines moving from right to left across the diagram. As one line, say the 16-plus line, moves across it will trace a logistic curve rising to its saturation level. It will be followed at a short distance by the 17-plus line, the 18-plus line, and then higher-education lines. But as one line reaches the end of its journey, the process of credentialization means that another one will be starting off. There is a process of continual movement. In contrast, if we turn from the growth in attendance at different ages to the position of different percentile groups, we find a completely static situation. If we assume that there is no change in the size or IQ distributions of the different classes, then the class differentials among, say, the brightest 5 per cent of pupils will remain absolutely unchanged. The top 5 per cent will be receiving more and more education as the process of credentialization continues, but class differences must necessarily remain as they are. If we consider, therefore, percentile groups rather than educational levels, the optimistic picture of increasing equality must be fundamentally revised. A strict meritocratic system will yield constant class differentials, and so will a non-meritocratic one such as our own if there is no move towards meritocracy.

SOCIAL CLASS AND EXAMINATION SUCCESS

We end this chapter by considering the relation between class origins and success in examinations at secondary schools. The examinations we have in mind are the School Certificate and Higher School Certificate which were later replaced by O-Level and A-Level.[8] The details appear in Table 8.12. We have already noted the larger class differences in proportions staying on to an extended secondary-school career: the class differences in examinations passed are therefore to be expected. What is more important to note is the *similarity* of the examination success rates in the different classes (a log distance of only 16 between the service- and working-class candidates at O-Level, and no distance at all at A-Level). This means that the differentials in examination success can almost wholly be explained by the differentials in staying on at secondary school. The relatively few working-class survivors to O- and A-Level competed on equal terms with their classmates from professional and white-collar families.

Essentially the same picture appears when boys are classified by different cultural backgrounds (i.e. are classified by parental education). This analysis appears in Table 8.13. Again there are big differentials in the percentages staying on from each 'educational class' and in the percentages securing credentials, while the success rates are in comparison very similar. Thus the log distance (comparing children whose parents attended private schools with those whose parents attended non-selective ones) is 120 in the case of attendance at 16, 187 in the case of attendance until 18, but only 22 in the case of the success rates in public examinations.

These similarities in success rates take on an interest, however, if we relate them to Bourdieu's argument that the educational system of capitalist societies, of which England and Wales must presumably count as an example, 'offers information and training which can be received and acquired only by subjects endowed with the system of predispositions that is the condition for the success of the transmission and of the inculcation of the culture'.[9] On this argument working-class boys, being bereft of the system of predispositions should, consequently, have lower success rates. Examinations, Bourdieu argues, denote successful acquisition of the dominant culture. The differences in the success rates shown by Tables 8.12 and 8.13 are undoubtedly in line with Bourdieu's thesis, but their smallness suggests that Bourdieu's postulated mechanism is not of great importance in explaining the differential attainment of service- and working-class children. To account for these differences we must look to the

Table 8.12

Social Class and School Examinations

Father's Social class	1 Percentage staying on until 16 or later	2 Percentage obtaining School Certificate or 1 or more O-Levels	3 Column 2 as a proportion of Column 1 (O-Level success rate)	4 Percentage staying on until 18 or later	5 Percentage obtaining Higher School Certificate or 1 or more. A-Levels	6 Column 5 as a proportion of Column 4 (A-Level success rate)
I, II (N = 1072)	70.0 *96**	58.1 *159*	0.83 *16*	28.2 *224*	26.9 *226*	0.93 *0*
III, IV, V (N = 2475)	32.6 *20*	24.2 *72*	0.74 *4*	7.7 *94*	6.9 *90*	0.90 *−3*
VI, VII, VIII (N = 4482)	26.8 *0*	11.8 *0*	0.71 *0*	3.0 *0*	2.8 *0*	0.93 *0*

* Figures in italic give log distances (see Chapter 3, p.37).

Table 8.13

School Examinations and Parental Education

	1 Percentage staying on until 16 or later	2 Percentage obtaining School Certificate or 1 or more O-levels	3 O-level success rate (Column 2 as a proportion of Column 1)	4 Percentage staying on until 18 or later	5 Percentage obtaining Higher School Certificate or 1 or more A-levels	6 A-level success rate (Column 5 as a proportion of Column 4)
One or both parents attended private secondary schools (N = 383)	74.7 *120*	61.9 *138*	0.83 *17*	33.7 *187*	30.8 *209*	0.91 *22*
One or both parents attended selective secondary schools[1] (N = 1205)	52.2 *85*	42.4 *100*	0.81 *15*	19.8 *134*	18.5 *158*	0.93 *24*
Both parents attended non-selective secondary schools (N = 6941)	22.4 *0*	15.6 *0*	0.70 *0*	5.2 *0*	3.8 *0*	0.73 *0*

[1] Defined as in footnote to Table 5.1.
* Figures in italic give log distances (see Chapter 3, p.37).

factors which lead to the early drop-out of working-class children from school, and as we have seen earlier in this chapter (Table 8.5) much of the explanation has to do with the type of school attended. As we showed, the pattern of working-class attendance at grammar schools is much more similar to that of the service class at grammar school than it is to either service- or working-class at non-selective schools. The type of school one attends would seem to be the single most important factor in determining how long one's school career will be.

We saw, of course, that there were still class differences *within* the grammar school in the patterns of our respondents' school careers, and it may be useful to see how these relate to examination success. The relevant figures appear in Table 8.14. A striking feature of this table is how much the log distances have been reduced now that we control for type of school. The class differential in attendance at 16 is reduced to 17, in O-Levels to 27, and in success rates to 11. Much the same picture appears when we classify respondents by parental education. Log distances are again much reduced.

Our conclusion, then, must be that differences in success rates, and hence Bourdieu's postulated mechanism, play a very small part in explaining differentials in academic achievement. True, Bourdieu might reply that his argument applies at earlier stages of the school career, that working-class boys obtain fewer places at grammar school and leave earlier because they do not have the necessary 'system of predispositions', and that those who stay on and successfully obtain academic credentials are a fortunate minority who have been assimilated by the dominant culture. Clearly our data cannot refute a reformulation along these lines. But we would reiterate that, as we said in Chapter 5, *'formal'* if not *'effective'* opportunity of acquiring educational skills is offered to many boys from 'unschooled' backgrounds. And we have now found that for a majority of these boys the formal opportunities were indeed effective. We do not wish to underestimate the inequalities which persist within our educational system, but we must not neglect the extent of educational opportunity either. Thus two-thirds of the boys at the grammar schools came from 'unschooled' backgrounds: in our terminology they were 'first-generation' grammar-school boys. And two-thirds of these 'first-generation' boys went on to obtain some academic credential. In Chapter 5 we quoted Bourdieu's statement that

the educational system reproduces all the more perfectly the structure of the distribution of cultural capital among classes (and sections of a class) in that the culture which it transmits is closer to the dominant culture and that the mode of inculcation to which it has recourse is less removed from the mode of inculcation practised by the family . . . . An educational system which puts into practice an implicit pedagogic action, requiring initial familiarity with the dominant culture, and which proceeds by imperceptible familiarization, offers information and training which can be received and acquired only by subjects endowed with the system of predispositions that is the condition for the success of the transmission and of the inculcation of the culture.[10]

We must now conclude that this reproduction is far from perfect.

Table 8.14

Social Class and School Examination: Grammar School Pupils Only

Father's social class	1 Percentage staying on until 16 or later		2 Percentage obtaining School Certificate or 1 or more O-Levels		3 Column 2 as a proportion of Column 1: O-Level success rate	
I, II (N = 376)	92.8	*17*	83.2	*27*	0.90	*11*
III, IV, V (N = 484)	82.9	*6*	71.9	*13*	0.87	*7*
VI, VII, VIII (N = 495)	78.4	*0*	63.2	*0*	0.81	*0*
One or both parents attended private secondary schools (N = 86)	86.0	*6*	75.6	*12*	0.88	*7*
One or both parents attended selective secondary schools[1] (N = 373)	89.5	*10*	81.0	*19*	0.91	*10*
Both parents attended non-selective secondary schools (N = 952)	81.3	*0*	67.0	*0*	0.82	*0*

[1] Defined as in footnote to Table 5.1.

* Figures in italic give log distances (see Chapter 3, p.37).

CONCLUSION

We have used our survey data in this chapter to consider two French contributions – from Raymond Boudon and Pierre Bourdieu – to the theory of social selection through education.

Raymond Boudon has argued that, at least in recent decades, selection against children of working-class origin has been more a matter of survival within the school system than one of disadvantaged initial access to that system. Our own evidence compels us to introduce a crucial modification to Boudon's thesis. We agree with him that the 'secondary' or survival effect repeats itself year after year, to attenuate the secondary-school presence of working-class boys. But whereas he assumed constancy of its effect, we have shown that during the secondary-school career the effect diminishes and that the survivors are increasingly assimilated to the pattern of survival, and also of performance, of the service-class pupils.

Further we have shown that while Boudon's secondary effects account for class differences *within* schools, primary effects still operated *between* schools under the tripartite division of secondary education through which most members of our sample had passed. It was the 11-plus 'branching' point that was decisive for class selection before the comprehensive movement supplanted the tripartite system. Under this system the primary effects of class selection outweighed the secondary ones. It was, in R. H. Turner's terms, more of a 'sponsored' than a 'contest' system, and it was the latter which Boudon had in mind in putting forward his exponential model of the relation between class and educational achievement.

Nevertheless, the 1944 Act and the general development of secondary education should have led to a closer approximation to a contest system. We should, in other words, be able to detect trends towards meritocracy in our cohort analysis. In fact, the analysis shows an increasing survival among boys of all classes after the War. In the case of working-class and intermediate-class boys the raising of the school-leaving age to 15 in 1947 seems to have provided only a temporary stimulus to an underlying longer-run trend. Yet the record is not one of simple linear progress towards meritocracy. Very roughly what seems to have been happening is that the service class has set a pattern of increasingly extended secondary schooling, following a path towards saturation (of approximately two-thirds) along a logistic curve which is trodden later first by the intermediate and finally by the working class.

On the side of examination success as distinct from length of schooling, our main conclusion is that, for those who survive to enter public examinations, class similarities rather than class differences describe the success rates. This finding enables us to comment on the other French contribution to theory put forward by Pierre Bourdieu. There are, of course, differences in examination success, but their smallness tells us that Bourdieu's postulated mechanism – the acquisition of the dominant culture of capitalist societies which is effectively accessible only to middle-class children – is of no great importance. In so far as it operated for those who passed through the British schools from the 1920s to the 1960s, it took the form of differential access to selective schooling, and not of differential performance. Even so, we would again emphasize the large numbers of 'first-generation' boys from unschooled backgrounds who successfully gained entry to grammar schools and profited from doing so by acquiring secondary school O-Level and A-Level qualifications.

NOTES

1. J. Floud, A. H. Halsey, and F. M. Martin, 'Educational Opportunity and Social Selection in England', in *Transactions of Second World Conference of Sociology* (1953), p.207.
2. J. B. Douglas *et al.*, *All Our Future* (Peter Davies, 1968), pp.27–8.
3. Boudon, op.cit., 1974, p.83: for a general critique of Boudon's work see R. M. Hauser, 'On Boudon's Model of Social Mobility', *American Journal of Sociology*, 81. 4 (1976), 911–28.
4. Boudon, op.cit., p.84.
5. R. H. Turner, 'Sponsored and Contest Mobility and the School System', *American Sociological Review*, 25 (October 1960), 855–67.
6. In order to minimize the number of respects in which the model differs from the real world we set our hypothetical survival rates equal to the figures for the intermediate class which actually obtained in the real world. What we have done, then, is to eliminate the class differentials but to remain true to the real world in other respects.
7. Despite the high R^2 we are not particularly confident about the estimates obtained since they may have been affected by the post-war 'bulge' in school attendance that we know, from our analysis in Chapter 7, was largely due to the decline in the size of the age-group. If we plot what we believe to be the 'underlying' trend and fit the curves, we obtain a series of estimates (all with somewhat higher R^2) that suggest an inflexion point no later than the early 1950s. Estimates of the saturation level are not very sensitive to this rather rough treatment of the data.
8. Too few of our respondents obtained the CSE which was introduced at the end of our period for the data to be usable in analysis. It should also be noted that we do not include such 'non-academic' examinations as City and Guilds, the Royal Society of Arts, etc., which were taken by boys in secondary modern and especially technical schools.
9. P. Bourdieu in Karabel and Halsey, op.cit., p.494.
10. P. Bourdieu, op.cit., p.493.

CHAPTER 9

The Tripartite System Assessed

In Chapter 8 we were inclined to conclude that 'the type of school one attends would seem to be the single most important factor in determining how long one's school career will be.'[1] This claim we inferred from contingency tables which showed that large class differences in length of school career (Table 8.2) were much reduced when we controlled for the type of school attended (Table 8.5). Thus we were able to show that 'the pattern of working-class attendance at grammar schools is much more similar to that of the service class at grammar school than it is to either service- or working-class at non-selective schools.[2]

However, while contingency tables may reliably indicate patterns of school attendance, we must also be cautious, as we demonstrated in Chapter 6, in drawing causal inferences from them. In Chapter 6, it will be recalled, an excellent basis for predicting a destination in the private or state sector of secondary education was whether or not a boy started in a private primary school. But it was not primary schooling in itself, so much as the material and cultural background of the family, which determined the choice of the private sector both at primary and secondary level. Introducing a hypothetical variable of parental values showed that the effect of private primary schooling on secondary schooling is small compared with the effect of the other variables included in our model. Similarly, an excellent basis for predicting the length of a boy's school career may be the type of secondary school which he attended, but we cannot safely conclude from a correlation that type of school *determines* length of school career.

The question of whether the school one attends affects one's educational career or whether it is ultimately a matter of family background is clearly a crucial one for the sociology of education. Jencks, studying the American *contest* as distinct from the British *sponsored* system, argued that 'differences between schools also have relatively little effect on students' eventual educational attainment.'[3] He concluded that

the most important determinant of educational attainment is family background. The impact of family background is accounted for partly by measurable economic differences between families and partly by more elusive non-economic differences. Except for family background, the most important determinant of educational attainment is probably cognitive skill . . . Qualitative differences between high schools seem to explain about two per cent of the variation in students' educational attainment. Unfortunately, we cannot say what qualities of a high school boost its college entrance rates and what qualities lower it. School resources do not appear to influence students' educational attainments at all.[4]

In a sponsored system we would, by contrast, expect school differences to explain much more of the variation in students' educational attainment. How much more is one of the central questions which we shall address in this chapter.

Apart from this comparison between the sponsored and contest systems of education, there are some important questions which are internal to the British tripartite system. The hope, especially after 1944, was that children would be allocated to different secondary schools, not on the basis of their parents' financial circumstances but on that of their individual aptitudes. And the traditional defence of tripartitism has been that it did allow the bright working-class child thus selected for grammar school to realize a talent which would be wasted under a comprehensive system where peer-group pressures would lead the able boy from the working class to drop out early. In essence, then, what these two arguments assert is that the school should, or does, have a degree of autonomy from the class character of society. It takes, and retains, able pupils irrespective of their class origins. This ideal-typical picture of a meritocratic sponsored system of educational mobility can be portrayed by a path diagram of the type used in Chapter 6.

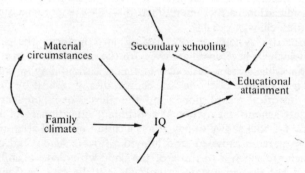

On this picture of the working of the tripartite system, the influence of social class and family background on educational selection and eventual attainment is entirely indirect, being mediated by ability. There are no direct paths from the background variables to schooling or attainments. It is, of course, an ideal-typical picture. Not even the most ardent advocate of tripartitism would expect these direct paths to be wholly missing, and the evidence from Chapters 4 and 8 on the primary and secondary effects of stratification indicates clearly that they will be present. Nevertheless, it is still of considerable interest to compare the size of the different paths from social origins to educational attainment, and to assess more precisely the degree to which the grammar school is independent of the class structure.

These direct paths take on an added interest in the light of G. H. Bantock's statement that

The implication of the sociologists is that there are numerous children who, for reasons of class, are being unfairly inhibited from going on to the education they deserve. My point is that many of these children are, for cultural reasons, likely to be inhibited from gaining the best of what is offered them even if they were to be offered 'chances' in these terms: and this because they have already been formed by historical socio-cultural forces which makes the segment of 'high' culture put before them pretty meaningless.[5]

Bantock is contrasting 'class' and 'culture'. He seems to be suggesting that it is the cultural background of the working class rather than their economic or material circumstances that makes them incapable of benefiting from selective education. In terms of our path model this means that the direct effect of family climate on educational attainment should be substantially larger than that of material circumstances, the latter effect, in an extreme formulation of Bantock's argument, presumably disappearing altogether. A further consequence would then be that the overall correlation between material circumstances and educational attainment could be wholly decomposed into various indirect paths running via family climate, ability, and schooling. Moreover, even if this is not an implication that Bantock himself would wish to draw from his arguments, it is sill important to know to what extent class differences in school leaving are due to material inequalities between the children's homes, and to what extent they are due to factors such as parental interest and encouragement and the value placed on educational achievement, factors which are more likely to be captured by our 'family climate variable.

The tripartite system is now passing into history. The answers to the questions which we have posed are thus, for the most part, an historical appraisal of a disappearing system, although one not without implications for present debates. The existence of the private sector, in any case, is by no means only a matter of historical record alone: and the success of its pupils compared with those in state schools is a matter of continuing educational and political significance. How far does ability to pay affect a child's eventual attainment? Does the child whose parents chose to send him to a private school end up with attainments which are superior to those of the child with identical abilities and home background but sent to a state school? Or is it the case, as Douglas's evidence suggests, that 'the pupils at the boys' public schools, once their ability and the circumstances of their families are taken into account, are no more successful, as judged by O-Level results and age of leaving up to sixteen and a half years, than grammar schools pupils'?[6]

To answer these questions we make use of multiple regression and path analysis in much the same way as in Chapter 6. First, we use multiple regression to look at the differences between the individual types of school, and in particular the differences between grammar schools and the three types of private school. Second, we construct a series of path models which will enable us to look at the overall working of the educational system as a whole and of the tripartite system in particular. Then, third, we compare Britain with America. In this way, we may throw light on the question of how far comprehensive reform affects the relations between class, ability, and educational attainment.

SCHOOL DIFFERENCES IN EDUCATIONAL ATTAINMENT

We know from Chapter 7 that there are substantial differences in the school careers and examination successes of boys at the different types of school. Table 9.1 summarizes the overall differences between schools in a form that enables comparison with the required regression analysis. This table, and the analysis in this chapter as a whole, deals only with the 1933–52 cohort, that is, with those who received their secondary education after the 1944 Act. We have

Table 9.1

School Type and Educational Attainment: Regression Coefficients
Model A

Type of School	Dependent Variable		
	School-Leaving Age (1)	O-Levels (2)	A-Levels (3)
HMC	2.35	0.83	0.57
Direct Grant	2.09	0.79	0.56
Grammar	1.59	0.70	0.32
Non-HMC	1.42	0.55	0.21
Technical	0.59	0.25	0.06
Comprehensive	0.63	0.19	0.07
Constant	15.13	0.07	0.01
R^2	0.479	0.471	0.263

restricted ourselves in this way because our primary focus in this chapter is on the working of the tripartite system.

Table 9.1 shows the coefficients obtained when various measures of school attainment are regressed solely on school type[7] (we call this Model A). The constant in column 1 of Table 9.1 shows the average school-leaving age of those respondents who scored zero on all the independent variables, that is, of those who attended secondary modern schools. The constant in column 2 gives the probability of a secondary modern boy obtaining O-Levels, and the constant in column 3 gives his probability of obtaining A-Levels. The other coefficients then give the *difference* between the secondary modern average and that of the relevant school type. For example, the average school-leaving age at grammar schools was 1.59 years higher than that at the secondary modern school, an extra 70 per cent of boys at grammar school obtained O-Levels, and an extra 32 per cent obtained A-Levels as compared with the secondary-modern boys.

These coefficients represent the differences between schools that we wish to explain. Despite the restriction of the sample to the 1933–52 cohort, the picture is essentially the same as that in Table 7.1. There are substantial gaps between the schools, and they are arranged in the familiar hierarchy. But what happens to these gaps when we add various background variables to our equations? Adding new variables will usually reduce the coefficients of the existing ones, and the extent of the reduction will tell us how much of the original difference between schools can be attributed to the differences in their pupils' scores on these added variables. To begin with we add the background variables used in Table 6.1, namely the five indicators of material circumstances, the seven indicators of parental education, and respondents' private primary schooling. We call this Model B. Together with the school-type variables this gives us nineteen independent variables altogether. It would be extremely cumbersome to give the coefficients for all nineteen variables. Instead, only the 'school type' coefficients are reported since these are the ones on which our interest focuses. They constitute Table 9.2.

Table 9.2

School Type and Educational Attainment: Regression Coefficients
Model B

Type of School	Dependent Variable		
	School-Leaving Age (1)	O-Levels (2)	A-Levels (3)
HMC	1.67	0.63	0.39
Direct Grant	1.59	0.63	0.43
Grammar	1.37	0.63	0.27
Non-HMC	0.92	0.39	0.08
Technical	0.50	0.23	0.04
Comprehensive	0.54	0.16	–
R^2	0.534	0.506	0.312

The coefficients in Table 9.2 are all reduced from those in Table 9.1, but some large gaps still remain. The gaps between the grammar, Direct Grant, and HMC schools at O-Level are entirely eliminated, confirming Douglas's conclusion. In other words, the advantage which the Direct Grant and HMC schools showed over grammar schools in Table 9.1 turns out to be wholly a matter of the difference in their social composition.[8] Gaps still remain, however, although much reduced, at A-Level and in length of school career.[9] Thus whereas the original difference in school-leaving age between boys at grammar and HMC schools was 0.76 years in Table 9.1, Table 9.2 shows that nearly two-thirds of this can be attributed to the background characteristics which we have included in Model B.

Comparison between grammar and secondary modern school on the other hand reveals a different picture. In the case of school career the original gap was 1.59 years, and this is reduced by less than one-fifth to 1.37 years if we control for social background. Similarly, the difference in the chances of obtaining O- or A-Levels is only slightly diminished when we control for background. Thus, whereas the superior performance of the élite private schools can largely be explained in terms of the social composition of their intake, the inferior performance of the secondary modern schools cannot be so explained. What all this means is that of two boys with identical social backgrounds and primary schooling, the one allocated to a grammar school did vastly better than the one sent to a secondary modern. By contrast, if one of them was sent to a grammar school and the other to an élite private school, the difference in their performance was very small.

We cannot, of course, ascribe the whole of the differences remaining between schools in Model B to the causal influence of the school. As we saw in Chapter 6, eliminating differences allows us to draw firm conclusions, but failure to eliminate them does not. There may still be many unmeasured characteristics of pupils and their homes that can account for the remaining differences. We must therefore follow the same procedure as in Chapter 6 and attempt to capture these unmeasured characteristics. We begin as before by using our data on brother's school career. We are not interested this time in the question of whether the parents value private as opposed to state education but in whether they promote school achievement. This is frequently held to be a major determinant of a child's success or failure at secondary school.[10] We can try to capture it by using two measures of brother's attainment, namely school-leaving age and examination successes.[11] True, we cannot treat these measures as proxies for parental attitudes in the way that we did with private schooling, for there will undoubtedly be processes of sibling rivalry, and sibling encouragement, influencing school achievement. However, this is of no consequence in the present case for we are interested in *any* non-school processes that might affect a respondent's attainment, whatever their source.

What we have done, then, is to construct Model C in which these two measures of brother's attainment are added to the nineteen independent variables of Model B. As in the equivalent analysis in Chapter 6, however, we must remember that we cannot directly compare the coefficients of Model C with those of Model B since the two models are based on different samples. In Model B we include all respondents born 1933-52, but in Model C we can include only those who reported a brother's school career. Since the sample is thereby reduced from 4247 to 2487 we would in any case expect some minor changes in the coefficients, quite apart from the changes brought about by the introduction of the 'brother variables'. Accordingly, we compare the coefficients of Model C with those obtained when Model B is estimated for the reduced sample of 2487 men who reported brothers. The two sets of results are reported in Table 9.3. The reduction in the size of the sample does account for some minor anomalies such as the superior performance of Direct Grant boys as compared with those of HMC schools. Their superiority in Model C is not due to the inclusion of the brother variables but to the change in sample, and the anomaly can, therefore, be ignored.

To assess the effect of these two extra variables, we must compare the coefficients in the two panels of Table 9.3. There is a particular contrast with the results of the comparable analysis in Chapter 6. In Chapter 6 the inclusion of the brother variables reduced the size of the primary schooling coefficient by nearly 50 per cent, here their inclusion reduces the size of the school type coefficients by less than 10 per cent. So parental values may explain why boys from private primary schools go on to private secondary schools, but parental interest and encouragement (if we may interpret the brother variables in this way) do not explain why boys at selective schools stay on so much longer and have such a superior chance of examination successes. School effects cannot be as easily dismissed as they were in Chapter 6.

To what, then, can we ascribe the remaining school differences? One obvious possibility is the intelligence of the pupils. Since, under the tripartite system, schools ostensibly selected pupils on the basis of their measured intelligence, it is clear that apparent school effects may be due to the differences in the intellectual qualities of their student bodies. Since ability is not correlated perfectly with family background and parental interest, the variables that we included in Models B and C will serve as imperfect proxies for pupil ability and we cannot therefore ascribe all the remaining differences to school effects. All

Table 9.3

Type of School	MODEL B Reduced Sample Excludes Brother Variables (see text)			MODEL C Includes Brother Variables		
	School-Leaving Age	O-Levels	A-Levels	School-Leaving Age	O-Levels	A-Levels
HMC	1.50	0.55	0.36	1.31	0.49	0.32
Direct Grant	1.58	0.61	0.40	1.46	0.57	0.37
Grammar	1.29	0.62	0.22	1.18	0.58	0.19
Non-HMC	0.84	0.38	0.07	0.72	0.34	0.05
Technical	0.39	0.20	0.02	0.38	0.20	0.02
Comprehensive	0.43	0.09	0.04	0.40	0.08	0.04
R^2	0.501	0.492	0.279	0.526	0.505	0.297

we can say at the moment, therefore, is that the coefficients in Table 9.3 give us an estimate of the *maximum* likely size of the school effects. The 'true' effects are likely to be substantially smaller.

FAMILY CLIMATE AND EDUCATIONAL ATTAINMENT

We have taken the problem as far as we can with regression analysis. To go further we must turn to path analysis, which may be used not only to penetrate further into the problem of unmeasured elements of family background, as in Chapter 6, but also to deal with the effects of intelligence. We cannot do this in our multiple regression analysis since we have no measures or even remotely plausible proxies for intelligence, but one of the strengths of path analysis is that it enables us to incorporate correlations drawn from other studies and to compute the resulting path coefficients. This technique was extensively used by Jencks and equally extensively criticized.[12] The principal criticism is that correlations derived from different studies will be based on different samples and on measures constructed in different ways. However, another strength of path analysis is that it is always open to the sceptical reader to vary the assumptions and compute a new set of coefficients. It will usually be possible to make plausible assumptions about the way in which the difference between the studies would affect the correlations and to change them accordingly.

However, before incorporating IQ into our model we can explore some simpler models analogous to those in Chapter 6. These will enable us to assess the role of family climate, and as we shall see, this is an essential step in completing the final model. We begin with Model Alpha.

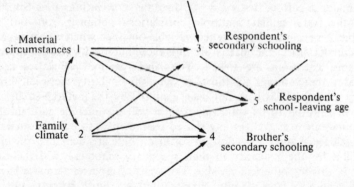

This model has the same basic structure as that employed in Chapter 6. We assume that brother's schooling has no direct causal effect on the respondent's schooling (and vice versa), and our knowledge of the correlation coefficients (together with an assumption about the value of r_{12}) enables us to estimate the effect of the hypothetical variable of family climate on the respondent's schooling. If we then assume that brother's type of secondary schooling has no effect on the respondent's school-leaving age, we can calculate the remaining coefficients.

The correlations from which we shall derive our path coefficients are given below. Since we need information on brothers to compute correlations with variable 2, for consistency all the correlations are based on the same sub-sample, those who reported data on a brother.[13] As in Models A, B, and C we are also restricting ourselves to the 1933–52 cohort.

		1	2	3	4
Family Climate	2	0.300			
Respondent's Secondary Schooling	3	0.439	(0.700)[14]		
Brother's Secondary Schooling	4	0.439	(0.700)	0.548	
Respondent's School-Leaving Age	5	0.459	(0.476)	0.647	0.413
		1	2	3	4
		Material Circumstances	Family Climate	Respondent's Secondary Schooling	Brother's Secondary Schooling

We have constructed variable 1, material circumstances, in the same way as before, basing the correlations in the matrix (except r_{12}) on the multiple correlations with the five members of the material circumstances group. Since we are also assuming, as before, that $r_{13} = r_{14}$, these two correlations are a compromise between the (very similar) multiple correlations obtained from our data.[15]

Variable 2 is again the hypothetical variable obtained when we set p_{34} at zero, and the correlations in the matrix are thus those obtained when the appropriate simultaneous equations are solved. The label 'parental values' is now less appropriate, representing all those sources of similarity between brother's secondary schooling that have not been captured by the material circumstances variable. In addition to parental values these will also include parental interest and encouragement as well as any shared characteristics of the brothers themselves. Intelligence and motivation, in so far as these are shared by the brothers and account for the similarity in their secondary schooling, will therefore be included in this hypothetical variable. For want of a better term we have used Blau and Duncan's label 'family climate', but we must reiterate our earlier warning that it is the method of construction, not the label itself, which is crucial in understanding the nature of these hypothetical variables.

Variables 3 and 4, on the other hand, are quite new. They are constructed in the same way, being four-point scales of secondary school type. The respondent (or his brother) scores 1 if he attended a non-selective school, 2 if he attended a technical school, 3 if he attended a grammar school, and 4 if he attended an independent or Direct Grant school. It is rather simpler to use a variable of this kind than a set of binary variables, and the correlations are not greatly different. Finally, variable 5 is respondent's school-leaving age, measured in the usual way.

We can now compute the path coefficients. They are:

Model Alpha

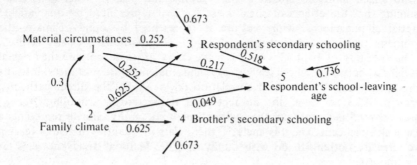

There are some striking similarities and differences compared with the equivalent path model in Chapter 6. First, the left-hand side of the diagram looks very similar. Material circumstances are much less important than family climate as determinants of respondents' and their brothers' secondary schooling. The absolute values of the path coefficients are, of course, different since the measures of schooling are different from those employed in Chapter 6, but it is none the less clear that, as before, the similarity between brothers is such that (assuming they have no direct effect on each other) we need to postulate unmeasured variables such as family climate to account for it.

Second, the right-hand side of the diagram gives a different picture from that which we had before. This time schooling has a large effect, while that of family climate almost disappears. The reason for the large effect of schooling lies in the relative sizes of r_{35} and r_{45}. In the equivalent model in Chapter 6 these two correlations were of very similar magnitude and we were able to show that the symmetry of the correlation coefficients imposed a symmetry on the path coefficients. In the present model, on the other hand, r_{35} is considerably larger than r_{45}, and the path coefficient therefore has a considerably larger value than the zero we have assumed for p_{54}.[16]

We can also see why p_{52} should be so much smaller now than it was in Chapter 6. Since

$$r_{45} = p_{53}r_{34} + p_{51}r_{14} + p_{52}r_{24} \qquad \text{Equation 9.1}$$

and r_{45} is relatively small (compared with the equivalent correlation in Chapter 6) while $p_{53}r_{34}$ is relatively large, it follows that there is not a great deal of work for the other two paths to do. In other words, the correlation between brother's secondary schooling and respondent's school-leaving age can be accounted for by the measured variables in our model, and there is thus no role for the unmeasured ones.

This analysis, therefore, confirms the results of our multiple regression investigations earlier in this chapter. Controlling for family climate fails to eliminate the school effect, and it remains as persistent as ever. The analysis also enables us to test our formulation of Bantock's argument. The testable inference that we were able to extract from Bantock was that it was not class *per se* but culture which inhibited children from 'gaining the best of what is offered'. Assuming that the effects of social class are best represented by our variable material circumstances, while culture is represented by family climate, the hypothesis to be tested is that $p_{51} < p_{52}$. This hypothesis is clearly refuted.

The enormity of Bantock's error is made clearer if we decompose the original correlation between school-leaving age and material circumstances into its component parts. Of the total correlation ($r_{15} = .459$), the direct path, p_{51}, represents 47.3 per cent, the indirect path via secondary schooling ($p_{53} r_{31}$) represents 49.5 per cent, and the 'indirect' path via family climate represents a meagre 3.2 per cent. On this analysis, then, class inequalities in school leaving have virtually nothing to do with family climate. Material disadvantage is far more important.

However, an objection to this line of reasoning is that its results partly reflect the rather arbitrary assumption which we made about the size of the correlation between material circumstances and family climate. But we can check this by varying our assumption. Reducing the correlation will have the effect of increasing p_{51} and reducing p_{52} still further, so we must investigate the effect of increasing r_{12}. Increasing it to .400 has barely any effect, reducing p_{51} to .211 and increasing p_{52} to .053. Increasing it further to .600 still has little effect. It reduces p_{51} slightly to .195 and increases p_{52} to .059. The size of the two path coefficients therefore is not sensitive to changes in r_{12}, and our conclusion must stand.[17] Economic factors, not cultural ones, would appear to be the major source of early leaving.

We can now extend our model by adding examination success at O-Level to the path diagram already constructed. We assume that examination success is the final variable at the end of the causal sequence, or in other words that the length of one's school career determines one's chances of obtaining O-Levels. On the face of it, this is a reasonable assumption, but we must remember that the pupil's (and the school's) estimate of his chances of obtaining O-Levels will also affect his decision to stay on at school. *Expected* examination success may thus affect the length of school career, while school career in turn will affect the *actual* success achieved.

With this caveat in mind, let us turn to this new model, which we term Model Beta. To compute the path coefficients we need the correlations between the five variables of Model Alpha and the new variable 6, O-Level success.[18] They are as follows:

$$r_{16} = .426$$

$$r_{26} = (.496)$$

$$r_{36} = .652$$

$$r_{46} = .417$$

$$r_{56} = .745.$$

As before, these correlations refer to the experience of those members of the 1933–52 cohort who reported data on brothers, all of them being based directly on our own data except r_{26} which is obtained in a similar way to r_{25}. With this set of correlations we obtain the following path diagram. For the sake of simplicity, we have excluded variable 4 (brother's secondary schooling) from our presentation (although the correlations with variable 4 were of course required for the computation of the path coefficients). We have again assumed that variable 4 has no direct effect on the later variables (5 and 6) in the model, and the effects of earlier variables on 4 are, of course, the same as in Model Alpha.

Model Beta

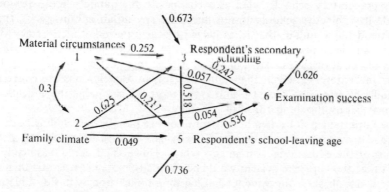

Model Beta confirms the picture that we had built up from earlier chapters. Table 7.1 showed, first, that the proportion of respondents staying on until 16 or later was closely related to type of school, second that the proportion obtaining O-Level was closely related to the proportion staying on, and third that there were none the less differences in the 'success rates' of the different types of secondary school. It can now be seen that these relationships continue to hold true even when material circumstances and family climate are controlled. The first of Table 7.1's findings is reflected in the size of the path coefficient p_{53}, the second in the coefficient p_{65}, and the third in the coefficient p_{63}. The school differences found in Chapter 7, then, are not to be wholly explained by the social composition of the different types of school. School effects remain.

Model Beta also makes it clear that the direct effects of material circumstances and family climate on examination success are minimal, confirming the result of Chapter 8. Social class and family climate affect examination success almost wholly *indirectly*, the paths running via type of secondary school and school-leaving age. Thus if we take the correlation between material circumstances and examination success we find that only 18 per cent is accounted for by the direct effect. Similarly in the case of the correlation between family climate and examination success the direct path accounts for only 8 per cent. On the other hand, the *indirect* path via type of school accounts for 24 per cent and 35 per cent respectively, and the path via school-leaving age accounts for 62 per cent and 52 per cent. This is a very striking result. It means that to an important degree social advantage is converted into academic credentials by the capacity of the advantaged families to keep their children longer at school.

ABILITY AND EDUCATIONAL ATTAINMENT

What happens when we introduce IQ into the analysis? There are two issues here of considerable interest. One is the effect it has on the path from secondary schooling to school-leaving age. It is certainly possible that the introduction of IQ will have the same consequences for the effect of secondary schooling as the introduction of parental values had for primary schooling in Chapter 6. This would mean that selective schools simply acted as a *channel* for able youngsters just as preparatory schools acted as a channel to the public schools. It would indicate that selective schools do not introduce any unfair advantages on those who attend them, unfair, that is, as judged by the criterion of meritocracy. The second issue is somewhat similar. It is that of the extent to which the *direct* effects of social origin indicated in Model Alpha are in fact mediated by IQ. The greater the extent to which these direct effects of Model Alpha are converted into indirect effects in Model Gamma, the more we can judge the educational system as fair by the standards of meritocracy.

One important point arises here. Up to now we have been including both the state and private sectors in our path analyses: we have been looking at the working of the educational system as a whole. However, it could reasonably be argued that the tripartite system would be distinctly more meritocratic than the private sector. Indeed our evidence in Chapter 4 point strongly in this direction. To assess the tripartite system, therefore, we need to exclude respondents who attended private schools from the analysis. What we propose to do, therefore, is to carry out two separate analyses. In the first (Model Gamma) we shall continue, as before, with all our respondents aged 20–39 who reported data on a brother. This will give us a picture of the system as a whole and will enable comparison with Models Alpha and Beta. In the second (Model Delta) we shall exclude those respondents who attended private schools. This will give us a picture of the tripartite system, and comparison between Models Gamma and Delta will also enable us to make some inferences about the operation of the private sector.

Let us begin, then, with the system as a whole. The correlation matrix which we use to compute the path coefficients of Model Gamma is as follows:

Family Climate	2	0.300			
Respondent's Secondary Schooling	3	0.439	(0.700)		
Respondent's School-Leaving Age	5	0.459	(0.476)	0.647	
Respondent's measured IQ	7	0.375	(0.700)	0.601	0.494
		1	2	3	5
		Material Circumstances	Family Climate	Secondary Schooling	School Leaving Age

The correlations between variables 1, 2, 3, and 5 are familiar, being derived from our own data or from earlier stages of our model building. The correlations with variable 7, IQ, are the new ones which we must import from elsewhere. Consider first r_{17}. The main component of variable 1 is father's class, and a variety of sources yield us estimates for the correlation between father's class and son's IQ. Thus Kerckhoff, in his reanalysis of Douglas's data, obtains a correlation of 0.265 between father's occupation and son's ability; and in his reanalysis of the Crowther Report's data he obtains a correlation of 0.336.[19] We have also carried out a reanalysis of Floud, Halsey, and Martin's data and obtained correlations of 0.280 and 0.339 for south-west Herts. and Middlesborough respectively. An estimate of 0.3 thus seems reasonable for the correlation between father's class and son's IQ. However, the variable we use in the path analysis, material circumstances, contains a number of additional components besides father's class. These will tend to increase the size of the correlation, although our experience elsewhere suggests that they will not do so very much. For example, the simple correlation between father's class and respondent's schooling (Variable 3 in the present model) is 0.364, whereas the multiple correlation with material circumstances is 0.439. We have therefore settled on 0.375 as a reasonable estimate of r_{17}.

Next, consider the correlation between IQ and family climate. An estimate can be made by constructing a simple path model which contains the variables material circumstances (Variable 1), family climate (Variable 2), respondent's IQ (Variable 7), and brother's IQ (Variable 8). If we have estimates for r_{12}, r_{17}, and r_{18}, and if we assume in the usual way that $r_{17} = r_{18}$, $r_{27} = r_{28}$, and $p_{78} = 0$, we can solve for r_{27}.[20] The only new information we need, then, is an estimate of the correlation between brothers' IQ. Burt gives a figure of 0.498, but recent exposés demonstrate that little reliance can be placed on Burt's claims.[21] However, there are American sources which give the slightly higher estimate of 0.52 and we must perforce use this.[22] We can now proceed to solve, and obtain 0.700 as our estimate of r_{27}, the correlation between IQ and family climate.

Peaker's study *The Plowden Children Four Years Later*[23] gives a firm estimate of the correlation between IQ and secondary school type. This study is a re-survey in 1968 of the national random sample of three groups of children carried out for the Plowden Committee in 1964. The middle of the three age groups used would seem to be the most appropriate for our purposes. This group was in their first year at secondary school in 1968, and the correlation between their test scores and school type was 0.585. Peaker used a three-point scale of secondary-school type: Direct Grant and independent, grammar, and other state secondary schools. This differs from our scale in its inclusion of the technical schools in the category of 'other state'. Fortunately, Peaker gives us sufficient information to recalculate the correlation using our own four-point scale. Not surprisingly, this increases the correlation slightly to 0.601, and this is the figure we use.

Finally, there is the correlation between IQ and school-leaving age. The only estimate we have been able to find is again Kerckhoff's reanalysis of the Crowther Report data and of Douglas's data. The Crowther estimate is 0.520, and the Douglas one 0.467. We have averaged these and use the resulting estimate of 0.494.

Solving for our path coefficients, we obtain the following results for Model Gamma.

Model Gamma

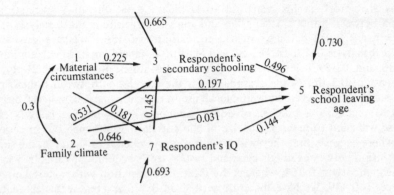

The most notable feature of Model Gamma is the relative unimportance of IQ. Its effects both on secondary schooling and school-leaving age are quite small compared with those of the other variables in the model. It does not have the central role which it might be expected to play in a meritocracy. Given the unimportance of IQ, moreover, it is not surprising that the other coefficients of Model Gamma are very similar to those of Model Alpha. This means that the direct effects of social origin exhibited in Model Alpha are not, after all, greatly mediated by IQ. Thus, of the overall correlation of 0.439 between material circumstances and secondary schooling, only 12 per cent is accounted for by the indirect path via IQ. Similarly, we find that the direct path from secondary schooling to school-leaving age is little affected by the introduction of IQ. In Model Alpha the path coefficient was 0.518; it has now fallen marginally to 0.496. The type of secondary school that one attends thus remains resolutely important as a determinant of the length of one's school career. The introduction of IQ into the model has not had the dramatic effects which the introduction of parental values had in Chapter 6.

Why, then, have the effects of IQ been so small? Take, for example, the effect of IQ on secondary schooling (p_{37}). The correlation between the two variables (r_{37}) is quite high at 0.601 and so a high path coefficient might have been expected. What has undermined this expectation? First of all, consider the way in which p_{37} is derived. From the basic theorem of path analysis we know that:

$$p_{37} = r_{37} - p_{32}r_{27} - p_{31}r_{17}.$$

Equation 9.2

We can see that p_{37} will be particularly sensitive not only to changes in r_{37} but also to changes in r_{27} and p_{32}, which in turn depends on r_{23}. Now both of these last two correlations derive from models in which we incorporate information on brothers. The crucial point is that the similarity between brothers' secondary schooling is such that a central role must be given to family climate rather than to IQ. This is easiest to understand if we consider what the implications of a meritocratic model, in which IQ played the central role, would be for the similarity between brothers. Suppose that the educational system was merito-cratic in the sense that the effects of social origin and family climate on secondary schooling were wholly indirect and mediated entirely by IQ. This would give us a path diagram of the following character where $p_{31} = p_{41} = p_{32} = p_{42} = 0$. We shall also assume that $p_{34} = p_{38} = p_{47} = p_{78} = 0$, that is, that brothers have no direct effect on each other.

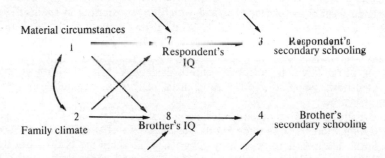

It can be shown that in this system

$$r_{34} = r_{37} r_{78} r_{84}.$$ Equation 9.3

Now we know that $r_{37} = r_{48} = 0.601$ and that $r_{78} = 0.52$. It follows that this system implies a correlation of 0.188 between brothers' secondary schooling, whereas in fact we know that the correlation is 0.548. A meritocratic edu-cational system, therefore, of the kind assumed here would lead to brothers being a great deal less similar than we know them to be in the real world. To account for the known similarity between brothers, therefore, we have to introduce direct paths from social origin and family climate to secondary schooling,[24] and Equation 9.2 shows that the moment we do so the direct path from IQ to secondary schooling must shrink. The minor role which our model ascribes to IQ, therefore, is a result of our taking brothers seriously.[25]

We have, then, reached an important conclusion. The British educational system has been much less meritocratic than has usually been supposed; IQ is a relatively unimportant determinant of the type of school one goes to, or of the length of one's school career. The introduction of IQ into the model has not transformed a class-stratified society into a meritocracy, and a comparison of Models Alpha and Gamma shows that the direct effects of social origin on secondary schooling are not greatly mediated by IQ. This means that among pupils with identical social backgrounds and family climates, those with superior measured intelligence have chances of getting to a selective school which are not greatly better than those of lower-ability pupils. Conversely, among pupils of identical measured ability, social origin is a good discriminator of pupils' chances of getting to selective schools.

From the effect of IQ on secondary schooling, let us turn to the determinants of the length of one's school career. Comparing Models Alpha and Gamma again, we see that introducing IQ has failed to eliminate, or indeed to modify seriously, the effect of secondary schooling on school-leaving age. This means that going, for example, to a grammar school really does make a difference to a child's school career. It confirms the results of the multiple regression analysis which we undertook in the first section of this chapter. Our results thus mean that, of two boys with *identical* origins and measured ability, the one allocated to a selective school will do substantially better than the other. Secondary schooling is not a mere transmitter of prior influences in the model (namely family background and measured ability). It introduces other influences which are by definition uncorrelated with those earlier ones and which are substantial in their effects[26] (witness the size of the residual path). It is up to the defender of the educational system to suggest what those influences are and to show that they are educationally relevant. Meanwhile, the critic can reasonably argue that the allocation of children to selective schools is largely made on educationally irrelevant criteria which then have substantial effects on a pupil's subsequent educational career.

Finally, the paths from material circumstances and IQ to school-leaving age in Model Gamma tell us something about the prospects of those who missed out at the initial allocation to secondary schools. That there are paths from these two variables suggests that there is indeed a 'second chance' for some. The statistical difficulty here (as elsewhere) is that there may be interaction effects that we have failed to capture in our model. If we assume that effects are additive, then we can say that, of people who attended non-selective schools, those with more favoured social origins and/or with higher measured intelligence, can expect a longer school career than those without. We can also see, since $p_{51} > p_{57}$, that the second chance is more significant for those with advantaged social origins. The small size of p_{57} means that the able boy, if unnoticed at secondary selection, has relatively little chance of extending his school career, although we should not forget that the 'alternative route' of further education may also be available to him. We shall examine this in Chapter 10.

IQ IN THE STATE AND PRIVATE SECTORS

The unimportance of IQ in Model Gamma could, of course, be a consequence of our inclusion of the private sector along with the state sector. It is possible that a highly meritocratic state sector exists alongside a private sector in which IQ plays little part, the coefficients in Model Gamma being an amalgam of these two conflicting tendencies. We must, therefore, attempt to separate the two sectors.

To construct a path model which relates only to the state sector we must obtain a new set of correlation coefficients. Correlations between variables 1 (material circumstances), 2 (family climate), 3 (secondary schooling), and 5 (school-leaving age) can be derived from our own data. We can use the same sample as for Model Gamma (that is, all respondents aged 20–39 who reported data on a brother), but excluding those who attended HMC and non-HMC independent schools. We *retain* those respondents who attended Direct Grant schools on the grounds that many of these would have been supported by local education authorities and would have been selected by competitive examinations.[27] The inclusion of the Direct Grant schools also makes it easier to make plausible estimates of the correlations with variable 7, IQ. We know that respondents at Direct Grant schools score highly both on IQ and on the other variables employed in our analysis.[28] To omit them would be to truncate the sample and would thus tend to reduce the correlations. Unfortunately, we have no way of knowing by how much they would be reduced since there are to our knowledge no estimates based on appropriate samples. True, the exclusion of the independent schools might also tend to reduce the correlations, but the effect is unlikely to be so great. Kalton's evidence suggests that boys at independent HMC schools have slightly lower average measured intelligence than those at HMC Direct Grant schools, and those at non-HMC independent schools would almost certainly also have a lower mean IQ. The exclusion of a group, therefore, who score highly on one set of variables (social origin, school-leaving age, or type of school), but relatively less highly on the other, IQ, would not have such a significant effect on the correlation. We have therefore felt able to keep the correlations with variable 7, IQ, at the same level as they were in the analysis required for Model Gamma.

The matrix of correlations is therefore as follows:

		1	2	3	5
Family Climate	2	0.300			
Respondent's Secondary Schooling	3	0.339	(0.649)		
Respondent's School-Leaving Age	5	0.411	(0.490)	0.641	
IQ	7	0.375	(0.700)	0.601	0.494
		Material Circumstances	Family Climate	Respondent's Secondary Schooling	Respondent's School-Leaving Age

We can now compute the path coefficients for Model Delta. They are:

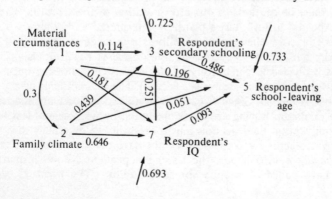

Comparing Models Gamma and Delta we see that the exclusion of the Independent schools has had some important consequences. First, the selection process is more meritocratic in the state sector than it was in the educational system as a whole. The effect of IQ on secondary schooling (p_{37}) is substantially larger in Model Delta and the effects of social background (p_{31} and p_{32}) substantially smaller than they were in Model Gamma. This indicates that the direct effects of social origin which were shown in Model Alpha are mediated to some significant degree by IQ in the state sector alone. We can show this more precisely by computing the amounts by which the direct paths from social origin fall when IQ is added. In the educational system as a whole p_{31} falls by 11 per cent when IQ is added, and p_{32} by 15 per cent. In the state sector the reductions are 29 per cent and 27 per cent respectively. These figures tell us what percentage of the *total* effect of social origin on secondary schooling is mediated by IQ.

By the 'total effect'[29] of, for example, material circumstances on secondary schooling we refer to the size of the path coefficient p_{31} when variable 3 is regressed solely on the background variables 1 and 2. The size of the 'indirect effect' of material circumstances via IQ is then given by the amount by which p_{31} falls when IQ is added as a determinant of secondary schooling. In the educational system as a whole the 'total effect' of material circumstances on secondary schooling is given by the value of p_{31} in Model Alpha, and to obtain the size of the indirect effect we then compare this with the value of p_{31} in Model Gamma. The change is from 0.252 to 0.225 and the indirect effect is thus 11 per cent of the total effect.[30]

Turning to the right-hand side of the path diagram we find a somewhat more surprising picture. IQ, rather than becoming a more important determinant of school-leaving age, actually becomes a less important determinant when we restrict ourselves to the state sector. Thus for the educational system as a whole the indirect effect of material circumstances on school-leaving age via IQ is 43 per cent of the total effect while for the state sector it is 32 per cent. Further, in the state sector the effect of IQ on school-leaving age is mediated to a greater extent by type of secondary school. The indirect effect via secondary schooling is 33 per cent of the total in the system as a whole but increases to 57 per cent when we limit ourselves to the state sector.

Given our doubts about the size of the correlations with IQ in the state sector, we must be cautious in our interpretation of these results. They are not ones we expected to find, but a plausible interpretation of them is possible. In the state sector, as we have seen, selection for secondary schooling is relatively meritocratic, but thereafter a considerable degree of rigidity exists. The school population is divided into relatively homogeneous educational groups which are sponsored for educational success (or failure). The *standardizing* effect of school type is what is crucial. Since virtually everyone at a secondary modern school left at the minimum leaving age, the correlation between school-leaving age and IQ for respondents at these schools must necessarily be extremely low.

The private sector by contrast does not have the same standardizing effect. Though *socially* homogeneous, the lesser independent schools in particular are likely to have pupils of a wide spread of ability. The eventual educational attainment is also relatively varied and there is thus more scope for IQ to have an effect on school-leaving age.

The comparison of Models Gamma and Delta brings out two important features of the sponsored system of educational attainment that existed within the state sector over our period. First, selection for secondary schooling is relatively meritocratic, but once in a particular type of school neither ability nor family climate have much impact on the length of a boy's school career. Class origins are somewhat more important, but above all it is the character of the school which is crucial. The pupils enter a relatively inflexible institutional structure. As innumerable parents have realized, the all-important thing was to pass the 11-plus. And it is no surprise that family climate appears to be a far more important determinant of success or failure in the 11-plus than the pupil's own measured ability. Even at this most meritocratic stage of the educational system, home background is the dominating feature.

THE SPONSORED AND CONTEST SYSTEMS COMPARED

We began this chapter by quoting Jencks's conclusion that variations in the quality of schooling explained only 2 per cent of the variance in eventual educational attainment. It will hardly surprise the reader to discover that the comparable calculation for Britain yields a much higher figure. What we can do is compare the amount of variance in school-leaving age explained by Model Gamma with that explained by a model which omits secondary-school type (but which is otherwise identical). The difference is 14 per cent. In Model Gamma we explain 51 per cent of the variance (a substantial proportion by the standards of most path analyses), whereas we explain only 37 per cent if type of secondary school is omitted.

Does this mean that we can go on, as Jencks is fond of doing, to say that equalizing schools would reduce the inequality in length of school career by 14 per cent? Certainly not. To do so would be to fall into the classic fallacy of supposing that relationships found to hold within a given system tell us what would happen if that system were changed. As one of us has written elsewhere:[31]

The nature of this fallacy is well illustrated by an example Jencks himself uses:[32] since the 1940 Census showed that schooling explained 21 per cent of the variance in income among men aged 35 to 44, 'statistical logic therefore implies that reducing the variance in years of schooling could never reduce the variance in men's income more than 21 per cent'. This statement, which on the face of it seems unimpeachable, actually conceals a number of important assumptions, the most crucial one of which is that it is actually possible to manipulate one variable without changing the ensemble of relations constituting the totality. Yet in the case cited here, it is highly questionable whether the absolute equalization of schooling would leave these relations untouched. Equalization of education might well upset the legitimating functions of schools and thereby set in motion a process that would change the values and relations among other variables, such as family background and income, that figure in the equation.

Similarly, in our case, 'equalizing schooling' through comprehensive reorganization would almost certainly 'set in motion a process that would change the values and relations among other variables that figure in the equation'. Most obviously the use made of the private sector by educationally ambitious parents would change. The effects of social origins and IQ in any new model of the comprehensive system could not therefore be inferred from those in the models we have already constructed.

Similarly, we cannot use our calculated regression coefficients to tell us about the effects of comprehensive reorganization. The regression coefficients indicate the chances of those members of our sample who actually attended these schools; they cannot tell us what the chances would be in some future state when all state schools were comprehensive. As we pointed out in Chapter 7, 'to examine the effects of changing a system, we must compare systems, not relations within a system.' This is an absolutely fundamental point. Though comparing systems is a hazardous enterprise, if used cautiously it offers useful lessons.

The comparison we can make most easily is with the United States since roughly comparable data are available. These two countries may be taken as representing a sponsored and a contest system. The difficulties with this kind of comparison are of course those involved in comparing any two studies: the nature of the samples and the construction of the variables may be different. In addition, and perhaps more important because it is less visible, there may be institutional differences other than the sponsored/contest one, and these may affect the results in ways we do not understand.

A comparison of the kind we have in mind has already been made by Kerckhoff.[33] He uses a model in which educational attainment is regressed on father's occupation, father's education, and ability. (Family size is also included in some of his analyses.) Type of secondary school is not included in the model since there is no strictly comparable variable in the American educational system. Kerckhoff's approach, therefore, enables us to compare the 'total' effects of ability on educational attainment in the two countries. We know from our own earlier analyses that the total effect of ability will be mediated to a very substantial degree by type of secondary school in England, and the direct effect of ability might thus be very much smaller in England than in the USA. But the question which Kerckhoff's approach enables us to tackle is whether the existence of a system of selective secondary schooling in England increases the total effect of ability on educational attainment. This is clearly an important question since it is after all the total effect which gives the best guide to the degree to which an educational system is meritocratic, and we would like to know whether comprehensive reorganization is likely to reduce the degree of meritocracy.

Kerckhoff relies for his comparison mainly on Duncan's analysis of 1964 data from American white males 25–34 years old, and on Douglas's data from a national sample of British males born in the first week of March 1946. His results can be presented in tabular form as follows:[34]

Path from:

	Father's Occupation	Father's Education	Ability	R^2
Britain: school-leaving age	0.229	0.202	0.362	0.349
USA: educational attainment	0.237	0.206	0.400	0.386

The outstanding feature is, of course, the similarity between the two countries. Despite the differences in their educational systems, Britain and America seem almost equally meritocratic. Indeed, if anything America seems slightly the more meritocratic, although it should be noted, as Kerckhoff points out, that if school qualifications rather than school-leaving age is used for Britain, the effect of ability becomes rather larger and that of father's occupation rather smaller. Over all it seems fair to conclude with Kerckhoff that 'the process by which the English assign youngsters to academic and non-academic forms of secondary education produces outcomes indistinguishable from those produced by the more open, competitive process in America. Thus the two societies use different mechanisms to produce the same outcomes.'[35]

We can now consider whether our own data enable us to shed any further light on the similarities and differences between Britain and America. The first thing we can do that was not open to Kerckhoff is to take account of brothers. We know that if we do so we shall reduce the effect of IQ on educational attainment: the question to be asked is whether the reduction is greater in America. The simplest way to investigate this is to compare the similarity of brothers' educational attainment in the two countries. If, for example, brothers were substantially more similar in the USA than in Britain, we could conclude that unmeasured aspects of family background were even more important than they were in Britain and the role of IQ would accordingly be even more reduced.

We have already seen that, in the case of our 1933–52 cohort, the correlation between respondents' and brothers' school-leaving age is 0.504. For America Blau and Duncan provide an estimate of 0.556 based on their sample of men of non-farm background reporting oldest brother's education.[36] In general, Blau and Duncan's correlations for their sample of adult males aged 20–64 are somewhat higher than our correlations for the 1933–52 cohort, and the correlation between brothers' attainment thus fits into this pattern. It means that the *relative* importance of the different variables within each country is likely to show the same pattern and this confirms Kerckhoff's conclusion about the similarity of the two educational systems.

The two educational systems, then, seem to be similar in the relative importance of social origin and IQ for educational attainment. There is, however, a further respect in which the systems may differ, and it is this which, we suspect, differentiates most clearly the effects of a sponsored and contest system. The point we have in mind is the *predictability* of educational attainment in the two systems. True, the amount of variance in educational attainment explained by the three variables of father's occupation, father's education, and IQ is much the same in the analyses based on Duncan's and Douglas's data. With

Duncan it is 39 per cent, and with Douglas 35 per cent. However, if we now add type of secondary school to the British analysis, the amount of variance explained will increase dramatically.

Kerckhoff does not give us the correlations needed to supplement his model in this way, but we can construct an analogous model from our own data. The correlations we use are as follows:

	Father's Class	Father's Education	IQ	Secondary School
Father's Education	0.431			
Son's IQ	0.300	0.223		
Secondary School	0.364	0.323	0.601	
School-Leaving Age	0.371	0.355	0.494	0.647

The correlations with IQ (with the exception of $r_{FED.IQ}$[37]) are the same as those of Model Gamma. The other correlations are based on those of our 1933–52 cohort who reported a brother's educational experience.

Regressing school-leaving age on the same three variables used by Kerckhoff leads to similar results: 33 per cent of the variance is explained. But if we next add type of secondary school to the model, the explained variance increases to 47 per cent.

For these members of our sample, then, the tripartite system entailed a considerable degree of rigidity in educational chances. Had they been going through a contest system of the American kind, their social origins and ability would, we may guess, have moulded their chances to much the same degree, but there would have been more scope left for uncorrelated factors.[38] We may, following Jencks, describe such factors as 'luck', although in that case we should also want to point out that luck is of even greater importance in determining who goes to selective secondary schools. Alternatively, we could claim that the contest system, on this showing, allows greater scope for 'late developers'. The lesser explained variance in the contest model, it could be argued, represents greater freedom of choice.

The distinction between 'luck' and 'freedom of choice' is not one which our data can illuminate, and we accordingly leave it to the reader to provide his own interpretation. However, there is one problem to which we can, and must, address ourselves. This is the role of streaming in sponsored and contest systems. It could reasonably be argued that children are allocated to streams in much the same way as they are allocated to different types of selective school, and that the consequences of such allocation are equally fateful. In other words, if we included a variable for streaming or tracking in the American model, the over-all similarity between the two systems might be restored.

Kerckhoff presents some relevant data on the division of high school students into college preparatory and other kinds of programme. He regresses choice of high-school programme on father's occupation, father's education, family size, and ability, and obtains a very similar pattern of coefficients to that obtained when he regresses type of secondary school on the same four variables for Britain. Unfortunately, he does not go on to show the effect of high-school programme on educational attainment, but as far as it goes, his analysis provides another demonstration of the similarity between the outcomes of the British and American educational systems, despite the differences in their institutions.

However, as Kerckhoff recognizes, the data for this part of his analysis are less satisfactory. In particular, his correlation coefficients between school type, ability, and social origin in Britain are markedly lower than the ones we have employed. Most noticeably, his correlation between school type and ability is only 0.478 compared with the estimate of 0.601 that we have used. Kerckhoff's estimate is based on a division of secondary schools into selective and non-selective (the data used being Douglas's), whereas ours is based on a fourfold classification using Peaker's data. We suspect that the difference in classification is largely responsible for the difference in the results, and that our higher estimate gives a more realistic picture of the workings of the British educational system. Using our estimates we find that 40 per cent of the variance in school type is explained by the three variables of father's occupation, father's education, and IQ, whereas Kerckhoff's four variables explained only 31 per cent of the variance in high school programme in the United States. The similarity between the two systems is not quite so great after all.

One crucial question remains. This is the *effect* of high-school programme and type of secondary school in the two systems. The hope of educational reformers in Britain has been that streaming, if it is employed at all, will be considerably more flexible than allocation to different types of school. We do not yet know whether this hope will be justified, but a cautionary note is perhaps in order. How streaming works will depend on the policies and practices of school teachers themselves, and if teachers have been habituated to the relatively rigid classifications of the tripartite system, these habits of thought may take some time dying.

CONCLUSION

We have used multiple regression and path analysis in this chapter to tackle some important questions about the effects of schooling. First we looked at the seven different types of secondary school and we saw the expected differences between them in their pupils' examination successes and length of school career. We then asked to what extent these differences persisted when we controlled for family background and, in a rough and ready manner, for family climate. The basic strategy of our analysis was the same as that used in Chapter 6, but the results were signally different. Large differences between grammar, minor independent, technical, comprehensive, and secondary modern schools persisted despite the inclusion of fourteen different measures of family background and family climate in our equation. Differences between grammar, Direct Grant, and major independent schools, on the other hand, were very much reduced or eliminated altogether. In other words, pupils of similar social origin had similar educational fates whichever of the latter three schools they attended but very different fates if they went instead to one of the schools ranked lower down the educational hierarchy.

Our provisional answer, then, was that schooling did indeed make a difference, but it was also clear that these apparent school effects which we had found might have been due to differences in the intelligence of their pupils. To check this we had to turn to path analysis and we had to incorporate data from other studies on the relation between intelligence and social background, schooling and school attainment. We found, first, that the school effects remained despite the inclusion of IQ in the model. This means that if we take boys of *identical* social origins and intelligence, the ones sent to more prestigious secondary schools ended up with substantially longer school careers and substantially improved chances of obtaining O- and A-Levels.

Next, we showed that the material circumstances of the home (as we had measured them) remained important as determinants of school careers even when we controlled for measured intelligence and type of secondary school, whereas family climate, for all its importance in determining which type of secondary school one went to in the first place, seemed to be of no importance in determining how long, or with what success, one would stay at a secondary school once there. This finding cast grave doubt on the arguments of writers such as Bantock who suggest that cultural reasons lie behind the failure of woking-class children to gain 'the best of what is offered them'. In so far as the two can be separated, our findings suggest that class not culture is important here.

Third, our analysis showed that IQ itself was surpringly unimportant. Its effects on secondary schooling and school leaving age were quite small compared with those of the other variables in the model. The introduction of IQ into the model did not therefore have the effect of transforming a class-stratified educational system into a meritocracy. This result is sharply at variance with thóse of other writers, but it follows clearly enough from our use of our data on brothers. We showed that in a meritocratic educational system brothers would be a great deal less similar than we find them to be in the real world, and that to account for this known similarity between brothers we have to postulate the existence of unmeasured family background factors, factors which prove to do much of the work that we might otherwise have attributed to IQ.

These main findings derive from our analysis of the educational system as a whole in the post-war period. Excluding the independent schools and confining our analysis to the state sector changes the picture a little but the main outlines stay much as before. Not surprisingly, the selection process for secondary schooling was somewhat more meritocratic in the state sector than it was in the educational system as a whole. More surprisingly, however, IQ becomes a *less* important determinant of school leaving age when we restrict ourselves to the state sector. This suggests that a greater degree of rigidity existed within the state sector. The pupils entered a relatively inflexible institutional structure; once allocated to a grammar or secondary modern school, intelligence had little effect on one's future career. The able working-class boys selected for grammar schools indeed had a good chance of doing well (at least as far as O-Level); but equally able boys (from whatever social class) selected for secondary modern schools had very little chance.

The rigidity of the tripartite system emerged too from the comparison between the British and American educational systems. Kerckhoff's work had shown that, despite the institutional differences, education was almost equally meritocratic in Britain and America. Comprehensive reorganization, we may conclude, will do little to increase (or reduce) equality of opportunity between the social classes. On the other hand, it may well reduce the predictability of educational careers. Some of the arbitrary injustices perpetrated by the tripartite system may be removed, although whether they will be replaced by 'luck' or 'freedom of choice' we cannot yet determine.

NOTES

1. Above, Chapter 8, p.144.
2. Ibid.
3. C. Jencks, *Inequality: A Reassessment of the Effect of Family and Schooling in America* (Basic Books, Inc., 1972), p.146.
4. Ibid., pp.158–9.
5. Quoted above Chapter 1, p.9.
6. Douglas, op.cit., p.187.
7. We have used three measures of attainment: school-leaving age, measured in years; O-Levels – binary variable where the respondent scores 1 if he obtained one or more O-Levels, zero otherwise; and A-Levels – again a binary variable where the respondent scores 1 if he obtained one or more. As measures of school type we have used six binary variables, one for each type (Headmasters' Conference, Direct Grant, grammar, non-Headmasters' Conference (independent), technical, and comprehensive) except secondary modern. The respondent scores 1 if he attended a given type of school and zero otherwise. A respondent who scores zero on all six variables must therefore have attended a secondary modern school, and there is no need for a seventh variable.
8. If we regress '5 or more O-Levels' on the same set of independent variables, some slight school effects still remain. The coefficients are 0.47 for HMC schools, 0.49 for Direct Grant schools, and 0.42 for grammar schools.
9. The differences at A-Level are largely a consequence of those in school leaving age. If we take boys from the service class who left school at 18 or older, we find that 81 per cent of those at grammar school, 84 per cent of those at Direct Grant schools, and 72 per cent of those at HMC schools obtained one or more A-Level pass.
10. For a summary of the evidence see O. Banks, *The Sociology of Education* (Batsford, 1968), ch.4.
11. 'Examination success' is represented by a four-point scaling of the highest qualification actually gained:

    4 = Degree or Dip.Tech. (level 'a' in the *Classification of Qualifications:* see Chapter 2, p.23).

    3 = Higher professional and technical qualifications (level 'b', ibid)

    2 = Lower professional and technical qualifications (level 'c', ibid)

    1 = School examinations: GCE (O- or A-Level) or School Certificate (Ordinary or Higher).

    0 = Otherwise.

    Note that 'non-academic' school examinations (clerical and commerical, RSA, etc.) are thus excluded, as are vocational examinations normally taken in further education courses, specifically City and Guilds, ONC/HNC and OND/HND (see question 3i, Appendix I and Chapter 2, p.23).
12. For criticisms of Jencks's *Inequality* see the symposia in *Harvard Educational Review* (Autumn 1973), and *American Journal of Sociology* (1974).
13. More precisely, we include only respondents who had been living in England and Wales at age 14 and who reported educational data on a brother who had left school by 1972.

14. Throughout this chapter we shall bracket correlations derived from the model itself.
15. The multiple correlation of respondent's secondary-school type with the group of 'material circumstances' indicators is 0.442, that of brother's secondary schooling 0.436.
16. More specifically, in the present model,

$$p_{53} = p_{54} + (r_{53} - r_{54})/(1 - r_{34}) = (r_{53} - r_{54})/(1 - r_{34}).$$

17. For a more general treatment see Appendix IV.
18. This is the same binary variable used in the first section of this chapter. See note 7 above.
19. Alan C. Kerckhoff, 'Stratification Processes and Outcomes in England and the U.S.', *American Sociological Review*, 39 (1974), 789–801.
20. One difficulty with this method is that we obtain our correlations with variable 2 from a variety of different models. The meaning of variable 2 thus changes since, as we have earlier emphasized, the meaning of a hypothetical variable depends on its method of construction. One answer to this problem, which is used by Jencks in his Appendix B, p.396, is to employ two hypothetical variables rather than a single one. Thus we might have one hypothetical variable which represent unmeasured sources of similarity between brothers' IQ, and another representing unmeasured sources of similarity between their school-leaving ages. The difficulty with this is that we then have to make more or less arbitrary assumptions about the size of the correlation between these hypothetical variables. Essentially our method of using a single variable amounts to the assumption that the correlation between the hypothetical variables is equal to unity.
21. See Dorfman, op.cit.
22. This is the weighted mean of seven US studies given by Jencks, op.cit. (1972), p.289.
23. W. Peaker, *The Plowden Children Four Years Later* (National Foundation for Educational Research, 1971).
24. Alternatively, we could allow brothers' characteristics to have direct effects, but this too will reduce the size of the direct path from IQ to secondary schooling. One could preserve the original estimate of $p_{37} = r_{37} = 0.601$ by allowing the residuals to variables (3) and (4) to be correlated. But this only postpones the issue: as soon as a variable is found that accounts for the residual correlation, the estimate of p_{37} will drop; unless, most improbably, this variable's correlation with IQ is precisely zero.
25. Not surprisingly, our results are seriously at variance with those of other writers who have produced path models of educational attainment without taking brothers into account. Thus Kerckhoff and Tyler (W. Tyler, *The Sociology of Educational Inequality*, Methuen, 1977, chapter 4), both using broadly the same data, construct models which ascribe a powerful effect to IQ. But neither takes account of brothers, and any attempt which either makes to do so will almost certainly weaken the effect of IQ.
26. For an interesting development of this aspect of the analysis, see K. I. Macdonald, 'Interpretation of Residual Paths and the Decomposition of Variance', *Sociological Methods and Research* (February 1979).
27. Inclusion of Direct Grant schools in the state sector clearly weights the outcome against our hypothesis that the sectors are distinct. If we can demonstrate a difference even under these conditions, it is a difference to be taken seriously.
28. See, e.g., Kalton, op.cit.
29. See Macdonald, op.cit., and for a lucid and thorough account of the principles of path analysis (from a standpoint which differs somewhat from our own) K. I. Macdonald and P. Dorreian, *Data Analysis for Social Science*, London: Methuen, 1979, chapter 5.
30. In the state sector we cannot use the estimates of Model Alpha and we must construct an equivalent to Model Alpha for the restricted sample of state sector respondents. The resulting value of p_{31} can then be compared with the value in Model Delta.
31. J. Karabel and A. H. Halsey, *Power and Ideology in Education* (Oxford University Press, New York, 1977), p.25.
32. C. Jencks, op.cit., p.160.
33. A. Kerckhoff, op.cit.

34. For simplicity we have here given results for the model that excludes a measure of family size. The coefficients are those based on Douglas's measure of school-leaving age, and Duncan's uncorrected correlations. For details, see A. Kerckhoff, op.cit., Table 3, and Appendix, pp.798–801.
35. A. Kerckhoff, op.cit., p.797.
36. Blau and Duncan, op.cit., pp.320–4.
37. This estimate derives from Douglas, as recalculated by Kerckhoff, op.cit., Table 2.
38. Rutter's recent work suggests that various characteristics of schools may play a considerable role in determining pupils' behaviour and performance in comprehensive schools. However there are some worrying problems in Rutter's work. See M. Rutter et al., *Fifteen Thousand Hours* (London: Open Books, 1979) and A.F. Heath's forthcoming review in the *Oxford Review of Education*.

CHAPTER 10

Post-Secondary Education

The metaphor of pathways and choices acquires a new significance at the end of the secondary stage of education. Individuals have a new freedom of responsibility thrust upon them when they reach the statutory school-leaving age. At this point they can choose to have done with the educational map: and half of our sample have done precisely that. But, for those with the will and capacity for further explorations in learning, there remains an expanding world of institutions beyond the secondary school. There is, in other words, formal freedom to go along a variety of paths extending from minimal and part-time in-firm training of short duration to the long journey through university and post-graduate education to higher academic and professional degrees.

Though the metaphor suggests an emphasis on individual choice at this stage in the educational journey, in carrying on the story from our account in previous chapters of primary and secondary schooling, we have already to be aware of the degree to which choices have been effectively settled by previous decisions in families and educational bureaucracies. For the moment we will take this previous experience for granted though later, in our analysis of the journey through post-secondary education, we shall return to the class origins of our respondents. Meanwhile, we shall ask how far the continuing development of the 'tertiary' stage of education has incorporated meritocratic principles.

Half, to repeat, have chosen to have done with formal learning and, for the remaining half, previous experience and attainment preclude many of the possible pathways of formal education. In this sense, what we have before us might be thought of as a transitional map between a traditionally 'elitist' to a future 'mass' or even 'universal' system of education beyond school. Indeed, the traditional stereotype, which we shall examine, postulated two educational territories. On the one there was a journey through the schools on the way to the universities for a small minority, typically composed of those born to the better-off families, who then entered professional, administrative, and managerial careers. On the other, which was used by the popular majority, primary, or more accurately elementary, education was terminal and led directly to manual and minor clerical employment. What we now have, however, is an evolving unification of the two maps which would presumably be complete in a world of universal post-secondary education. Meanwhile the university maintains its place as the most prestigious and remunerative educational destination and the metaphor is applied to the varied forms of part-time further education in the concept of the 'alternative route'[1] which by-passes the sixth form of the grammar school or its contemporary equivalents on its way to the many stations of vocational qualification.

THE STRUCTURE OF POST-SECONDARY EDUCATION

Post-secondary education, which has grown more rapidly than the primary and secondary schools during the period covered by our 1972 respondents, has a ramified structure and various phrases are used in the literature to describe its array of learning opportunities including higher education, further education, and adult education. For the purposes of this chapter we have used a simplifying division into three types - the university, the college of education, and part-time further education. This threefold division is useful in that it arranges the varied types of post-secondary experience into a hierarchy of educational and occupational opportunities and distinguishes between full-time and part-time courses: and it loosely fits the boundaries of recognized institutions at least as well as the conventional categories of official statistics. The university and the college of education have fairly clear boundaries and are dominantly, though not exclusively, full-time courses. The category of 'further education' is less satis-factory because, though it includes most post-school education except that offered in universities and colleges of education, it also includes some full-time courses, and, what is most confusing, it embraces the advanced work undertaken at a great number of technical and commercial colleges and schools of art which, in official statistics, count as higher education.

The university and the college of education also fit the metaphor of maps and journeys in the sense that they remain educational pathways at the end of which a transition is made to an occupational journey. In the case of the university a range of professional and administrative occupations is then involved, while the colleges of education have been monotechnic, preparing for the teaching pro-fessions. Travellers, moreover, along both these educational routes have relatively seldom dropped out. It has sometimes been said of the British university, and particularly of traditional Oxford and Cambridge, that the army principle was always applied of 'fit for service fit for pension'. Those who were admitted seldom left without the appropriate qualification after three years: and similarly for the teacher trainee after two years.

There is not, by contrast, the same assured journey and abrupt transition in the case of part-time further education. Almost half of our sample have attended part-time courses in evening classes or day release or block release at technical colleges or other institutions of further education. An additional 9 per cent have taken part-time in-firm training or correspondence courses.[2] In most cases they started their courses soon after leaving school: typically while holding their first jobs or in the jobs they entered on starting a trade apprenticeship. Thus the metaphor is of less certain application here, and part-time further education is in some ways best treated as part of an occupational rather than an educational career. In this book, however, we treat it tentatively as an educational destination, or rather a set of destinations, recognizing its heterogeneity, its fluidity of membership, and its low rates of course completion, and in this sense also making appropriate reservations about the appropriateness to it of the concept of an alternative route.

As David Raffe has observed, 'One difficulty with the concept of an alterna-tive route deserves to be underlined. There is some ambiguity as to what it is that further education provides the alternative *to*. It has generally been regarded as a social alternative as well as an educational one: as an alternative to the benefits of a high-status home background as well as an alternative to the highest levels of full-time education.'³ Yet the social and the educational concepts of the alternative route are not strictly parallel, as will be suggested below, and the apparent analogy between them can be misleading. We shall try to clarify this ambiguity later in this chapter by exploring the social and educational origins of those who follow the route through part-time further, as distinct from full-time higher, education.

FROM SCHOOL TO POST-SECONDARY EDUCATION

Putting together the experience of all the men in our sample, it appears that all paths from the schools to the post-secondary institutions carry some traffic, but some are much more heavily used than others as may be seen from Table 10.1. Approximately two-thirds of those who attended elementary or secondary modern schools compared with not much more than one-quarter of public school and grammar school boys ended their educational journey at the school exit.

There is, moreover, a general pattern of close connection between prestigious schools and prestigious forms of post-secondary education. Access to the university almost exactly parallels the academic hierarchy of the schools, though towards the end of the period covered by our data comprehensive schools had begun to emerge as an amalgam of the grammar, technical, and secondary modern schools. It emerges, further, that the hierarchy of access to the university is steep with 37.2 per cent of HMC leavers going on to university compared with 0.4 per cent of the elementary- and secondary-modern-school boys.

Access to further education seems, by contrast, to be fairly equal as between types of school. But, recalling the arguments advanced in Chapter 4, it would be false to infer that the pattern necessarily reflects a more meritocratic admission policy in these institutions. It is rather a reflection of their lower position in the queue for post-secondary places and apparent equality of access is in fact the residual effect of class-associated selection in the universities and colleges of education. If all forms of post-secondary education are combined (which is in effect to look at column 1 of Table 10.1), the familiar academic-cum-social hierarchy reappears, except that the HMC schools fall slightly below the grammar and direct-grant schools.

All this appears from a view of access as outflow from schools to colleges. The inflow picture (Table 10.2) brings into view the important fact that, despite the hierarchy of access, even the universities have drawn the majority of their entrants from the state schools, mostly, of course, the grammar schools. Moreover, nearly two-thirds of students at colleges of education come from grammar schools. Though the HMC and Direct Grant schools are the second most important sources for the universities, the technical schools hold this position with respect to colleges of education and part-time further education colleges. Altogether then, the majority of post-secondary, and especially non-university, education has been fed from the state schools. A summary description in terms of typicalities would be that the university undergraduate is an ex-grammar-school boy, and this is even more true in the case of colleges of education, while the part-timer in further education has come from a secondary

Table 10.1

Secondary School to Post-Secondary Education

School type	No post-secondary education	Part-time further education	College of Education	University
HMC (N = 199)	27.6	33.7	1.5	37.2
Direct Grant (N = 135)	23.7	42.2	5.2	28.9
Grammar (N = 1411)	24.3	53.0	5.5	17.2
Non-HMC (N = 206)	38.8	47.1	1.5	12.6
Technical (N = 988)	44.8	52.4	1.4	1.3
Comprehensive (N = 121)	39.7	55.3	0.8	4.1
Elementary and Secondary Modern (N = 5450)	58.5	40.9	0.3	0.4
All (N = 8510)	49.2	44.4	1.4	4.9

Table 10.2

Secondary School Origins of Students at Different Post-Secondary Institutions

School type	No post-secondary education	Part-time further education	College of Education	University
HMC	1.3	1.8	2.5	17.6
Direct Grant	0.8	1.5	5.8	9.3
Grammar	8.2	19.8	65.0	57.5
Non-HMC	1.9	2.6	2.5	6.2
Technical	10.6	13.7	11.7	3.1
Comprehensive	1.1	1.8	0.8	1.2
Elementary and Secondary Modern	76.1	58.9	11.7	5.2
	100.0	100.1	100.0	100.1
N	4188	3781	120	421

modern or elementary school, and this is even more true in the case of those who opt out of formal schooling altogether at the end of the secondary stage. All this, however, is consistent with a hierarchical array of chances for post-secondary education because of the pyramid of numbers who pass from the secondary schools.

DEVELOPMENTS OF THE ROUTE FROM SCHOOL TO POST-SECONDARY EDUCATION

Since Tables 10.1 and 10.2 present data from our sample as a whole, they disguise the fact that the map has changed with the expansion of education beyond school. Nevertheless, they suggest that the binary conception with which we began is over-simple, and further that the two separate systems of secondary schools – the one preparatory to higher education and the other terminal – had already passed into history if they ever existed. In fact our cohort figures show that, in the period since the First War which our sample covers, the distinction between the selective and non-selective schools was not that of transit and terminal but of different probabilities of entry to a growing and increasingly varied set of post-secondary destinations. At one end a minority of grammar- and private-school boys went straight to work and only a comparable minority went on to the universities. At the other end an admittedly tiny minority went on to the universities from the elementary schools, and a substantial minority went to part-time further education.

The expansion of post-secondary education shifted, but did not transform, this pattern. If we compare our oldest (born 1913–22) with our youngest (born 1943–52) cohorts we find that nearly one-third of the earlier products of non-selective schools were already going on to some form of education beyond school, and that a similar proportion of those who had private secondary education after the War were leaving school to go straight into employment. In the years between, the universities roughly tripled their intake from every type of school, and the other forms of post-secondary education nearly doubled their intake from technical, elementary, and secondary modern schools. Thus each successive cohort took advantage of more post-secondary opportunity. The question is not whether a binary system was destroyed so much as how the new opportunities were distributed among those who had taken different routes through the primary and secondary schools.

This question is most economically answered by using a multiple regression analysis of the type we used in Chapters 3 and 6 to estimate the predetermination of entry to private primary and selective secondary schools. The same set of independent variables from social background and primary schooling are used with the addition of type of secondary school. The dependent variable is whether or not the respondent went on to university.

The main result of the analysis (confined to those born 1933–52) is that, among all the factors of background and schooling, the crucial determinant of access to the university is A-Level qualification. The explanatory strength of the variables we have used is reasonably strong in that $R^2 = 0.46$. The β coefficient for A-Levels is 0.478, and no other variable has a coefficient of more than twice its standard error, except that of attendance at a Direct Grant school. This

Table 10.3
Social Class and Post-Secondary Education

Father's Social Class		No post-secondary education	Part-time further education	College of Education	University
I, II	(N = 1072)	29.6 −63*	47.6 13	2.7 110	20.1 241
III, IV, V	(N = 2475)	43.8 −23	49.8 18	1.7 64	4.6 94
VI, VII, VIII	(N = 4482)	55.4 0	41.8 0	0.9 0	1.8 0
All	(N = 8029)	48.4	45.1	1.4	5.1

* Figures in italic give the log distances. For definition see above, Chapter 3, p.37.

exception is significant negatively in that it shows no peculiar advantage in attendance at HMC or other private schools: the coefficient for Direct Grant schooling is 0.146. The boy who attended a Direct Grant school had a 10 per cent better chance of going on to the university than a grammar-school boy of similar social background and primary schooling. We may also specifically note that a boy who attended comprehensive school had the same chance of getting a university place if he had the same A-Levels and the same background as a boy who went to any other type of school other than Direct Grant.

SOCIAL ORIGIN AND POST-SECONDARY EDUCATION

Table 10.4

Social Composition of Post-Secondary Institutions

Father's Social Class	Part-time further education	College of Education	University
I, II	14.1	25.9	52.4
III, IV, V	34.1	38.4	27.9
VI, VII, VIII	51.8	35.7	19.7
	100.0	100.0	100.0
N	(3620)	(112)	(412)

Turning now from educational to social background we can look directly at class of origin in relation to post-secondary education. The basic information is presented in Tables 10.3 and 10.4. Looked at in inflow terms (Table 10.4) the university is dominantly a service-class institution, part-time further education dominantly working class, and the college of education more evenly based but with its typical student from the intermediate class.

The outflow table (Table 10.3) records class chances of access to these institutions. The familiar class gradient of educational chances reappears with service-class boys enjoying a log distance of 241 in access to the university, and 110 in access to the college of education, compared with a boy from the working class. Given this class selection for the more prestigious forms of higher education the log distances are much reduced for part-time further education and reversed for direct translation to the labour market with no further educational experience. A more detailed examination of class differences (not shown in the table) reveals further that boys from the entrepreneurial and agricultural labouring classes are 'out of line' in the sense of being relatively cut off from post-secondary education by comparison with those near to them in the conventional social hierarchy.

Again it is worth remarking on the absence of a class differential of access to part-time further education that this is properly interpreted not as a case of 'class-blind' admission but as a consequence of class queueing for the more desired forms of higher education. To take this point further, it is possible, though we have not included the relevant table, to recalculate class distributions in post-secondary education cumulatively on the assumption that colleges of education rank above part-time further education, and the university above

Table 10.5

Class Inequalities at Different Stages of the Educational System

Father's Social Class	Percentage attending[1] selective secondary schools	Percentage obtaining[2] O-Level	Percentage obtaining[2] A-Level	Percentage attending[3] University
I, II	71.9 *111**	58.1 *159*	26.9 *226*	20.1 *241*
III, IV, V	39.6 *51*	24.2 *72*	6.9 *90*	4.6 *94*
VI, VII, VIII	23.7 *0*	11.8 *0*	2.8 *0*	1.8 *0*
All	35.0	21.8	7.3	5.1

Notes: [1] For details see Table 4.4.
[2] For details see Table 8.12.
[3] For details see Table 10.3.

* Figures in italic give the log distances (see Chapter 3, p.37).

both. The results show that access to post-secondary education has a similar pattern of class inequality to that which we found for access to the various forms of secondary education. When the ratios are arranged cumulatively the extent of class bias in selection even for the lowliest forms of further education is made clear, and the class gradients are steeper than in Table 10.3. There are, however, differences in the steepness of the class gradient. Taking grammar schools 'and above' as the equivalent at the secondary stage of universities and colleges at the post-secondary stage, the selective advantages of the service-class boy are increased at the later stage of educational opportunity, while the disadvantages of the working-class boy are worsened. On this calculation, then, it appears that the class discriminatory post-secondary stage does not merely reflect earlier class selection but also adds to it.

These processes are summarized in Table 10.5 which confirms that class inequalities are cumulative at each successive stage of the educational career. Thus the log distances from the working class to the intermediate and, to a markedly greater extent, the service class, increase from entry to secondary education through O-Level and A-Level courses, and again at the gate to the university.

An inflow table (10.6) accordingly shows the increasingly service-class character of institutions or courses of study which are placed at the later stages of educational selection.

Table 10.6

The Class Composition of Successive Stages of Educational Selection
(percentages)

Father's Social Class	Selective[1] Secondary Schools	O-Levels	A-Levels	University
I, II	27.4	35.5	49.1	52.4
III, IV, V	34.9	34.2	29.4	27.9
VI, VII, VIII	37.7	30.2	21.5	19.7
All	100.0	99.9	100.0	100.0

Note: [1] For details see Table 4.5.

However, it must also be noted from Table 10.5 that the percentage point difference between the classes *decreases* steadily as the educational ladder is ascended, for example in the case of service-class and working-class boys from 48 percentage points at entry to selective secondary schools to 18 points at entry to university. This apparent contradiction arises from the fact that the later and more severely selective educational institutions are a minority experience for all classes. It remains the case, none the less, that there is additional class bias in selection for the university even after the hurdles of the previous stages. In our discussion of survival rates among boys of different social origins in Chapter 8, we pointed to the enormous drop-out of working-class boys at the minimum school leaving age, and went on to point to the diminution of these differences at the sixth-form stage with the surmise that assimilation of the working-class minority was virtually complete. But it is now clear that assimilation is not completed at the top of the secondary schools. The survival rates for the three classes from age 17 to 18 were 0.60, 0.51, and 0.50. The survival rates from 18 to university entry are 0.70, 0.60, and 0.60.[4] Thus the gap between the service class and the other two classes remains.

The question therefore arises as to whether university selection is less meritocratic than selection at the earlier stages. To tackle this question we must first glance back at the concept of IQ handicaps introduced in Chapter 4.[5] These are the differences between thresholds of IQ which have to be reached by boys of different class origin in order to gain admission to an institution given its class composition and the distribution of IQ between classes.

MERITOCRACY AND THE UNIVERSITY

From our analysis in Chapter 4 we concluded that selective schools within the state sector were more meritocratic in their admission than were private schools. For example, the HMC schools set a threshold IQ of 126 for service-class boys, and 137 for working-class boys – a handicap of 11 points compared with a grammar-school handicap of 7 points.

Table 10.7

'IQ Thresholds' at Different Stages of the Educational System[1]

Father's Social Class	Age 16	Age 17	Age 18	University
I, II	101.6	109.6	116.8	120.8
III, IV, V	108.3	116.4	121.9	125.6
VI, VII, VIII	111.5	119.9	124.3	127.4
Service-class/working-class IQ handicap	9.9	10.3	7.5	6.6

Note [1] For details see text.

An analysis of the university in the same terms appears in Table 10.7 with figures also for survival to ages 16, 17, and 18. The thresholds for all classes rise at each successive stage of survival or selection, and a regular pattern of class discrimination is maintained throughout the process. But the most striking feature of the table is that, by contrast with class inequalities as shown in Table 10.5, the IQ handicap falls among the survivors to age 18 and the entrants to the university. The handicaps rose from the point of entry to grammar school to the point of sixth-form entry largely because of the heavy drop-out of working-class boys at the minimum school-leaving age. But why do they then fall? The explanation is seen most easily with the aid of the diagram below (Figure 10.1).

Figure 10.1 shows what would happen if survival rates for all classes were constant and set at .5. Let line A represent the IQ threshold of those staying on from each class into the sixth form. It indicates a gross class inequality of the kind that occurs in the real world, with a large proportion of service-class children staying on and a small proportion of working-class children

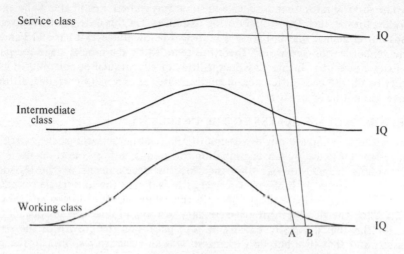

Service class

IQ

Intermediate
class

IQ

Working class

A B   IQ

Fig. 10.1.

staying on. Line B then represents the IQ threshold of those staying on for a second year in the sixth form. Since we have set the survival rate at .5, only half the service-class children to the right of line A will also be to the right of line B. But since there were already a large number of children to the right of line A, we have to move a considerable distance to the right before we have eliminated half the children. In the working-class case, however, there are only a few children to start with to the right of line A, and we are already well into the tail of the distribution. Hence we only have to eliminate a small number of children to reach the half-way mark, and we need only move a small distance to reach line B.

What this means is that identical survival rates in the different classes could lead to a marked narrowing of IQ handicaps (depending, of course, on the starting values), and that the difference between survival rates might have to increase progressively if the IQ handicaps were to remain constant. In practice, as we have seen, the survival rates start off markedly different from each other but then tend to converge until there is a relatively small gap between them. It should now be clear how such a pattern could generate narrowing IQ handicaps.

We can now sum up the impact of selection on class chances at university level and compare it with earlier stages. The crucial point is that while the class distances (shown in Table 10.5) are at their largest at university level, it would be wrong to infer that class bias is strongest there. The distance at university entrance is largely a consequence of earlier decisions in the educational process. Even if universities were completely neutral as between classes, for example accepting all those who were qualified, i.e. who had A-Levels, the log distance of service from working class would necessarily be 262 (the log distance at A-Level). Only if universities positively discriminate in favour of the working class could this class differential decline.

The survival rates, therefore, give in some ways a better estimate of the extent of class bias at each stage than do log distances. On this criterion the university does not eliminate bias but it does reduce it below the level it has at 15 and 16. The school-leaving age would therefore seem to be the crucial stage for public policies aimed at reducing class inequalities of educational opportunity. On the other hand, the class difference in survival rates at university entrance, although small, cannot be ignored.

TRENDS IN CLASS ACCESS TO THE UNIVERSITY

We can now complete our discussion of the relation between social origin and university entrance by an examination of trends, using cohort analysis in a comparable manner to our discussion of the development of the secondary school in Chapter 4. Table 10.8 reflects the fact that the universities expanded throughout our period but especially in the 1960s, i.e. for those born 1943-52. Comparing the development of secondary schools (Table 4.9) it appears from Table 10.8 that university expansion kept pace with the growth of the service classes, and that 'Robbinsian expansion' was an effective response to the post-war baby boom. For this group, it will be recalled from Chapter 4, the building of grammar-school places fell behind.

Table 10.8

Attendance at University by Birth Cohort

Father's Social Class	(percentages)			
	1913–22	1923–32	1933–42	1943–52
I, II	7.2	15.9	23.7	26.4
	208*	258	233	214
III, IV, V	1.9	4.0	4.1	8.0
	75	120	58	95
VI, VII, VIII	0.9	1.2	2.3	3.1
	0	0	0	0
All	1.8	3.4	5.4	8.5
N	(1846)	(1879)	(1856)	(2246)

* Figures in italic give log distances; see Chapter 3, p.37.

The familiar picture also emerges, as with educational expansion generally, that though the fastest *rates* of growth almost always accrue to the working class, the greatest absolute increments of opportunity go to the service class.

If, however, we look at the expansion in relation to the numbers qualifying at the end of the secondary-school stage (Table 10.9), the picture is more like that of secondary-school expansion itself. There is an inverted U-curve, i.e. just as in Table 4.9, all classes experienced a rise in the proportion going on to university in the 1923-32 birth cohort. The proportion then stayed constant in the 1933-42 cohort and then dropped for the 1943-52 cohort as the number of secondary-school-qualified leavers outpaced university expansion. And, while

Table 10.9

Percentage of Respondents with A-Levels or Higher School Certificate who Attended University

Father's Social Class	1913–22	1923–32	1933–42	1943–52
I, II	41.2	74.3	72.9	57.8
III, IV, V	46.2	59.1	63.3	46.7
VI, VII, VIII	60.0	76.9	59.4	45.1
All	45.2	68.5	66.7	51.3
N	(42)	(73)	(138)	(353)

this was happening, the working class was less able to hold on to its previous gains so that the distance between classes increased.

PART-TIME FURTHER EDUCATION

We can now return to the question of the 'alternative route' and concentrate attention on part-time further education. Our interest in this concept has to be set in the context of the more general theme of this book, viz. the impact on the social distribution of educational chances which has been made by a national programme of educational expansion in the twentieth century.

A general pattern has been unfolded in our discussion. The origins of the modern educational system may be described as a minimal education for the majority, with further opportunity for the minority. For a minority within that minority the golden road to high opportunity was provided by selective secondary education (private or public), and the universities. Educational expansion has developed the system in two main ways – by raising the output of children qualified to go beyond secondary education, and by differentiating the opportunities available to those, whether qualified or not, who stayed past the minimum school-leaving age.

All forms of post-secondary education have been selective in the simple sense of not being universal. The pattern of selection has, moreover, just as in selective secondary education, been class related in that there has been a correlation between social-class origin and selective educational destination. Expansion was expected to reduce that correlation or, to use a different terminology, to reduce the steepness of the class gradient of opportunity, and eventually to make it a plateau on which the classes would be more nearly representative of their numbers in the population at large.

The shape of class stratification, though changing, has remained that of a pyramid in the period we are considering. This, together with the minority character of extended or selective education, accounts for the double, and apparently contradictory, appearance of outflow and inflow tables from the same data. Outflow tables like Table 10.5 show the correlation between class origin and educational attainment, the higher the origin the higher the attainment. Inflow tables like Table 10.6 show the class composition of educational groups or institutions, the larger numbers of the lower strata counter-balancing or overturning their low proportionate contribution to 'reduce' service-class exclusiveness.

We have seen the general pattern applied to the flow from origins to post-secondary destinations in the earlier part of this chapter. The evidence gives some support to the idea of part-time further education as an alternative route within the general pattern of class (and school) related access (outflow) combined with a much less dramatically skewed class composition of the post-secondary institutions such that part-time further education has over half of its recruits from working-class families (Table 10.4).

It was the main concern of the Crowther Committee to develop further education as an alternative route to that provided by the sixth form of the grammar school. As David Raffe notes, 'They described further education as a "practical" alternative to the "academic" education available in the grammar school or the university. It was a route for the student who had been missed by selection at 11 or whose talents and interests had been dormant during most of his academic schooling. Further education, it was thus supposed, recruited proportionately fewer of its students from among those who had reached the highest levels of academic education.' Table 10.10 supports this verdict.[6] It shows (in column (1)) the proportions with different levels of school achievement who went on to part-time further education. Either of the two measures used may be depicted as a 'V' with its maximum in the middle ranges of the academic hierarchy. Those with the highest levels of school achievement were less likely to enter than those who did less well at school. Sixth-formers (at least those who left with A-Level or Higher School Certificate), were less likely to go on to part-time further education than were those leaving with O-Level or Ordinary School Certificate.[7] Those who left school with four years more than the statutory school-leaving age which applied to them were less likely to go to part-time further education than those with three years of extra schooling, and similarly those with three years' extra schooling were less likely to do so than those with two. The proportions move downwards again for those with no further years of schooling.

Nevertheless, it is equally clear from the inflow analysis (column (2)) that part-time further education has recruited mainly from those with the lowest level of school success and not from the top of the academic hierarchy. In other words, those leaving school with no examination passes have been less likely than the average to enter part-time ccourses, but they none the less constitute a majority. So, for the majority of the population, part-time further education has been an alternative to higher attainment within the academic sector.

The authors of the Crowther Report tended to identify educational with social inequality and to believe that support for the educationally under-privileged was tantamount to support for the socially underprivileged. This belief still persists and is associated with the concept of the alternative route. On this view, if part-time further education provides a special route for those with less academic education, it is thereby providing a special route for those from less favourable home backgrounds. We have already seen that educational opportunity for the more prestigious levels of post-secondary education is fairly heavily weighted in favour of the service class. This is not so for part-time further education looked at separately. The heaviest use (outflow) was by boys

Table 10.10

School Achievement and Part-time Further Education

Years at School beyond Minimum Leaving Age		Percentage Attending Part-time Further Education	
		Outflow Analysis (1)	Inflow Analysis (2)
None	(N = 5646)	39.8	59.3
One year	(N = 1270)	61.5	20.6
Two years	(N = 751)	62.2	12.3
Three years	(N = 602)	39.0	6.2
Four years	(N = 260)	21.5	1.4
			99.8
Examinations Taken Successfully at School		Outflow Analysis	Inflow Analysis
None (N = 6688)		42.2	74.4
One or more O-Levels, or Ordinary School Certificate (N = 1235)		66.2	21.6
A-Level or Higher School Certificate (N = 606)		24.8	4.0
			100.0

from the intermediate classes, though an analysis in terms of our eight-class schema shows that the entrepreneurial group (Class IV) was a relatively low user (42.2 per cent) even by comparison with the manual-working Classes VI (45.4 per cent) and VII (also 42 per cent). The highest rate of participation was among th sons of foremen and technicians (Class V – 55 per cent), and the lowest among small-holders and agricultural workers (Class VIII – 21 per cent). So a truncated view of post-secondary education again shows the V-pattern for our three main classes, but this does not eliminate the familiar pattern of correlation between class and post-secondary education *as a whole* which is shown for each of our four birth cohorts in Table 10.12. Table 10.11 enables us to see the relation between class of origin and use of part-time further-education courses for boys with different school-leaving qualifications.

It is in this form that the social and educational aspects of the idea of an alternative route can be most clearly seen. What stands out from Table 10.11 is that part-time further education is a frequently used educational alternative for poorly qualified boys from the service class. Indeed, among those with neither O-Levels nor Ordinary School Certificate the use of part-time further education is proportionately highest in this class. For the moderately qualified working-class use of part-time further education is highest, and for those with A-Levels the position is held by the intermediate class. By and large, class differences of access to this type of post-secondary experience

Table 10.11

*Percentage Attending Part-time Further Education by Social Class
and School Achievement*

Father's Social Class		None	Examinations Taken Successfully at School	
			One or more O-Levels or Ordinary School Certificate	A-Level or Higher School Certificate
I, II	(N = 1072)	53.6	62.3	20.8
III, IV, V	(N = 2475)	47.7	67.3	29.1
VI, VII, VIII	(N = 4482)	39.4	69.4	27.8

are very small, and educational opportunity would be much more unequal if it did not exist. In this sense it is a social as well as an educational alternative.

Table 10.12

*Percentage Attending Part-time Further Education
by Social Class and Birth Cohort*

Father's Social Class	1913–22	1923–32	1933–42	1943–52
I, II	50.0	46.2	59.3	45.1
III, IV, V	40.3	41.7	55.1	57.2
VI, VII, VIII	29.9	36.9	46.4	50.8

*Percentage Attending Any Form of Post-School Education
by Social Class and Birth Cohort*

Father's Social Class	1913–22		1923–32		1933–42		1943–52	
I, II	60.6	*65**	64.4	*50*	77.1	*44*	73.9	*30*
III, IV, V	43.5	*32*	48.0	*21*	60.4	*19*	67.4	*21*
VI, VII, VIII	31.5	*0*	38.9	*0*	49.9	*0*	54.6	*0*

* Figures in italic give log distances (see Chapter 3, p.37).

Trends in class access to part-time further education and to post-secondary education as a whole are shown in Table 10.12. From the evidence it emerges that for part-time further education class access has slowly changed with expansion from the familiar positive correlation of class and opportunity to an *inverse* relation for those born after the Second War. Thus in the earlier decades it was not usefully seen as an alternative route for the working class so much as an extension of class-biased educational opportunity. For the last cohort, the alternative-route description is more accurate. Yet *any* description has to be placed in the context of the whole structure of educational opportunity beyond school, and then it appears that expansion has brought a slow and steady diminution of class inequality. The log distance of the service from the working class falls from 65 to 30. In the same process the gap in rates of journeying decreased. An extra thirteen of every 100 service-class boys travelled educationally beyond school compared with an extra twenty-three working-class boys.

CONCLUSION

The analysis of entry to university, college of education, and further education completes our story of social origins and educational destinations. The first part of the analysis is depressingly familiar. The boy from a privileged school or from a privileged social background had a much higher chance than his unprivileged contemporary of gaining a place at university. These inequalities, however, were very largely a consequence of earlier decisions in the educational process: seventy per cent of service-class boys who stayed on at school until 18 went on to university; sixty per cent of those from the intermediate and working classes did so. For those who survived in school as far as 18, therefore, the chances of going on to university were very similar. It is the earlier inequalities of access to selective schools and to the sixth form that are crucial.

The question then arises whether part-time further education provides an 'alternative route' for those who missed out at earlier stages of the educational career. We found in answer that the boy from the *middle* ranges of the academic hierarchy was the most likely to go on to further education although, moving from an outflow to an inflow analysis, we also saw that the majority of recruits actually came from the *lowest* academic levels. In these senses, then, further education does constitute an educational alternative. But is it also a social alternative? Again, we found that the boy from the intermediate classes was more likely than his service- or working-class contemporary to make use of part-time further education, although this must be qualified by another finding that further education was a particularly frequented route for poorly qualified boys from the service class. If FE gives a second chance to those who had missed out at school, it is a second chance that the service class is not slow to utilize. In general, however, (apart from Class VIII which trailed far behind the others) class chances of access to further eduation were notably equal and educational opportunity would have been a great deal more unequal if it did not exist.

Sustained expansion has been the story of the university over the four cohorts covered by our survey. Unlike the case of the selective schools which failed to keep pace with the increase in the birth rate, the 'Robbinsian expansion' was an effective response to the post-war baby boom and all three social classes saw a steady improvement in their chances of going on to university throughout our period. As so often before, however, the fastest *rates* of growth went to the working class but the largest *absolute* gains to the service class.

But even this relatively encouraging picture of sustained expansion must be qualified by the important finding that the growth of places in higher education did not keep pace with the growth in school attendance and school examinations. If we look at the proportion of boys with A-Level or Higher School Certificate who went on to university, we find the same inverted U that we found with selective schools. Chances fell back in our youngest cohort for the qualified members of all social classes and inequality between generations once more is added to the familiar inequality between social classes.

NOTES

1. On which see D. Raffe, op.cit.
2. These are excluded from our analysis.
3. op.cit., p.50.
4. These survival rates are in fact calculated as a percentage from a given class attending university divided by the percentage staying on at school to age 18 or later, whereas some boys go to university at 17. But calculating the percentage of boys with A-Levels who go on to university gives a similar result.
5. See above Chapter 4, p.59.
6. Raffe, op.cit., p.52. We are indebted to David Raffe for the analysis which follows.

CHAPTER 11

Retrospect and Prospect

INTRODUCTION

We asked at the outset whether education can change society. Then, in the course of a long analysis of the experience of men living in England and Wales in 1972, we circumscribed and refined the question. Now, in this final chapter, we can put the question again, treating it first as a matter of history; but second, in the light of that history, as a prospect for future policy.

In brief political retrospect our study may be said to document the judgement on British education made by Anthony Crosland in 1956. He saw the school system in Britain as 'divisive, unjust and wasteful' and went on to say that

The least we can ask for is that all ordinary children, irrespective of social background, should enjoy a good primary and secondary education in decent buildings, with classes of reasonable size, and up to a reasonable age. This the children of better-off parents enjoy in the independent schools. But many working-class children, owing to the appallingly low quality of parts of the State Educational system, are still enjoying nothing of the sort . . . .[1]

Improvements in building, staffing, and a lengthening of school life have taken place over the period we have studied. Nevertheless, we can add with Crosland that

. . . we shall still not have equality of opportunity so long as we maintain a system of superior private schools, open to the wealthier classes, but out of reach of poorer children however talented and deserving. This is much the most flagrant inequality of opportunity, as it is cause of class inequality generally, in our educational system; and I have never been able to understand why socialists have been so obsessed with the question of the grammar schools, and so indifferent to the much more glaring injustice of the independent schools.[2]

Since the mid-1960s, of course, the picture has been complicated by expansion in higher and comprehensive reorganization of secondary education, in both of which developments Crosland played a part as Secretary of State for Education and Science. We shall include them in our own retrospect and prospect.

CHILDREN AND SCHOOLS 1913–1972

In one sense our historical description has consisted of elaborating a metaphor. We have thought of educational institutions as a map on which individuals have given starting-points from which they are required or choose to move to one of a diverse set of educational exits into working life. The account of journeys in these terms has been unavoidably complicated. Even so, we have had perforce to simplify our cartography. Our social and educational classes, measures of family attitudes, types of school and academic qualifications all do scant justice to a more complex reality. The map, moreover, changed during the time which elapsed from the childhood of our oldest to the adolescence of our youngest respondents: yet we have had to condense them by using four decennial birth cohorts and, hence, to simplify the variety of routes and modes of transport. If our survey data and the patience of our readers had permitted larger-scale mapping to reveal the great variation of local conditions, it would have been still clearer that both the points of origin and of destination shifted and multiplied as the country changed its occupational structure, raised its income, and elaborated its secondary and post-secondary educational provision. The simplified panorama, however, is that each year brought in more children embarking on longer journeys with the acquiescence or encouragement of parents who were themselves increasingly experienced educational travellers.

In order to appraise the territory we have surveyed we may first retrace the history of the supply of children which, looked at from another angle, is an evolving demand for education. Fluctuations in fertility turn out to have been both considerable in themselves and consequential for the distribution of educational chances among successive age groups. The absolute numbers of children in the population represented by our four cohorts (Figure 11.1) form a U-curve

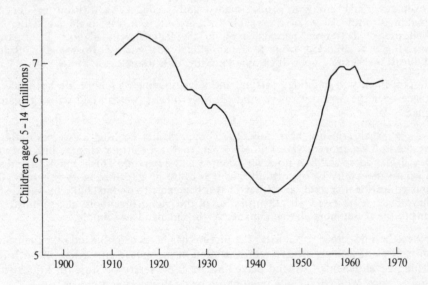

Fig. 11.1. Child Population of England and Wales (children aged 5–14 incl.).

of supply over time. Educational expansion was therefore in that respect an easier policy to achieve between the wars than after the Second War until the mid-1960s. This demographic description enabled us also to show shifts in the numbers and proportions of children of defined social class and familial origin. It emerges that there were trends towards the amelioration of early childhood in the double sense that the typical child of the later cohorts was more likely to come from a service-class home or, if from the working class, to have been born into rather better material circumstances, to have had rather better-educated parents and fewer siblings. As a supplier of children, the service class increased from less than 1 in 10 in the first cohort (born 1913-22) to approximately 1 in 5 in the fourth (born 1943-52) (Table 2.2). Material goods in any case became less certain discriminators between families both across and within classes (Table 11.1).

Table 11.1

*A Review of Changing Experience from 1913 to 1972:
Percentage of each age-group having the specified attribute*

	Born			
	1913-22	1923-32	1933-42	1943-52
At Respondent's age 14				
Class origin: service	9.1	10.2	12.2	17.7
intermediate	28.5	27.4	29.7	30.3
Domestic amenities: telephone	7.4	9.7	16.3	25.4
refrigerator	2.2	3.8	16.2	46.4
inside lavatory	37.2	50.9	61.3	82.1
fixed bath or shower	37.5	56.8	67.7	86.4
House tenure: owned	19.6	24.7	27.5	36.0
Council house	18.7	26.6	31.9	39.2
Number of siblings (average)	3.3	3.0	2.5	2.2
Father's Education				
Private primary	3.1	3.0	2.8	3.3
Private secondary[1]	2.3	2.3	3.3	4.0
Selective secondary[2]	6.6	9.8	14.3	23.1
Any exam or qualification[3]	1.9	2.0	2.7	5.3
Respondent's Own Education				
Private primary	5.2	5.1	7.1	5.7
Private secondary[1]	5.0	5.4	7.5	7.3
Private, excluding Direct Grant	3.7	3.8	5.8	5.5
Grammar school	10.6	13.6	20.2	21.0
Any selective secondary[2]	29.0	36.2	38.2	34.4
School-leaving age (average)	14.5	14.6	15.4	15.8
Ordinary School Certificate/O-Level	11.9	14.2	23.1	34.0
Higher School Certificate /A-Level	2.1	3.6	6.9	14.4
Entered university	1.8	3.4	5.4	8.4
N (= 8529)	(2035)	(2053)	(1990)	(2451)

[1] Independent schools (whether HMC or not) and Direct Grant schools.
[2] Including technical schools.
[3] This is equivalent to the variable father's higher education (FHE) used in Chapters 3, 6, and 9.

The structure of schools, into which the demand for education had to be fitted, was also expanded and transformed. Children stayed longer in schools and went on in larger proportions and numbers to post-secondary education. The rates of change varied. The private sector of both primary and secondary education expanded in proportion to the number of children in the intermediate post-war years, but thereafter attendance at private primary schools fell away and private secondary schooling ceased to grow.[3] Meanwhile, various forms of selective secondary education expanded before and even after the Second War, but it should be noted that the expansion was greatest and sustained longest in the case of grammar schools, whereas the proportion of children in technical schools fell among those who reached the secondary stage after the war. The net result of these state and private developments in secondary education in relation to the fall and rise of fertility was that chances for some kind of selective secondary schooling rose in the first three and fell back in the fourth cohort: the percentages in succession were 29, 36, 38, and 34. There was net expansion but its progress was not linear. These figures are significant given that the structure of secondary schooling before, and especially after, the 1944 Act was dominated by a tripartite division of state schools, that is, between grammar, technical, and what came to be called secondary modern schools. Only among our youngest cohort was there the beginning of the development of comprehensive secondary schooling.

Finally, we should recall that post-secondary schooling in universities, colleges of education, and further education also expanded throughout the period, and indeed, despite its large size, with an accelerated rate for the youngest cohort. Accordingly, the cost of the education of the average boy rose throughout the period in terms of both the amount of money spent on him and the length of his educational career. But investment was proportionately higher at the higher levels of secondary and post-secondary education. Thus, what is essential for the understanding of theories concerning equality and social selection, the nature of educational expansion was such as to maintain, and indeed to increase, the cost of the longest compared with the shortest possible educational career.

At the same time, the return to education in terms of the passing of public examinations followed a similar rising curve in that the higher qualifications increased at the greatest rate in relation to the supply of children. In short, looking at averages over time, it is clear that we have been studying a period of remarkable progress in the formal education of the population as a whole. Educationally at least we have certainly been living through 'the century of the child'.

CULTURAL CAPITAL AND EDUCABILITY

This description of the recent history of childhood in England and Wales, though like all descriptions incipiently theoretical in the classifications it uses and the data which it attends and neglects, tests no theories; it merely checks received chronological accounts. Our fundamental theoretical concern has been with the question of whether education can change the class character of childhood. A strong strand in liberal traditions of political and social thought it that it can. We began this book with a recognition of the cautious optimism of political arithmeticians on this issue.[4]

But against the optimism of the liberal educational reformers has to be set the pessimism of the Left and the Right. On the Left writers such as Bourdieu

have argued that the educational system serves merely to reproduce the distribution of cultural capital. Those who can receive what the school has to give are
those who already are endowed with the requisite cultural attributes – with the
appropriate cultural capital. A parallel argument comes from the Right. Bantock
argues that many working-class children are 'for cultural reasons likely to be
inhibited from gaining the best of what is offered them even if they were to be
offered "chances" in these terms; and this because they have already been
formed by historical socio-cultural forces which make the segment of "high"
culture for them pretty meaningless.'[5] Their political differences do not prevent
them from arriving at the same hypothesis: the culture of the working class (as
opposed to their measured IQ or material circumstances) will inhibit them from
taking advantage of what the school has to offer.

To test this hypothesis we looked first at the proportion of 'first-generation'
grammar- and technical-school boys. In our sample as a whole, the great majority
of those who attended selective secondary schools came from homes where both
parents had been to non-selective schools. Eighty per cent of boys at the
technical schools and two-thirds of those at the grammar schools came from
homes with no tradition of formal academic schooling (Table 5.2). Even at the
apex of the educational system, 88 per cent of the boys at university came from
families in which neither parent was a graduate, and 41 per cent from homes in
which neither parent had been to selective schools. The state system of
education, therefore, gave 'superior' education to vast numbers of boys from
'uneducated' homes. It is the dissemination rather than the reproduction of
cultural capital that is more apparent here. And even within the private sector
there has been a large minority of boys from these less educated backgrounds.
Only the independent HMC schools could really be said to maintain a 'cycle of
privilege' in which cultural capital is reproduced among those from educated
homes.

In other words, the educational system has undoubtedly offered chances of
securing cultural capital to large numbers of boys to whom the ethos of the
grammar and technical schools was new. But did 'historical socio-cultural forces'
mean that these chances were largely spurious, that there was *formal* but not
effective opportunity for these first-generation grammar-school boys? The
answer is an unequivocal No. As we have noted, two-thirds of our respondents
at grammar school were 'first generation', and two-thirds of these went on to
secure some kind of academic credential. Moreover, their chances of success
were very little different from those of second-generation grammar-school boys.
The kind of education which the parents had received was of little value as a
predictor of success or failure in the grammar schools (Table 8.13).

It might be objected that our use of the variable 'parental education' does
scant justice to the notion of cultural capital, but another method yields the
same result. We used path analysis in Chapter 9 to explore the determinants of
educational attainment, incorporating two measures of family background which
we labelled 'material circumstances' and 'family climate' respectively.[6] Our estimate of the effects of material circumstances are based on multiple correlations
between the various dependent variables and a group of five measured
independent variables: father's class, domestic amenities, owner occupation,

council-house tenancy, and number of siblings. In contrast, 'family climate' is a hypothetical variable representing all those sources of similarity between certain measured specified characteristics of brothers that have not been captured by the material circumstances variable. It could represent parental interest and enouragement, linguistic competence, genetic endowment, or indeed income, in so far as these factors are not picked up by the variables in the 'material circumstances' group. 'Family climate' is thus a rag-bag, but it is a capacious rag-bag which is likely to provide ample room for the variables which Bourdieu and Bantock have in mind, in so far as these are distinct and separable from social class: and if they are not separable from social class, their arguments reduce to triviality. It will give us then an estimate of the *maximum* effect which the parents' cultural capital is likely to have on the respondents' cultural capital.

The results are clear. Cultural capital influences selection for secondary school, but thereafter its importance is minimal. The effect of 'family climate' on the respondent's school-leaving age or examination success is wholly indirect, being mediated by type of secondary school and, to a lesser extent, by IQ. Among boys who attended the *same* type of secondary school 'family climate' does not discriminate between the academic successes and failures. IQ is slightly better as a discriminator, and 'material circumstances' better still, although we should note that none of these variables, not even 'material circumstances', is a particularly powerful discriminator among boys within a given type of school.[7]

At all events, it would seem to be class, not culture or IQ, which is the more important source of, for example, early leaving from grammar school. Our evidence holds no comfort for those who would believe that class differences in educational attainment reflect a fair distribution of opportunities to those with the intellectual ability or cultural capacity to profit therefrom.

We can go further still. Our evidence suggests that 'the pool of ability' - the number of children with the capacity to obtain O-Levels, A-Levels, or university degrees - was larger than is usually supposed. We have tested a theory of the demand for education, which assumes that the numbers staying on to take O-Levels and A-Levels would continue to grow until all those believed by themselves and their teachers to have the ability to qualify in fact do so. The theory predicts that the demand for education will follow a logistic curve, a curve shaped like an elongated S, and that the demand will be saturated when the 'pool of ability' is exhausted. Though the dangers of extrapolation must again be emphasized, logistic curves derived from this theory explain 99 per cent of the variance and predict that eventually 80 000 boys each year would stay at school until the age of 17 and 55 000 to the age of 18 (Table 7.5). In comparison, however, official figures[8] show that by the end of our period the actual numbers staying on were of the order of 73 000 and 48 000 respectively. Wastage of talent therefore continues and was massive over most of the period with which we have been concerned. Given that by the 1970s the number of boys obtaining at least one A-Level was actually somewhat larger than the number staying on until eighteen, we may reasonably conclude, assuming current conceptions of educability, that *at least* 7000 boys each year could have obtained A-Level passes but were not in fact remaining at school long enough to do so. Further back in time, of course, the wastage was much greater. In the early 'sixties it was running at an annual rate of around 30 000, and in the early 'fifties it would have been well over 40 000.

These figures bring out clearly the enormous strides that have been made since the Second War in the provision of sixth-form education, but this past progress cannot be a source of current complacency. We have shown that the chances of becoming an undergraduate have declined for boys with A-Levels. Two-thirds of them went on to university in the 'fifties, but only half of them did so in the 'sixties (Table 10.9). The expansion of the universities failed to keep pace with the expansion of the sixth forms – a reminder of one of the recurrent features of the British educational system – inequity between generations caused by educational inflexibility. Able children unfortunate enough to have been born in years of baby boom were at a serious disadvantage in the competition for university places compared with their siblings born a few years earlier or later.

At university level, then, there is a double wastage. There are the children who could have obtained A-Levels, but failed to stay at school long enough. And there are the children who obtained A-Levels but failed to find a university place because of the unresposniveness of our system to changes in the demand for education. Our evidence also shows that much of this was a wastage of working-class talent. We found in Chapter 8 that the service class demand for sixth-form education had already reached saturation level by the end of our period. Thirty-eight per cent of the service class were already staying on until the age of 18 in our youngest cohort, and this was the same figure as our predicted saturation level. Assuming that these were the cleverest 38 per cent of the service class, then boys with measured IQ at least as low as 113 were staying on until 18 and obtaining A-Levels. Our IQ assumptions entail that 14 per cent of working-class boys had measured IQ scores above 113, but only 6 per cent in fact stayed on until 18 (Table 8.11). It follows that the proportion of working-class boys reaching A-Level, and *pari passu* securing places at university, could comfortably be doubled without any necessary lowering of standards. At the time that our youngest cohort was of university age, the working class was obtaining less than half the number of places which, by service-class standards, it was entitled to.

EQUALITY OF OPPORTUNITY

So far then, our retrospective view is that the optimists rather than the pessimists deserve support. The optimism in question has been essentially liberal. But the main legacy of the liberal tradition is, of course, a combined intention and prediction that modernizing the education system would mean realizing the principle of equality of opportunity. This educational policy, it might reasonably be demanded, should be evaluated in the terms of the liberal tradition in which it was formed. However, equality of opportunity is a phrase with many different meanings. A minimal definition of it can be described as formal equality of opportunity with the implication that no legal barrier exists to prevent a child from entering any form of education in the way that Jews were once kept out of Oxford and Cambridge, or black Africans are excluded from white South African universities. In this minimal sense formal equality of opportunity existed in the British schools throughout our period. The real debate, at least in the years before 1944, turned on strengthening the definition to take account of inequalities of circumstances, and especially financial ones. It was these, whether in the form of school fees or earnings forgone where boys stayed on beyond the statutory leaving age, that were in dispute: and the 1944 Act brought the final elimination of fee paying in state selective secondary schools. If, therefore, we define equality of opportunity in a second way to include the elimination of financial barriers then the reduction of these through the expansion of free places before 1944 and their total abolition after 1944 was clear progress towards equality of opportunity. At the same time, however, the existence of the private sector at both primary and secondary level, and the absence of maintenance grants for secondary-school children beyond the statutory school-leaving age, prevented full realization of this stronger definition of the ideal aimed at through liberal reform.

It is also important and relevant to this second definition of equality of opportunity to notice the financial implications of a developing non-financial selective system. As we have seen, the 1944 Act continued the growth of selective secondary schooling and, particularly in the 1960s, there was expansion of higher education on a selective basis. The costs of the different forms of education have been such that success in the selective process did not diminish but, if anything, widened the distance between those who got most and those who got least out of the public purse towards the cost of their schooling.

Given, then, that the selective stakes became, if anything, higher it is all the more crucial to note the actual distribution between social classes of educational costs, educational experience and examination results. In consequence, the third definition of equality of opportunity on which we have concentrated is one which compares the relative chances of access to schools and qualifications which were, *substantively* as distinct from *formally*, open to the children of different social classes. In effect, taking the word 'equality' to have its normal meaning in common speech, the definition now shifts from equality of opportunity to equality of outcome.

This third meaning of equality of opportunity in the sense of equality of access to superior forms of education yields a much less comforting picture. At the secondary-school stage access has been more unequal at the higher levels of the academic hierarchy as we have defined it.[9] Class differentials are most extreme in the case of the independent HMC schools; a boy from the service class had nearly forty times the chance of his working-class peer of entering one of these schools (Table 4.4). In the case of the Direct Grant schools his chance was twelve times as good, and in that of the grammar schools it was three times as good. Only in the technical schools has there been equality of class chances, and even this apparently more equitable distribution of opportunity has had much more to do with their lower standing in the academic pecking order than with the fairness of their methods of selection; relatively few boys from the service class went to the technical schools simply because so many had already gone to notionally superior secondary schools.

In general, then, class chances of access vary according to position in the academic hierarchy. The only clear exception is that of the minor independent schools. We have ranked these below the grammar schools (a position confirmed by their O-Level and A-Level records), but the service-class boy had nearly eighteen times the chance of the working-class boy of securing a place at one. Another possible exception is that of the major independent schools. We placed these at the head of the academic hierarchy. Though on most criteria of academic achievement they are virtually indistinguishable from the Direct Grant schools, they are socially far more exclusive. The private schools represent a bastion of class privilege compared with the relatively egalitarian state sector. The hybrid Direct Grant schools, before they were abolished, uncomfortably straddled the divide.

Class differentials in access are necessarily reflected in school differences of class composition. Only the technical schools contained anything resembling a representative cross-section of the population, while the HMC schools remained socially the most exclusive. About 90 per cent of those at the private schools came from the service and intermediate classes. In contrast, over one-third of boys in the state grammar schools came from the working class (Table 4.5). Admittedly, the grammar schools may have served more to assimilate these working-class boys into middle-class life and culture than to break down class boundaries, but the social experience they offered must undoubtedly have been significantly different from that of the private sector. Tawney's judgement accordingly retains its force:

A special system of schools, reserved for children whose parents have larger bank accounts than their neighbours, exists in no other country on the same scale as in England. It is at once an educational monstrosity and a grave national misfortune. It is educationally vicious, since to mix with companions from homes of different types is an important part of the education of the young. It is socially disastrous for it does more than any other single cause, except capitalism itself, to perpetuate the division of the nation into classes of which one is almost unintelligible to the other.[10]

This picture of unequal access to the superior secondary schools has remained depressingly constant over time. For the selective secondary schools as a group, chances of access rose at all levels of the class structure in the middle of our period, leading to some slight narrowing of class differentials, but they then fell back again to levels very like those of a generation earlier. Thus the likelihood of a working-class boy receiving a selective education in the mid 'fifties and 'sixties was very little different from that of his parents' generation thirty years earlier (Table 4.9).

If we disaggregate selective schooling into its component types of school, however, we find a more complex pattern. Chances of private schooling traced the inverted U that was followed by selective schools as a whole. Twenty-six per cent of the service class attended some form of private secondary school – HMC, non-HMC, and Direct Grant – in our earliest cohort. This percentage crept up to 27 and then to 29 in the succeeding two cohorts, only to fall back to 25 among the most recent cohort. The working-class percentage followed a parallel but lower path, starting at 0.5, rising to 2.3, and falling back to 1.1.

With the grammar and technical schools, on the other hand, an inverted J rather than an inverted U provides a better picture of the path. Grammar-school chances steadily improved for all three social classes among the first three cohorts, followed by small and uneven retrogression in the final cohort (Table 4.12). As a result, class differentials narrowed appreciably; in the first cohort the service-class boy's chance was over four times that of his working-class contemporary, but in the final cohort it was little more than twice as high. But what was given to the grammar schools was taken away from the technical schools. Here the inverted J is turned the other way round. Small increases at the beginning of our period were followed by a long and steady decline, and what the working class gained through the expansion of the grammar schools, they largely lost through the decline of the technical schools. Over the period as a whole 100 working-class families sent an extra eight boys to grammar schools, but eight fewer to technical schools.

So much, then, for patterns of entry to the secondary schools. But what of exit? The short answer is that class differentials widen at each rung up the educational ladder. The boy from the working class was much more likely than his service-class contemporary to drop out of school as soon as the minimum leaving age was reached, was less likely to continue his school career into the sixth form, and less likely to enter a university or some other form of education after school. As we have shown, there was a persistent class difference in survival rates, and inequalities thus increased. A service-class boy in our sample was four times as likely as his working-class peer to be found at school at the age of 16, eight times as likely at the age of 17, ten times as likely at the age of 18, and eleven times as likely to enter a university (Tables 8.2 and 10.3).

On the other hand, despite the continuing class differences, survival rates also show a tendency to converge. The scondary effects of stratification, as Boudon termed them, although reasserting themselves on each higher rung of the educational ladder, do so with less and less vigour. For the school population as a whole, the biggest difference is at the minimum school-leaving age; over three-quarters of our working-class respondents dropped out at this stage whereas about three-quarters of those from the service class stayed on. But at the gate of the university the gap narrowed appreciably. Of those who had survived long enough in the educational system to secure at least one A-Level or Higher School Certificate, 63 per cent from the service class went on to university, while the working-class percentage was not so greatly lower at 53 per cent. *For those who survive*, inequalities of opportunity are much reduced, although not entirely eliminated. They are, however, a small and select band. Less than one in forty of our working-class respondents acquired Higher School Certificate or an A-Level pass compared with one in four from the service class (Table 8.12). The convergence of the survival rates, therefore, occurs too late in the school career to be relevant to more than a tiny handful of working-class children. Inequalities of opportunity have already done their damage at earlier stages of the school career.

However, patterns of exit from the secondary schools offer a slightly more encouraging trend than patterns of entry. Sustained expansion replaces the inverted U. The picture is at its most encouraging if we focus on the percentage staying on until 16 or later. In the earliest cohort a boy from the service class had nearly six times the chance of his working-class contemporary of being found in school at the age of 16: in the final cohort his chance was less than three times as high (Table 8.10). But even this optimism must be tempered by the finding that while the *rate of increase* was greater for the working class, their *absolute* gains were less. Thus for every 100 working-class boys there were an extra twenty-two staying on until 16 or later by the end of our period; but for every 100 service-class boys there were an extra twenty-six staying on. In this sense, then, the difference between the classes had actually widened until, in 1974, the raising of the school-leaving age brought statutory equalization.

The proportion of 18 year olds staying on at school again shows steady expansion with larger absolute gains going to the service class (Table 8.11). An extra twenty-two service-class boys for every 100 stayed on till 18, but for the working class the increment was a meagre three per 100. In consequence, relative chances as well as the absolute differences widened.

In summary, school inequalities of opportunity have been remarkably stable over the forty years which our study covers. Throughout, the service class has had roughly three times the chance of the working class of getting some kind of selective secondary schooling. Only at 16 has there been any significant reduction in relative class chances, but even here the absolute gains have been greater for the service class. If the 'hereditary curse upon English education is its organisation upon lines of social class',[11] that would seem to be as true in the 1960s as it was in 1931 when Tawney wrote.

EMBOURGEOISEMENT

There is a particular version of the issue of equality which is of some importance in the history of social science applied to public policy. Elsewhere,[12] one of us has traced liberal optimism back to Alfred Marshall who, in 1872, argued that a measure of equality could be realised through public policies of educational expansion. This theory of educational embourgeoisement was in fact a general one, embracing occupational as well as educational experience. Its main thrust was towards specifying the conditions for widespread prosperity and an elevated general level of civility. But one of its principal components was the historical prediction that a programme of educational expansion would reduce the differences between classes which had traditionally distinguished the entry of their children to the labour market. The theory has been attacked in recent years from a variety of theoretical standpoints. Marxists like Bowles and Gintis have argued that the elaboration of schooling in American merely reflects the increasing complexity of the division of labour so as to remain in strict correspondence to the class-determined hierarchy of authority of a capitalist economy and to prepare children for their places in that hierarchy.[13] Radical liberals like Christopher Jencks[14] or Raymond Boudon[15] have also, in their different ways, argued that class inequalities are generated and maintained by social forces beyond the reach of egalitarian educational reform.

These arguments can now be tested under the actual circumstances of educational expansion. The orthodox liberal thesis, which has dominated official policy in Britain in this century, would require an assimilation of the educational standards of the working class to those previously confined to the middle class. We can test it from our survey evidence by two methods. First we can compare the educational attainments of working-class boys with those of service-class boys born earlier, and second, we can examine whether there has been convergence between the classes in the number of years spent in school by their members. Taking the highest qualification offered by the educational system as the university degree, it was shown in Chapter 10 (Table 10.8) that the proportion of graduates in the working-class 1943-52 cohort was less than half that obtained by the service class in its 1913-22 cohort (3.1 per cent compared with 7.2 per cent). Moreover, although the graduate output of each class was rising throughout our period, and although the proportionate increase was greater for the working class than for the two other classes, if we use the absolute percentage increases it appears that, far from converging, the working class has actually fallen further behind both of the other classes in the proportion of its children who become university graduates. An extra 2 per cent of working-class children found their way to the universities compared with an extra 19 per cent of the service class and 6 per cent of the intermediate-class children. The distance of the working class from each of the other two classes was greater for those born after the Second than those born before the First War.

To take such a high point of educational achievement (which is attained in any case by only a minority of any class) is to apply the most stringent test to the educational embourgeoisement thesis. If instead we take, as our standard, survival to age 16 in secondary school, the thesis looks slightly more promising, as we have seen in our discussion of trends in class chances.[16] After the First War half of the sons of the service class, one in seven of the sons of the intermediate class, and less than one in ten of the working class stayed at school beyond the age of 16 (Table 8.10). By the post-Second War years service-class attendance at 16+ had levelled off at nearly four out of five, the intermediate class had reached the service-class norms of the inter-war years, and the working class was establishing the inter-war norms of the intermediate class. A slow and incomplete process of educational embourgeoisement can be discerned. Perhaps the classes might eventually have converged? Our tentative and conservative estimates in Chapter 8, though subject to a considerable margin of error, suggest that by the end of the century there would have been a substantial narrowing of class differentials to perhaps 20 percentage points between the service and the working classes. However, what in fact, and significantly, happened was that in 1974 there was 'enforced saturation': the minimum statutory leaving age was raised to 16.

Throughout a century of educational expansion working-class children have dropped out in higher proportions at the earlier stages, leaving a decreasing minority which is, admittedly, bourgeois in the sense of assimilating more and more closely to a dominantly middle-class group of survivors. Our data on school examinations illustrate the tendency. For those of different class origins who survived to enter public examinations it is the similarities rather than the differences in success rates that are striking. The possibility of assimilation or embourgeoisement is thus demonstrated. Nevertheless, the mass movement of embourgeoisement envisaged by liberal optmists has certainly not materialized.

Our second measure – the average age at which the average boy in each class and cohort left full-time education to go to work – tells a sad story (Table 11.2).

Table 11.2

Average Age on Taking Up First Job, by Father's Social Class
(Men aged 25 or more in 1972[1])

Father's Social Class	Year of Birth			
	1913–22	1923–32	1933–42	1942–47
I, II	16.8	17.3	18.4	18.1
III, IV, V	15.0	15.2	15.9	16.2
VI, VII, VIII	14.4	14.5	15.5	15.6
N =	1879	1900	1891	1158

[1] Of the men aged 25 or more in our sample, only 0.2 per cent had not yet started work in 1972. Among those aged 20–24, this figure rises to 8 per cent; the youngest men have therefore been excluded from this table.

The class differences were the same in the 1960s as they had been in the 1920s despite a relatively favourable demography, economic growth, and rising educational investment. Moreover, a class inequality with respect to the quality of education provided at all stages of schooling has persisted over and above the class differences in educational survival. The private schools have been almost exclusively middle-class preserves throughout their existence and children of working-class origin have been disproportionately distributed, even as survivors, to the less prestigious forms of secondary school and to part-time post-secondary colleges as opposed to full-time universities. In short, interpreting educational embourgeoisement to mean that, as education expanded, the typical educational careers of children from different social origins would converge, the result is disappointment. Instead what we have shown is that certain types of educational experience, such as attendance at some kind of secondary school or beyond a traditionally defined and low terminal age, have been legally enforced for all classes after having become the norm of the middle class. But meanwhile further differentiations have been built at later stages of the educational process with the effect of maintaining class differences of educational experience.

MERITOCRACY

There is yet another way through which we have approached the issue of equality. In adopting our third meaning of equality of opportunity - equality of access between the social classes to superior forms and levels of education - we will undoubtedly have raised some liberal and conservative hackles. But if we now assess the British educational system by the criterion of meritocracy we are judging it much more according to its own professed goals and by a yardstick acceptable to most right-wing, if not left-wing, commentators. Merit is commonly held to constitute a claim on social rewards and opportunities over and against the claims, for example, of citizenship or rank or market power. Expressions of the liberal tradition in advanced industrial countries have characteristically justified the granting of opportunity to merit on grounds of efficiency in industry, government, and administration. As governmental bureaucracies developed in the nineteenth century selection of entrants on merit increasingly replaced patronage, nepotism, and purchase. This movement, which can be traced to colonial administration especially in India, had a metropolitan milestone in the Northcott-Trevelyan reforms of the Civil Service. Merit in this context was educationally defined and the examination emerged as an instrument for detecting potential capacity for the performance of an expanding range of occupational tasks. This is what is meant by the general sociological thesis of a transition from ascriptive to 'achievement' criteria in occupational selection. The theory of meritocracy evolved from this liberal movement, and the definition attached to it by Michael Young is summarized in the label or slogan 'IQ plus effort'. As we have indicated, our data do not yield measures of the complex amalgam of mind and character which would fully represent any of the possible definitions of merit. In practice, we are confined to a definition in terms of measured intelligence and even here, as we explained in Chapter 4, our IQ distributions between classes are estimated. We have thus been working with a simplified definition of merit. Moreover, simplification apart, the meaning of measured intelligence in the context of explaining and justifying educational selection procedures is highly contentious.[17] There is an unresolved debate as to how far measured intelligence is cause and how far effect of class membership. There is continuing disagreement as to how far past social selection has, in association with assortative mating, produced *genetically* distinct classes. The position taken on these issues affects the significance to be attached to our results.

At one extreme it could be argued that a true measure of merit would show it to be randomly distributed between classes. If so, the measure of bias against meritocratic principle would be to compare *actual* with *random* allocations to selective schools or advanced courses. We would, in other words, simply use the Index of Association to show, for example, that the working class actually got 6 per cent of the places in HMC schools, whereas under meritocracy it would have got 56 per cent. At the other extreme it might be held that actual allocation exactly reflect the (accumulated and projected) merit of the children of diverse familial and class origins. Merit is what the system expresses. But what we have done is to define merit as it was understood by most of those who were influential in the development and control of the schools between the 1902 Act and the 1960s, in terms of measured IQ.

We start with estimates of the distribution of IQ scores among children of the three broad social classes which we have distinguished. We then assume an academic-social hierarchy of educational institutions running from the most exclusive private schools with membership of the Headmasters' Conference at the top, down to the unselective state secondary schools at the bottom. We then assume that this hierarchy of institutions constitutes a pecking order for selecting the most talented available children (i.e. those with the highest IQ scores). This gives us a model from which we can calculate the proportionate share of places which would go to each class in a fully meritocratic system of selection. Finally, we juxtapose meritocratic allocation against actual allocation to gauge the degree to which the real world approximates meritocracy. The model and reality bear some resemblance in their differences of access as between classes. But, even on the assumptions we have used, which, to repeat, give a minimal estimate of non-meritocratic influences on allocation, there is a shortfall of meritocratic justice to working-class boys, especially in the most exclusive private schools.

Our model indicates that in a fully meritocratic educational system 58 per cent of boys from the service class would have been selected for some form of selective secondary schooling, whereas in practice an extra 14 per cent were selected. Conversely, the model predicts that 28 per cent of the working class would have been selected in a fully meritocratic system, whereas in fact 4 per cent fewer were given places (Table 4.7).

A shortfall of 4 per cent may not sound a very grave departure from meritocracy, but in absolute terms it represents a very large number of working-class boys who were deprived of a selective education to which they were, in fact, entitled. During our period the annual in-take into state selective schools fluctuated between 250 000 and 300 000 boys. Of these, rather more than one half were from the working class. A misallocation of 4 per cent of the working class, therefore, represents a total of around 6000 boys from the working class who were denied their meritocratic due *each year*. Misallocations of this scale are hardly trivial.

We must, however, be careful to remember the limitations of our IQ estimates in drawing inferences about the total number of misallocated boys. To measure the mean IQ of the different classes we have had to draw on the results of other studies and compromise between different definitions of social class. While the order of magnitude of our estimate is reasonable, the margin of error involved could be substantial and the estimates of misallocation could be significantly changed by quite small adjustments to our IQ assumptions. If we stretch the estimated mean IQ of the three classes further apart, the number of boys wrongly allocated is reduced; and if we bring them closer together the apparent unfairness of the selection processes is increased.

A comparison of the degree of meritocracy at eleven plus with that at 16-plus or at university entrance can be made, however, without depending on precise IQ estimates. On the unassailable assumption that the mean measured IQ of the service class is higher than that of the intermediate class, which is in turn higher than that of the working class, our findings will not be affected.

With these cautions, the main conclusions from our analysis are as follows. At entry to secondary school the private sector is consistently less meritocratic than the state sector. In competition for places at technical and grammar schools, working-class boys suffered a handicap in comparison with boys from the service class equivalent to 7 IQ points. In competition for places at the non-HMC schools the handicap widens to 9 points, for places at the Direct Grant schools to 10 points, and for places at the private HMC schools to 11 points.[18] Moving through the school career, the working-class/service-class IQ handicap is 9.9 points at age 16, 10.3 points at age 17, 7.5 points at age 18, and 6.6 points at entry to the university (Table 10.7). Access to the sixth form has, therefore, been a crucial point of social selection in the period we have studied. It is here, taking the educational system as a whole, that departure from meritocracy and consequential wastage of talent has been at its maximum. What is extracted from the pool of talent depends, in J. W. B. Douglas's metaphor, much less on its content than on the effectiveness of the pump. Douglas showed that the pump was leaking badly at the points of secondary selection and early leaving. Our study confirms this hydraulic view of selection through education, although we would note that the leaks were actually somewhat worse at entry to the sixth form than at the minimum leaving age. For example, we saw in Chapter 8 that, in the post-war period, the working-class grammar-school boy was highly likely to stay on for the extra year and secure some O-Levels; it was after O-Level that the most serious wastage occurred.

Perhaps the most important result of our analysis of meritocracy, however, is that the 1944 Education Act brought England and Wales no nearer to the ideal of a meritocratic society. The working-class/service-class IQ handicap was much the same after the Act as it had been before, the apparent reduction in the final cohort being due to a fall in the mean IQ of the expanded service class. The wholly admirable aims of the Act had been to ensure that 'the places in secondary schools are filled by the ablest candidates for admission' and to prevent the possibility that 'a parent by paying only one-third of the cost of education can buy a place in a secondary school for his child, possibly to the exclusion of an abler child whose parent is not in that position'. In the event, however, the more affluent parents were relieved of the need to pay even one-third of the cost. Secondary education was made free in order to enable the poor to take more advantage of it, but the paradoxical consequence was to increase subsidies to the affluent.

DOES TYPE OF SCHOOL MATTER?

The final major issue to which we have addressed ourselves is that of the structure of the educational system. Does it matter what type of school one attended? Does it matter whether the educational system is organized along comprehensive or selective lines? Does it matter whether there is a private sector or not? The furore which attends current debates about comprehensive reorganisation and the future of the private schools suggests that many people would answer with a vociferous 'Yes' to all these questions, but research findings from the other side of the Atlantic suggest that this may simply be a storm in a British tea cup. Jencks concluded that 'differences between schools seem to have very little effect on any measurable attribute of those who attend them'.[19] True, he also made the point that 'Some schools are dull, depressing, even terrifying places, while others are lively, comforting, and reassuring. If we think of school life as an end in itself rather than a means to some other end, such differences are enormously important.' But few of the British protagonists have been solely concerned with schooling as an end in itself. Schooling is more often seen as a means to other ends, most notably to educational attainment and its associated job prospects. If certain sections of British society have been particularly attached to the grammar and private schools, it is not perhaps so much out of a disinterested concern for the quality of school life as out of a belief that these schools offer a more certain route to the educational credentials that putatively bring success in our society. Is this belief warranted?

We began our answer to this question in Chapter 6 by tackling the seemingly innocuous (if technically thorny) issue of the effect of primary schooling. Boys who went to private primary schools were much more likely than their state-educated contemporaries to go on to private secondary schooling. Controlling for the material circumstances of the home and the education of the parents, the type of primary school attended has a large (statistical) effect on the respondent's secondary-school destination. But does this mean that going to a private primary school actually confers advantages on children in the competition for places in the private secondary schools? Is the parent who aspires to send his son to one of these schools well advised to spend his money on primary-school fees, or can he 'take the Cash and let the Credit go?'.

Our unambiguous answer to the anxious parent is that he should take the cash. It transpired that in all probability the respondent's type of primary education was highly correlated with various *unmeasured* attitudes and values held by the parents and thus acted as a proxy for them. The 'effect' which our first analyses attributed to primary schooling was almost certainly an effect of home background, not of schooling. To paraphrase Jencks, 'differences between state and private primary schools seem to have very little effect on any measurable attribute of those who attend them.'

We were able to reach this conclusion because we had data on *brother's* schooling. Brothers, it emerged, were remarkably similar in their primary schooling; the correlation was 0.731. To account satisfactorily for so high a correlation it is necessary to postulate the existence of various unmeasured background factors, and the algebra of path analysis shows that these unmeasured factors must correlate highly with the measured variables of primary and secondary schooling. The correlation between these two schooling variables thus turns out to be a spurious one.[20]

On the other hand, the same technique of analysis revealed that the type of secondary school attended remained important as a determinant of the length of one's school career and hence of one's examination success. The introduction of the hypothetical variable of family climate into our models substantially reduced the effects of IQ – a result we had not expected – but its impact on the effects of secondary schooling was minimal. Primary schooling may not matter, but secondary schooling does.

We made a more detailed investigation of the effects of secondary schooling using conventional multiple regression techniques. The path model tells us about the *average* effect of secondary school, but a high average can be consistent with low specific effects of individual types of school, particularly if the type of school caters for only a minority of the school population. Multi-variate analysis enabled us to look at these specific effects. The boy at a private HMC school after the Second War typically stayed on at school twenty-eight months longer than the boy at a secondary modern school, twenty-one months longer than a boy at technical school, eleven months longer than a boy at a minor private school, nine months longer than a grammar-school boy, but only three months longer than a boy at a Direct Grant school (Table 9.1). Differences in the proportions of boys obtaining O-Levels and A-Levels followed very much the same pattern.

But these differences between types of school turn out to be very largely a consequence of their differing social composition. In other words, boys of the *same* social background at HMC, Direct Grant, or grammar types of school had very similar O-Level records; and while those at HMC or Direct Grant schools were more likely to stay on after O-Level than were grammar-school boys, the differences were not great. At A-Level some differences appear, but these are almost entirely a result of differences in school-leaving age. We would conclude, then, that the parent who had a choice between these three types of school would have gained very little from the extra expense of fees at the private school, while even a free place at a Direct Grant school was not of enormous benefit. For those who were affluent enough to afford the fees and lucky enough to have clever children the choice was not very important.

For the affluent parents of less able children, however, the choice was probably much more significant. The comparisons here must be between the minor private schools and the secondary modern schools. The differences between the typical lengths of school career of pupils at these types of school was eleven months, and even for boys of similar social background was nine months. The social composition of these schools, then, is less important as an explanation of their academic success and failure. Nine months is an estimate of the *maximum* possible effect of the minor private schools' effects on their pupils, but its size leaves open the possibility that these schools had some kind of causal effect on their pupils' careers. The existence of the private sector, then, may well have conferred a substantial benefit on those parents of less able children who were able to afford school fees. Thus, to paraphrase the 1943 White Paper on Educational Reconstruction, 'the system under which fees are charged in one type of post-primary school and prohibited in the other continued throughout our period to offend against the canon that the nature of a child's education should be determined by his capacity and promise and not by the financial circumstances of his parent.'

Choices within the state sector itself were not made by the parents but by the educational authorities and they were choices of decisive consequence for the unfortunate pupils who were of borderline ability. For boys of similar social background the average educational career in a grammar school was fourteen months longer than that in a secondary modern, and ten months longer than that in a technical school. These are again maximum estimates, but coupled with the results of our path analysis of the state sector, they show that for boys of similar ability and background allocation between the three main types of state school was enormously consequential. As we argued in Chapter 9, at the age of 11 the pupils entered an inflexible institutional structure and there was relatively little hope of a second chance for those who missed out at this stage. The tripartite system has certainly played its part in the diffusion of cultural capital and gave effective educational opportunities to many able working-class children, but it has done so at the cost of much individual injustice. The able boy allocated to a secondary modern school was denied educational opportunities that were available to his luckier or more affluent contemporaries.

What, then, is the future prospect? Comprehensive reorganization proceeds apace, curtailment if not abolition of the private schools is still on the political agenda, post-secondary education continues to expand, if more slowly, and the age-old question of equality is still with us. We end, therefore, with a prospective word on each of these issues.

COMPREHENSIVE REORGANIZATION

Perhaps the main future hope for education in England and Wales is that one *structural* problem, which lay at the centre of the more general problem of class inequality of educational opportunity, is now settled. In 1965, 92 per cent of state-secondary school children were in schools organized along tripartite lines. By 1976 the comprehensive schools accounted for 76 per cent, with only 8 per cent in grammar, 2 per cent in technical, and 15 per cent in modern schools. The tripartite secondary system was, as we have shown, neither a class solvent nor an engine of meritocracy: it added educational to class rigidity. The future lies with the comprehensive schools where these rigidities may be eased.[21]

Meanwhile, of course, the transition from a tripartite to a comprehensive system is still incomplete and the price of friction and reorganization remains heavy. Moreover, and of importance far beyond their numerical strength, the private schools still exist and exact their uncalculated but enormous toll of reduced political pressure from middle-class parents, of stimulus from expert teachers and response from motivated children. The private market starves the comprehensives of the resources they need to attain high standards.

Thus private schools remain a serious threat to more open and equal opportunity in state schools. Though the trend is one of continuing proportionate decline of private schooling, it could be reversed, and the more that class bias is eliminated from state schools, the more tempting it is for middle-class parents to flee to the private sector. The fact that the decline has been accounted for largely by falling recruitment to those private schools that are not recognized as efficient by the Department of Education and Science reinforces the fear that, especially under restrictive conditions of educational spending by the state, the advantages of a bought education might become greater in the future than in the past. Class inequalities of opportunity might thereby widen.

Educationally, the integration of the private sector into a national system, so that it ceases to play a class-discriminatory role, is essential if the ideals of either meritocracy or equality are to be realized. It emerged from an elaborate analysis in Chapter 9 that the state sector along tripartite lines was distinctly better at identifying and selecting talented boys than were the private schools.

Yet at the same time we have also established that the tripartite division added itself as a self-fulfilling prophecy to the formidable rigidities imposed by class and family background, differentiating grammar from secondary modern school boys by their length of school career. Of no less importance, therefore, is the task of developing comprehensive secondary schools with high standards and flexible internal organization. Tripartitism was premissed on both distinct types of school and distinct types of children. Comprehensive theory drops both assumptions. The danger here, of course, is that of jumping from the frying pan of segregated schools into the fire of comprehensives, residentially segregated and internally streamed in such a way as to produce the same patterns of socially based educational inequality. Our comparisons between Britain and the USA hold out this warning. There are diverse social sources of distorted educational selection. The comprehensive school cannot be isolated from, for example, the effect of housing policies. Only within a wider social framework can we assess the weight of professional responsibility borne by teachers for the internal arrangements of comprehensive schools. Their task is, in any case, of heroic proportions. They have both to extract the valuable elements of a previously class-distorted curriculum and to encourage all children to escape the limitations of their own backgrounds. Old prejudice against the learning of practical skills by able service-class boys or of literary knowledge by working-class boys of average ability stand in the way of a common curriculum.

In this connection we would put particular stress on an infrequently remarked feature of the tripartite system. The decline of the technical schools was, in our view, one of the tragedies of British education after the Second War. It is fashionable in some quarters to bewail the passing of the grammar school, while the fate of the technical school has gone largely unlamented. But the potentialities of the technical schools may have been rather greater than those of their more famous rivals. The 1943 White Paper included the remark that

too many of the nation's abler children are attracted into [grammar schools] which prepare primarily for the University and for the administrative and clerical professions; too few find their way into [technical] schools from which the design and craftsmanship sides of industry are recruited. If education is to serve the interests both of the child and the nation, some means must be found of correcting this bias.[22]

Our data cannot tell us whether any of the failings of Britain's past economic performance can be attributed to the withering away of the technical schools and to their replacement by the more narrowly academic and less vocational grammar schools, but a link may well exist.

At all events these past battles for educational ideals and ethos may hamper the progress of the new comprehensive schools. Some may be overburdened with notions of excellence carried over mechanically from previous existence as a grammar school. In others the merits of the technical-school tradition may be lost. In yet more of them neither grammar nor technical excellence may be strong enough to make an impact. The comprehensive school embodies the ambitious ideal of fostering a variety of excellence on the basis of a common culture. The architects of the tripartite system were certainly wrong to suppose that there could be three types of secondary school, 'of diversified types but of equal standing', but perhaps they were right to see that the ideals of the grammar school were not the only educational ideals worth pursuing. We believe that, if the comprehensive movement is to achieve the goal of an educated society with a common culture there must be a *common curriculum* as well as common schools. But it must also be a curriculum that appeals to the members of all social classes and to individuals of diverse as well as little talent. On this view the vocational ethos of the technical schools and the literary and scientific ethos of the grammar schools, as well as the popular ethos of the modern schools, have to find a place. These issues are not ones on which we can derive authority from our present study, but the question 'What kind of curriculum?' must be central to the educational agenda.

POST-SECONDARY EDUCATION

Education beyond school also both offers ground for cautious hope and invites reform. Expanded enrolment since the War has taken in increasing proportions against a background of rising absolute numbers in the relevant age groups. Nevertheless, past selection processes, especially to the highest education in the universities, cannot satisfy either meritocrats, or still less egalitarians. Reasonable men may reasonably doubt that universities could ever be equally open to all, irrespective of ability; but so far they have not even been equally open to the talents. The possiblity of satisfying either meritocratic or egalitarian demands depends on reform both earlier in education and more widely in society. In particular, the continuing class-related drop-out between the statutory leaving age and entry to higher education calls obviously for incentives through maintenance grants to 16–18-year-olds. Even so, the further expansion of post-secondary education cannot expect to escape the logic of logistic curves which have shown us in this book how the long-run path to equality passes in the shorter run through terrain of initially *increasing* inequality. That knowledge lends all the more urgency to decisions on priorities in the allocation of resources. Our analysis of recent changes and, especially, of trends in school-leaving age shows that the supply of places is a major obstacle to equalization of opportunity. The 'pool of ability' is clearly not a limit. While we would not wish to challenge the general truth that he who learns earliest learns best, with its inference, much emphasized in the past decade, that a 'positively discriminatory' pre-school programme could reduce educational inequality, we cannot ignore the evident contribution to be had from the reform of post-secondary schooling. The considerable creation of 'cultural capital' through the development of secondary schooling is a foundation for egalitarian movement in education beyond school that has so far been inadequately used.

It is even tempting to argue that we should reduce investment in pre-schooling, and probably fruitless attempts to make secondary schooling more responsive; instead, we should expand further and higher education. But the difficulty here is that we have a post-secondary tripartite system which appears to be even more inflexible and divisive than its secondary precursor. Universities, as our analysis has shown, have been notably unresponsive to changes in demand (they have restricted supply so tightly as to preclude our developing a 'rational choice' model to explain changing attendance rates: indeed, the logistic curve has barely left its base level). To produce change here may well be difficult. Universities in Britain value their relative independence from the vulgar persuasions of 'the economy', whether represented by central or local government. Internally, they are the epitome of sponsored education: the old army adage 'fit for service, fit for pension' applies almost as much to students as to staff. This puts an excessive burden on selection procedures, and hence distorts the curriculum and organization of those schools that would supply candidates.

Other post-secondary institutions have been afflicted by the relative deprivation characteristic of tripartite systems. Whatever their nominal parity of status, the less selective can gain parity of esteem only, it appears, by mimicry of the practices and aims of the more selective. Thus as technical colleges have metamorphosed into polytechnics or universities, we are in danger of losing in post-secondary as well as secondary education the distinctive contribution of the technical ethos.

A concern for equality will require a broadening of 'alternative routes' to post-secondary education, and in particular the provision of truly open recurrent education. The latter involves radical change of organization, curriculum, and aims. Ten years' experience has shown how difficult it is for the Open University to sustain the paradox of its title. Prospective students have no automatic right to maintenance grants, while course fees rise. We cannot be surprised that, isolated and inadequately funded, in this sense, the Open University tends to develop the second rather than the first part of its title. Plans for recurrent education have, in any case, to be drawn to a vastly greater scale. Building a structure of recurrent education should certainly not be made to await completion of its pre-school foundations.

EXPANSION AND EQUALITY

Returning finally to the major educational fact of the past seventy years – the programme of continuous expansion – we must ask what are the future prospects for this, now venerable, strategy. Our retrospect might be held to have demonstrated that expanding a traditional structure of opportunities guaranteed failure to equalize. Those who want equality of outcome between classes might then gloomily extrapolate from the past and conclude that this ideal is beyond the reach of public policy. Such an inference would be false. We must avoid the error of generalizing from the experience of a particular history to some supposed universal imperative of social policy.[23] The record gives no warranty to easy optimism: but neither does it endorse defeatism. With the relatively clear vision of hindsight we can strike a balanced view of the pessimistic and optimistic theories that have been brought to the interpretation of trends in modern education.

In the first place, the more extreme forms of pessimism have received no comfort from our analyses. The growth and spread of educational qualifications bears witness to a larger and deeper pool of educability than some policy makers ever envisaged, and the actual history of rising norms of educational attainment discredits both the Black Paper pessimism of the political right and the parallel despondency of those who predicted from the political left that working-class children were doomed to be incapable of grasping any opportunities apparently offered to them by educational expansion.

Where the pessimists have been on firmer ground is in their scepticism, on the right that a common culture could be formed through mass education in the tastes and style of the Victorian gentleman, and on the left that any school organization could be proof against the imported influences from class and family which militate against a school-based common culture and against a differentiation of individual achievement unrelated to class background.

Both of these more realistic pessimisms may be expected to carry over to any conceivable future in Britain. The evidence from capitalist and communist countries alike is overwhelmingly that stratification along class, ethnic, status, or cultural lines heavily conditions both what knowledge is regarded as socially valuable and the eagerness and capacity of the children of the different strata to receive it. In their more unguarded and romantic hopes, the British reforming optimists in education have pictured all children as earnest seekers after grammar-school scholarship and all teachers as middle-class Fabians devoted to the peaceful transformation of middle-class privileges into a universal common culture.

The realities are different but they are by no means all grim. There are educational, demographic, economic, and even class forces which in future might favour high educational standards more equally spread. Even though inequality survived the 1944 Education Act and may find accommodation in a comprehensive system, we cannot yet conclude that class differences are immutable.

One reason for optmism is that it is above all the conditions of 'supply' and 'demand' that determine changes in class differentials. Class chances of access to selective secondary schools became more equal as the number of places increased in the immediate pre- and post-war years. But they then widened again as the children of the 'baby boom' years passed through into the secondary schools. But if the programme of building selective schools had kept pace with the growth in the size of the school population, differentials, too, might have remained constant. Scarcity of places was the crucial factor. There is no short cut to equality of class chances. Trying to equalize access to a limited stock of grammar and technical schools had little effect: making secondary-school places free merely increased the subsidy to the more advantaged social classes. But building more grammar and technical schools would have had more effect, as indeed it did in the pre-war years. Equality and expansion might have gone hand in hand.

Nevertheless, expansion has its difficulties beyond those of cost. While the *ratio* of class chances may decline, the *difference* between them may none the less increase. In the inter-war period the working class increased their chances of securing a place at a selective secondary school from 20 to 26 per cent, while the service class increased theirs from 70 to 77 per cent. The rate of increase was greater for the working class, but the absolute gain was greater for the service class.

We have seen this pattern of development many times, and some of the examples are quite dramatic. For example, class chances of access to the university remained more or less constant over our period, but the absolute gains for the service class were massive compared with those for the working class. There is no universal law linking expansion to equality. Rates of increase and absolute gains depend on the starting-points and saturation levels. If the working-class starting-point is very low (as it is in the case of university entrance) there can be a high rate of growth but low absolute gains. A higher starting point on the other hand, may yield a lower rate of growth but, providing it is still well short of the saturation level, the absolute gains can be large, and class differences can decline.

So we arrive at a modified generalization relating expansion to equality. In the *early* stages of educational growth expansion will lead to *greater* inequality; only in the *later* stages will it reduce inequality. This applies both to inequality between classes and to the overall inequality of schooling itself. Looking at the 'share' of schooling going to percentile groups rather than social classes we saw in Chapters 7 and 8 that there was an underlying trend towards inequality throughout our period (albeit interrupted by the raising of the school-leaving age). But we also saw (extrapolating along our logistic curves) that after the end of our period this underlying trend would have been reversed and a limited movement towards equality would occur. So now, for the first time in our history, we stand on the threshold of a period where a sustained policy of expansion could at last attain what for so long has escaped the intentions of reform. The fall in the size of the school population will make equality of opportunity easier to achieve, but educational retrenchment will just as surely postpone it. An attempt to trim the size of the universities to match the reduced size of the age group will leave class inequalities much where they stand at present. An attempt to starve the sixth forms of staff and resources might have the same effect. We repeat: there is no short cut to equality.

There is another problem, too, which might sabotage egalitarian reform. This is credentialism. We argued in Chapter 8 that if there is a process of 'credentialization' such that higher levels of educational attainment are required as more pupils attain the lower levels, the trends towards equality revealed by our logistic curves could be fundamentally misleading. Differentials may narrow at one level, while widening at a higher one. Thus there may be increasing equality of *schooling* as the service class reach their saturation level, while the working class continue to increase their consumption of school education. But access to universities and to post-graduate professional training may show a different picture. As the working class clear one hurdle, so another one is set up in their path, leaving the service class always one flight ahead.

There are two ways of looking at this problem. One is to regard education as a consumer good to be valued as an end in itself. To have achieved some measure of progress towards equalization of schooling by raising the working-class average towards the service-class saturation level is worth while in itself. On this view, more schooling is better than less schooling, irrespective of what is happening to higher education or professional training courses.

Alternatively, education may be seen as a stepping stone to a job. If employers fill the most desirable jobs with the most qualified applicants, one's relative, not absolute, educational level becomes all-important. Educational expansion could be consistent with constant class chances of obtaining a fixed number of desirable jobs. In practice, as we saw in Chapter 7, the number of service-class jobs did not remain fixed, and there was hence little 'educational inflation'. The great increases in the numbers obtaining O- and A-Levels did not lead to any marked devaluing of these qualifications (Table 7.4).

While not deciding between the 'means' and 'ends' view of education, it is important to see that the implications of educational expansion may be different according to which goal is set. If we seek to equalize access to an élite stratum, defined in *relative* terms as the top 5 or 10 per cent of jobs, then educational expansion is likely to prove an inadequate tool. But if we seek to equalize access to schooling on the grounds that the benefits of schooling are desirable in themselves, then expansion provides an answer, and indeed it is possibly the only answer.

The least we can say is that the egalitarian potential of expansion has yet to be fully exploited. The prospect for further expansion rests partly on the demographic fact of reduced numbers since birth-rates fell in the mid 1960s. For a century before that educational expansion had to contend with fertility which was not only higher but also inversely correlated with class.

Economic trends by contrast are widely described as crisis and chaos. Moreover, economic growth does not guarantee a surplus to be distributed to pupils and students. Even so, the economy may reasonably be expected to afford higher average material standards of life for children, parents, and teachers than were contemplated by those who framed either the 1902 or the 1944 Education Acts. And if the future does not bring economic growth then at least the politically more difficult policy of redistributing resources to education remains. The political will to pursue this policy should be strengthened by a true assessment of the experience of expansion. Expansion can bring us higher standards more fairly shared. Education has changed society in that way and can do more. It does so slowly against the stubborn resistance of class and class-related culture. But it remains the friend of those who seek a more efficient, more open, and more just society.

NOTES

1. C. A. R. Crosland, *The Future of Socialism* (Jonathan Cape, 1956), p.258.
2. Ibid., pp.260–1.
3. The proportion of children in independent and direct grant schools (excluding nursery and special schools) was 9.4 per cent in 1950, 7.9 per cent in 1960, 6.2 per cent in 1970, and 5.5 per cent in 1976. These are official figures for single years. Our own survey estimates in Table 11.1 are averages over a ten-year age-group, and thus are not directly comparable.
4. Above, Chapter 2, p.2.
5. Quoted above, p.9–10.
6. We would remind the reader that it is not the labels attached to these variables but their method of construction that is crucial.
7. Within the grammar school 'material circumstances' account for only 14 per cent of the variance in school-leaving age.
8. *Statistics of Education, 1971*, vol. 2, Table A gives the number of boys leaving maintained secondary and Direct Grant schools in 1970–1.
9. For details of our definition, see above Chapter 4, pp.55–6.
10. R. H. Tawney, quoted above pp.4–5.
11. R. H. Tawney, op.cit., p.142.
12. See above, Chapter 1, p.14 n.5.
13. See Bowles and Gintis, op.cit. (1976), see above p.2.
14. See C. Jencks, op.cit. (1972), see above p.12.
15. See R. Boudon, op.cit. (1974), see above p.12.
16. See above (this chapter), pp.203–4.
17. For a general discussion of the issues involved see A. H. Halsey (ed.), op.cit. (1977), pp.187–200.
18. See Chapter 4, p.59. These handicaps, it will be remembered, represent the degree to which the lines A, B, C, D, and E in Figure 4.1 have to be tilted away from the vertical

in order to secure complete agreement between our model and the real world. They are not to be taken as evidence of deliberate discrimination exercised by the schools but may result from differences in the pattern of applications to the different types of school.

19. Quoted above, p. 148.
20. Every first-year sociology student knows that he must not draw causal inferences from correlations because of the risk of spurious correlation, and every third-year student can think of half a dozen variables which, had the researcher had the foresight to have included them in his design, could conceivably have rendered the observed correlations spurious. But it is one thing to suggest such variables, quite another to show what effect they have. Our technique of using data on brothers, however, does permit more stringent empirical tests of the spurious correlation hypothesis. Our technique depends, of course, on various assumptions which we have detailed in the appropriate chapters, but it does give us much more leverage on the problem of unmeasured variables than any other with which we are familiar. Had we not used it we would have drawn some radically different conclusions from the present study, and we suspect that if other investigators employed it, certain 'well-established' findings might be undermined.
21. This concluding passage was written before the advent of the Conservative government on May 3rd 1979. That event casts doubt on the future completion of comprehensive reorganisation. The scheme for 'assisted places' is, in effect, a re-invention of the hybrid direct grant school system, blurring the distinction between state and private education. At all events the announced policies of the new administration would impel us to underline our remarks on the prospects for education and equality without a policy of expansion.
22. Cmd 6458.
23. For a criticism of Jencks from this point of view, see J. Karabel and A. H. Halsey, op.cit. (1977), pp.23–6:

Appendix I: Extracts from the Oxford Mobility Project 1972 Questionnaire

INSTRUCTIONS ON EDUCATION QUESTIONS ARE ON PAGES 226-9

3a. PRIMARY SCHOOLING

Now I would like to ask you about your schooling up to the
age of 11. Did you go to an ordinary (elementary or primary)
school or did you go to a private school?

Ordinary 1

{ Private .... 2 }   GIVE NAME(S)

{ Both .... 3 }   AND LOCATION(S)

Foreign Schools (excluding Ireland) ... 4

Other (Specify) 5

3b. SECONDARY SCHOOLING

I want to ask you about your schooling *after* the age of 11.
What schools did you go to then? (Any others?)

CIRCLE ALL
WHICH APPLY

Stayed at exact same school 01

Elementary school 02

Central/Intermediate/Higher Elementary/
   Senior School 03

All Age school/Advanced division 04

Secondary Modern/Junior Secondary school/
   Vocational school (Republic of Ireland–South) 05

Comprehensive (including Multilateral and Bilateral
   schools) 06

Technical school 07

{ Grammar school .... 08 }

{ Direct Grant/Grant Aided .... 09 } GIVE

{ Independent (fee-paying) school .... 10 } NAME(S)

{ Scotland only: Senior Secondary school .... 11 } AND

{ Scotland only: Higher Grade .... 12 } LOCATION(S)

{ Republic of Ireland (South) only: }

{   'Secondary' school .... 13 }

Special School (e.g. Open Air, Blind, Deaf, ESN,
MH, Maladjusted)d) SPECIFY TYPE AND GIVE
NAME AND LOCATION 14

_____

_____

All Foreign Schools 15
Other (Specify) 16

_____

_____

3c. FEES

Did your family ever pay fees for your schooling?

No 1
Yes . . . . 2 – GET DETAILS
(Between what ages were fees paid?)

_____

_____

3d. AGE WHEN LEFT SCHOOL . . . .

☐ TICK HERE IF DON'T KNOW EXACT AGE BUT
KNOW IT WAS SCHOOL LEAVING AGE

IF ATTENDED ONLY FOREIGN SCHOOLS AFTER AGE 11
(Q.3b) – SKIP TO Q.3i
IF UNDER 14 WHEN LEFT SCHOOL OR BOX TICKED – SKIP
TO Q.3f

3e. SCHOOL EXAMS (Hand Card A to Informant)

Did you pass any of these exams *before leaving school*?

Number of Passes

Certificate of Secondary Education (CSE) 01
School Certificate 02
Matriculation 03
Higher School Certificate 04
General Certificate of Education – O level . . . . . 05 _____
General Certificate of Education – A level . . . . . 06 _____
Clerical and commercial qualifications, such as
typing, shorthand, book-keeping, RSA
commercial certificate 07
Scotland: O levels/O grade/Day School Higher/
Intermediate Certificate . . . . 08 _____
Scotland: Higher Leaving Certificate . . . . 09 _____
Republic of Ireland (South): Intermediate
Certificate 10
Republic of Ireland (South): Leaving Certificate . . 11
Foreign (Specify) 12

_____

_____

Other (Specify) 13

_____

_____

NONE 00

3f. FURTHER EDUCATION

Did you at any time go on to any further education or training, either full-time or part-time? (What was that?) (Hand Card B to Informant)

CIRCLE ALL
WHICH APPLY

No further education 00
Apprenticeship of any kind 01
Articled to a Profession (e.g. accounting,
   surveying, law) 02
In-firm training 03
Day-Release or Block Release 04
Sandwich Course 05
Part-time Vocational training (but not in-firm,
   day-release or block-release) 06
Other part-time (leisure interests) 07
Correspondence Course (vocational) 08
Correspondence Course (leisure interests) 09
Full-time 10

GIVE FULL DETAILS: Always give full details on field, length and nature of training, and kind of institution (for example, University, Polytechnic, Teacher Training, WEA, Adult Education Residential College, College of Further Education, etc.). RELATE the codes circled to these details as explained in the instructions (page 47).

_____

_____

_____

_____

_____

_____

ASK Q.3g *ONLY* IF INFORMANT HAD FULL-TIME FURTHER
EDUCATION   IN ALL OTHER CASES – SKIP TO Q.3h

3g. TERMINATION OF FULL-TIME EDUCATION

When did you finish your full-time education?

AGE   OR   YEAR

3h. QUALIFICATIONS

(Hand Card C to informant) Did you take any of these exams *after* leaving school?

	Completed	Age achieved	Started never completed or failed	Started still working on it
Certificate of Secondary Education (CSE)	01	_____	01	01
School Certificate	02	_____	02	02
Matriculation	03	_____	03	03
Higher School Certificate	04	_____	04	04
General Certificate of Education – O level	05 ____ (No.)	_____	05	05
General Certificate of Education – A level	06 ____ (No.)	_____	06	06
Scotland: O levels/O grade/ Day School Higher/ Intermediate Certificate	08 ____ (No.)	_____	08	08
Scotland: Higher Leaving Certificate	09 ____ (No.)	_____	09	09
Republic of Ireland (South): Intermediate Certificate	10	_____	10	10
Republic of Ireland (South): Leaving Certificate	11	_____	11	11
NONE	00		00	00

3i. QUALIFICATIONS (Hand Card D to Informant)

Have you any of these qualifications? (Any others?) (Did you ever start any?)
ALWAYS ASK: Any not on this card?
ALWAYS EXPLAIN: I am interested even in qualifications that you may not be using now and may never have used very much.

	Started never completed or failed	Started still working on it	Period working on it (Give starting and finishing date)
Ordinary trade apprenticeship 01	01	01	_____
TICK ONE: ☐ INDENTURED ☐ OTHER ☐ Don't know			
Qualifications gained in Armed Forces 02	02	02	_____
Specialised vocational qualifications, as for example in horticulture, building, catering, management, retailing and salesmanship 03	03	03	_____
Any other trade, vocational or occupational qualifications 04	04	04	_____
Clerical and commercial qualifications such as typing, shorthand, book-keeping, RSA and similar commercial certificates, RSA language certificate . . 05	05	05	_____

	Completed	Started never completed or failed	Started still working on it	Period working on it (Give starting and finishing date)
City and Guilds	06	06	06	_____

TICK ONE:
☐ CERTIFICATE/INTERMEDIATE
☐ FINAL   ☐ Don't know
☐ FULL TECHNOLOGICAL

Ordinary National Certificate (ONC) or Diploma (OND)	07	07	07	_____
Higher National Certificate (HNC) or Diploma (HND)	08	08	08	_____

PROBE: ENDORSEMENTS/GRADUATESHIP OF INSTITUTION

☐ Yes (GIVE DETAILS BELOW)
☐ No   ☐ Don't know

Professional qualifications including membership of a professional body (includes A.M.T.E.E./A.M.I.M.E./ A.C.C. and fully qualified solicitors . . .	09	09	09	_____
University Degree – First (including such as medical/dental/veterinary qualifications)	10	10	10	_____
Diploma in Technology (Dip.Tech.) . . .	11	11	11	_____
University Degree – Higher (such as M.Sc., Ph.D., D.Sc.)	12	12	12	_____
University Diploma (excluding teaching diploma and excluding Dip.Tech.)	13	13	13	_____
Qualifications or Certificates – Art, Music, Drama, Elocution, (Specify Grade)	14	14	14	_____
Nursing qualifications (SRN/SEN) . . .	15	15	15	_____
School Teaching qualifications such as Dip.Ed., Certificate of Education	16	16	16	_____
Others (SPECIFY BELOW)	17	17	17	_____
NONE	00	00	00	

DETAILS OF QUALIFICATIONS, e.g. kind of degree (and the University from which obtained), type of teaching or nursing qualification, name of professional body, name and grade of certificate, etc. For Apprenticeships – give field. RELATE each qualification to the form of further education by which it was obtained as explained in the instructions (page 228-9).

_____

_____

_____

_____

_____

_____

_____

EDUCATION QUESTIONS

We ask about the education of the informant, his father, mother, wife, and one of his brothers. The same basic question is used for each, although there are minor variations which are noted below. Note that we have attempted in the precodes to provide for those educated in Scotland and Ireland.

a. 'Ordinary' schools include primary schools (post-1944) and 'elementary' schools (pre-1944). These schools may be 'church' (denominational) schools, which may be 'maintained', 'aided' or 'controlled' by local education authorities. 'Ordinary' schools include 'national' schools in Ireland. Occasionally very old respondents who attended 'elementary' schools may report that they paid a penny or twopence a week. This does not make them private schools for our purpose.

'Private' schools are those in which most children attending pay fees (even though the informant may not have done so). They include the so-called 'preparatory' schools attended by children up to the age of 13 before going on to the independent so-called 'public' schools. They also include the now extinct 'junior' departments (for children under 11) of grammar schools.

b. Note that we want you to code all categories which apply. In the case, for example, of a man who went to a preparatory school until age 13, and then went to another school, you would code 'private' in (a); you code 'stayed at same school' plus the appropriate code for the school he attended next in (b).

Primary Schools – Elementary schools were State or Church schools controlled by local education authorities (see above) for children aged 5 to school leaving age. They were renamed and re-organised after 1944. After that date, children up to the age of 11 attended 'primary' schools, and children over 11 attended 'secondary' schools. There were still, for some years after 1944, a number of un-reorganised all-age schools, especially in rural districts, taking children for both the primary and secondary stages in their schooling.

Central, Intermediate, Higher Elementary and Senior schools are pre-1944 schools in the general class of 'elementary' schools.

Grammar and Technical schools are selective schools and admit children on the basis of an examination at the age of 11 plus, or in some cases at 13 plus. Secondary Modern schools do not select their pupils but receive those who do not gain admission to either grammar or technical schools. In Scotland these non-selected children sometimes proceed to the 'advanced' division of an all-age school.

Comprehensive schools are for children over the age of 11; there is no selective entry. They were established soon after 1944 but only in the last 5 years have they admitted more than a tiny proportion of secondary school children.

Multilateral and Bilateral schools are combinations of two or more of the types of school, grammar, technical and modern, sharing a common site and facilities and working under a centralised direction.

Secondary Schools – Grammar, technical, modern and comprehensive schools are post 1944 schools in the general class of 'secondary' schools.

Direct Grant schools are schools having 25% at least of their pupils recruited from state primary schools with free places. The rest of the places are fee-paying. These schools get their money directly from the Central Government and not from a local education authority. Sometimes informants are not certain if a school was a Direct Grant school. In such cases, please code 'Direct Grant' but also write in the name of the school and the location.

Independent schools include both the public schools and other private fee-paying schools. 'Fee-paying' refers to the school, not the student, i.e. a school in which most students pay fees even though the informant may not have done so.

Scottish Senior Secondary schools is a separate category because in some areas they may be similar to English grammar schools, whereas in other areas they are more nearly equivalent to the English comprehensive.

Irish 'Secondary' schools are state schools in Ireland in which fees were paid until a few years ago. They should not be taken to include all secondary education in Ireland, as they were attended by a relatively small proportion of the population. You should always PROBE to be certain it is this particular type of school to which the informant is referring, and not secondary schooling generally.

Special schools are for children who are handicapped in such a way or to such a degree as not to be suitably educated in ordinary state schools. Please try to get the name and location of the school and ALWAYS specify the type (e.g. Open Air, Blind, Deaf, ESN, MH, Maladjusted).

There is a place to write in the details (type, name and location) of any school which is not provided for. These are schools which could have been attended only by a fraction of 1% of the population: state boarding schools (get name and local authority), army schools, fee-paying local corporation schools (in Scotland), etc.

You will find that most schoos fit readily into these categories. If a school has changed type, e.g. grammar school becoming a secondary modern school, you should code according to what it was when the informant attended it. If it changed whilst he was there, code it according to what it was when he entered. If you do not know which code is applicable, please circle the code(s) you think applies and write the name and location of the school at the side.

c. For those for whom fees were paid, find out between which ages fees were paid. We are not interested in fees paid by lodges, scholarships, etc., but only fees paid by the family. Nor are we interested in the penny or twopence a week sometimes paid by the parents of very old informants.

d. Those who attended school before 1921 may have left at age 12 when part-time working was permitted. Statutory school leaving age was raised to 14 in 1921 and to 15 in 1947. If the informant knows that he left at the school leaving age, but does not recall the exact age, tick the box.

e. The form of this question varies slightly. For informants we ask 'Did you pass any of these exams before leaving school?' and ask later if any of these exams were passed after leaving school. But for parents, brothers and wives, we only ask the question once: 'Did you pass any of these exams?' This is an important distinction so you must read the question exactly as it appears on the page. Passing the exams 'before leaving school' means that the informant was entered by the school. Occasionally he may have actually left the school a few months before taking the examination, but so long as the school entered him for it, it counts as 'before leaving school.'

In 1950 the system of examinations at the end of secondary schooling was changed. Up to that time, the examination taken at 15 or 16 was School Certificate, which was either passed or failed as a whole. If you got a high standard you could also get Matriculation (meaning the minimum entry requirements to university) on the same examination. This was followed by a two year course in the sixth form leading to the Higher School Certificate which school children normally took before entering the university.

After 1950 School Certificate was replaced by the General Certificate of Education O level. In this you can take as many subjects as you like, there is no passing or failing as a whole, and therefore we want to know the number of passes. The post-1950 equivalent of Higher School Certificate is the .General Certificate of Education A level. The Certificate of Secondary Education is a lower level qualification than the General Certificate of Education.

In the case of the Scottish exams we ask the number of passes. This will not always apply; although the present exams are similar to English O and A levels, they have not always been so. If the informant says that the examination he took was passed as a whole, just tick on the line for number of passes.

'Scotland: O levels/O grade/Day School Higher/Intermediate Certificate' all refer to examinations roughly equivalent to the English O levels and usually taken one year past the school leaving age. Informants occasionally confuse them with School Certificates given to show school attendance for a specified period, so you should PROBE to establish if this is the case. The Higher Leaving Certificate is roughly equivalent to English O levels and here too you should PROBE as needed to be certain that it is not being confused with a mere certificate of attendance given the student when he leaves school.

Clerical and commercial qualifications can be taken in Institutions of Further Education, Night Schools, Technical Colleges etc., but may also be taken in Secondary schools in some cases.

We are not interested in S (Scholarship) exams. These exams are usually taken in conjunction with A levels, but should not be included when counting the number of passes.

'Additional' examinations in such subjects as Maths, should be counted as O levels.

PROBE in this question for other exams, e.g. Civil Service clerical and executive exams and G.L.C. or other local authority exams.

f. Further Education – In some cases, several codes may apply to the same experience. For example, an apprenticeship would almost certainly be full-time and might include sandwich courses – so you would circle 1, 5 and 8. You would then put an 'a' by each of the codes and on the line for details repeat the 'a' and give field and length.

If there were another educational experience, e.g. an evening course in art appreciation, you would circle 7, put a 'b' by it and note the details under 'b'.

g. (i) in the case of the Informant.

When you come to qualifications you must then relate them to the form of further education by which they were obtained. In the case cited above, you would circle 'Ordinary trade apprenticeship', and then put an 'a' by it to indicate that the further education details recorded under 'a' apply to this qualification. EVERY QUALIFICATION (excepting Category 2, qualifications gained in the Armed Forces) SHOULD BE RELATED IN THIS WAY TO THE FURTHER EDUCATION QUESTION.

Accept all qualifications the informant tells you about, even if you think them irrelevant or not really a qualification. We can always eliminate anything irrelevant in the office.

Appendix II: Publications from the Oxford Mobility Project

HOPE, K. (ed.), *The Analysis of Social Mobility: Methods and approaches.* Oxford: Clarendon Press, 1972.

RIDGE, J. M. (ed.), *Mobility in Britain Reconsidered*, Oxford: Clarendon Press, 1974.

GOLDTHORPE, J. H., and HOPE, K., *The Social Grading of Occupations: A New Approach and Scale*, Oxford: Clarendon Press, 1974.

HALSEY, A. H., 'Education and Social Mobility in Britain Since World War II'. In *Education, Inequality and Life Chances*, vol. 1, Paris, OECD 1975.

GOLDTHORPE, J. H., 'Mobilité Sociale et Intérêts Sociaux', Sociologie et Sociétés, vol. viii, 1976.

GOLDTHORPE, J. H., and LLEWELLYN, C. 'Class Mobility in Modern Britain: Three Theses Examined', *Sociology*, vol. 11, no. 2, 1977.

GOLDTHORPE, J. H. and LLEWELLYN, C., 'Class Mobility: Intergenerational and Worklife Patterns', *British Journal of Sociology*, vol. 28, no. 3, 1977.

HALSEY, A. H. (with J. Karabel), 'Introduction – Educational Research: A Review and Interpretation'. In J. Karabel and A. H. Halsey, *Power and Ideology in Education*, New York: Oxford University Press, 1977.

HALSEY, A. H., 'Towards Meritocracy? The Case of Britain', in J. Karabel and A. H. Halsey, *Power and Ideology* in Education, New York: Oxford University Press, 1977.

THORBURN, P., 'Political Generations: The Case of Class and Party in Britain'. *European Journal of Political Research*, vol. 5, 1977.

HALSEY, A. H., 'Mobility and Education', in A. H. Halsey, *Change in British Society*. Oxford: Oxford University Press, 1978.

RAFFE, D., 'The "Alternative Route" Reconsidered: Part-Time Further Education and Social Mobility in England and Wales', *Sociology*, vol. 13, no. 1, 1979.

GOLDTHORPE, J. H., *Social Mobility and Class Structure*, Oxford: Clarendon Press, 1980.

Appendix III: On Fitting the Logistic Curve by Least Squares

by Peter Clifford
Mathematical Institute, Oxford

The logistic curve

$$Z(t) = a_1 + a_2/(1 + \exp(-(t - a_3)/a_4))$$

where a_1, a_2, a_3, and a_4 are parameters is frequently used to fit growth data. One of the earliest references is the work of Pearl and Reed (1920). Typically, growth data consist of increasing values Y_1, $Y_2 \ldots Y_n$ at times $t_1, t_2 \ldots t_n$. The best fit of the curve to the data according to the criterion of least squares is obtained when the parameters a_1, a_2, a_3, and a_4 are adjusted so as to minimise

$$\sum_{i=1}^{n} (Y_i - Z(t_i))^2 \qquad \text{Equation III.1}$$

In principle the minimum may be computed by standard iterative techniques. In practice difficulties may arise when bad initial values are put into the computer program, and to obtain a measure of protection against this defect complicated partial derivatives must be computed (Oliver, 1966). The purpose of this note is to show that the optimisation problem with four parameters a_1, a_2, a_3, and a_4 can be reduced to one with only two parameters, namely a_3 and a_4. To see this write $W(t) = 1/(1 + \exp(-(t - a_3)/a_4))$ then, for any given values of a_3 and a_4, $W(t)$ can be computed and the minimum of

$$\sum_{i=1}^{n} (Y_i - a_1 - a_2 W(t_i))^2$$

with respect to a_1 and a_2 will be given by

$$\sum_{i=1}^{n} (Y_i - \bar{Y})^2 (1 - R^2) \qquad \text{Equation III.2}$$

Here R is the correlation between $W(t_i)$ and Y_i, and $\bar{Y} = \sum_{i=1}^{n} Y_i/n$ so that

$$R^2 = \frac{(\sum_{i=1}^{n} (Y_i - \bar{Y}) W(t_i))^2}{\sum_{i=1}^{n} (Y_i - \bar{Y})^2 \sum_{i=1}^{n} (W(t_i) - \bar{W})^2}$$

where $\bar{W} = \sum_{i=1}^{n} W(t_i)/n$.

The values of a_1 and a_2 for which the minimum is attained are given by

$$a_2 = \sum_{i=1}^{n} (Y_i - \bar{Y}) W(t_i)/ \sum_{i=1}^{n} (W(t_i) - \bar{W})^2$$

and $\quad a_1 = \bar{Y} - a_2 \bar{W}.$ $\qquad$ ·Equation III.3

Since $W(t)$ depends on a_3 and a_4, it follows that R^2, a_1, and a_2 depend on a_3 and a_4. Now Equation III.2 represents the minimum of Equation III.1 for any fixed values of a_3 and a_4. It follows that the minimum of Equation III.1 with respect to a_1, a_2, a_3, and a_4 is given by the minimum of Equation III.2 with respect to a_3 and a_4, or equivalently the maximization of R^2. Since only two parameters are involved this maximization can be obtained most instructively by tabling R^2 for a variety of values of a_3 and a_4 and finding the largest value of R^2 by inspection. Once a_3 and a_4 are found, a_1 and a_2 can be obtained from Equation III.3 by substitution. This informal method has the virtue of exposing the interdependence of a_3 and a_4 near the maximum and it is thus possible to identify the range of values of a_3 and a_4 for which tolerably good fits are obtained.

REFERENCES

Pearl, R., and Reed, L. J., 1920, 'On the rate of growth of the population of the United States since 1870 and its mathematical representation', *Proc. Nat. Acad., Sci. U.S.A.*, vol. 6, pp.275–88.

Oliver, F. R. 1966, Aspects of the maximum likelihood estimation of the logistic growth function, *J. Amer. Statist. Ass.*, vol. 61, pp.697–705.

Appendix IV: Path Analysis

by Peter Clifford
Mathematical Institute, Oxford

This Appendix deals with a number of problems which arose whilst performing the path analyses in Chapters 6 and 9. The main reference sources on path analysis were unable to illuminate these problems. To provide solutions, a fairly detailed study of path analysis is required. The discussion which follows makes use of standard statistical terminology and assumes some familiarity with elementary statistical techniques.

Firstly, it seems appropriate to provide a translation of the specialized vocabulary of path analysis. Path analysis involves the calculation of the coefficients in multiple linear regression. If a variable X_{n+1} is to be predicted by a set of variables $X_1, X_2, \ldots, X_n$, then the linear combination of $X_1, X_2, \ldots, X_n$ which has the greatest correlation with X_{n+1} is called the multiple linear regression of X_{n+1} on $X_1, X_2, \ldots, X_n$, and the correlation R_{n+1} is called the multiple correlation coefficient. If all the X's have variance 1 and the linear combination L_{n+1} is written as $L_{n+1} = P_{n+11} X_1 + P_{n+12} X_2 + \ldots P_{n+1n} X_n$, then the typical coefficient P_{n+1k} is called the path from X_k to X_{n+1}. The quantity $X_{n+1} - L_{n+1}$ is called the residual. It is uncorrelated with L_{n+1} and has standard deviation $\sqrt{(1 - R_{n+1}^2)}$, called the residual path. The paths can be calculated in a straightforward manner. If $\mathbf{A}_n$ is the matrix of correlations of the variables $X_1, X_2, \ldots, X_n$, and if $\mathbf{V}_n$ is the vector of correlations between X_{n+1} and $X_1, X_2, \ldots, X_n$ then $\mathbf{P}_n$, the vector of paths from $X_1, X_2, \ldots, X_n$ to X_{n+1}, is obtained by solving the system of equations $\mathbf{A}_n \mathbf{P}_n = \mathbf{V}_n$.

In path analysis it is frequently the case that the variables have some hierarchical structure. For example, if X_1 and X_2 are variables representing parental attributes and $X_3, X_4, X_5 \ldots$, are successive measures of the respondent's educational development, then X_3 depends on (X_1, X_2), X_4 depends on (X_1, X_2, X_3), X_5 depends on (X_1, X_2, X_3, X_4), and so on. Calculation of the paths of interest, that is, the vectors $\mathbf{P}_3, \mathbf{P}_4, \mathbf{P}_5 \ldots$, is facilitated by certain aspects of this hierarchical structure. Specifically, the matrix $\mathbf{A}_{n+1}$ is just the matrix $\mathbf{A}_n$ with an extra row and column. Rao (1973)[1] gives a formula for the inverse of the matrix $\mathbf{A}_{n+1}$ in terms of the inverse of the matrix $\mathbf{A}_n$. Applied successively, this enables the paths to be obtained with great computational economy.

HYPOTHETICAL VARIABLES

Up to this point we have assumed that all correlations are known or can be determined empirically. However, when one of the variables, say X_2, is hypothetical, some method has to be devised to enable the unknown correlations r_{2k} between X_2 and X_k to be determined. We suppose that X_1 and X_2 are parental variables and $X_3, X_4, \ldots$, have a hierarchical structure. Initially we shall consider the case in which X_1 and X_2 are uncorrelated. We shall suppose that for the

---

[1] C. R. Rao, *Linear Statistical Methods* (Wiley, New York, 1973).

respondent's brother there is a further set of variables $X_3{}^B, X_4{}^B, \ldots$, and that the correlation matrix of $X_1, X_2, X_3{}^B, \ldots, X_n{}^B$ is the same as the correlation matrix of $X_1, X_2, X_3, \ldots, X_n$. Our main assumption is that for each k, the respondent's residual

$$Z_k = X_k - P_{k1} X_1 - P_{k2} X_2 - \ldots - P_{kk-1} X_{k-1}$$

is uncorrelated with his brother's residual

$$Z_k{}^B = X_k{}^B - P_{k1} X_1 - P_{k2} X_2 - \ldots - P_{kk-1} X_{k-1}^B$$

(The assumptions made in Chapters 6 and 9 that there is no direct path from brother's to respondent's schooling etc., and vice versa, are, of course, instances of this main assumption.)

We can then write

$$X_k = P_{k1} X_1 + P_{k2} X_2 + \ldots + P_{kk-1} X_{k-1} + Z_k \qquad \text{Equation IV.1}$$

$$X_{k-1} = P_{k-11} X_1 + P_{k-12} X_2 + \ldots + P_{k-1k-2} X_{k-2} + Z_{k-1} \qquad \text{Equation IV.2}$$

Using Equation 2 to eliminate X_{k-1} in Equation 1 we may successively reduce Equation 1 to

$$X_k = C_1 X_1 + C_2 X_2 + W_k \qquad \text{Equation IV.3}$$

where C_1 and C_2 depend on the paths contained in the vectors $\mathbf{P}_3, \mathbf{P}_4, \ldots, \mathbf{P}_k$, and W_k is a random variable depending on $Z_3, Z_4, \ldots, Z_k$. A similar reduction of $X_k{}^B$ leads to

$$X_k{}^B = C_1 X_1 + C_2 X_2 + W_k{}^B \qquad \text{Equation IV.4}$$

where $W_k{}^B$ depends on $Z_3{}^B, Z_4{}^B, \ldots, Z_k{}^B$. Observing that W_k is uncorrelated with $W_k{}^B$ and that both are uncorrelated with X_1 and X_2, we have the simple consequences that

$$r_{1k} = C_1 \qquad \text{Equation IV.5}$$

$$r_{2k} = C_2 \qquad \text{Equation IV.6}$$

$$r_k = C_1{}^2 + C_2{}^2 \qquad \text{Equation IV.7}$$

where r_k is the correlation between X_k and $X_k{}^B$.

It follows that the unknown correlation r_{2k} is given by

$$r_{2k} = \sqrt{(r_k - r_{1k}^2)} \qquad \text{Equation IV.8}$$

We have shown that if there are two uncorrelated parental variables then the assumption of uncorrelated residuals enables the unknown correlations r_{2k} to be obtained. The general case of correlated X_1 and X_2 presents no further problems. Suppose X_1 and X_2 have correlation a, then X_2 has to have the form $aX_1 + Z\sqrt{(1 - a^2)}$ where Z is uncorrelated with X_1. Knowledge of X_1 and X_2 is equivalent to knowledge of X_1 and Z. But Z is uncorrelated with X_1, so that by the preceding arguments the correlation between Z and X_k must be $\sqrt{(r_k - r_{1k}^2)}$. Since $X_2 = aX_1 + Z\sqrt{(1 - a^2)}$, it follows that the correlation between X_2 and X_k is $ar_{1k} + \sqrt{(1 - a^2)}\sqrt{(r_k - r_{1k}^2)}$.

We now have all the correlations necessary for path analysis, and it is worth noting that the missing correlations which have now been provided will not be affected by expanding or reducing the set of hierarchical variables $X_3, X_4, \ldots, X_n$. It is thus in order to take the correlations derived from Model Alpha in

Chapter 9 and employ them in the expanded Model Gamma. Thus the correlation between X_2 (family climate) and X_3 (respondent's secondary schooling) is not affected by the addition of the intervening variable IQ in Model Gamma.

Nor is it necessary to perform separate path analyses for each value of a. Let us denote the path from X_j to X_i obtained with $r_{12} = a$ by $P_{ij}(a)$. Once the analysis for $a = 0$ has been done we will have determined the linear combination of $X_1, Z, X_3, \ldots, X_{k-1}$ which is maximally correlated with X_k. This linear combination is given by

$$P_{k1}(0) X_1 + P_{k2}(0) Z + \ldots + P_{kk-1}(0) X_{k-1} \qquad \text{Equation IV.9}$$

But for the general case $Z = (X_2 - aX_1)/\sqrt{(1 - a^2)}$ so that the maximally correlated linear combination of $X_1, X_2, \ldots, X_{k-1}$ is

$$P_{k1}(0) X_1 + P_{k2}(0) (X_2 - aX_1)/\sqrt{(1 - a^2)} + \ldots$$
$$+ P_{kk-1}(0) X_{k-1} \qquad \text{Equation IV.10}$$

$$= P_{k1}(a) X_1 + P_{k2}(a) X_2 + \ldots + P_{kk-1}(a) X_{k-1} \qquad \text{Equation IV.11}$$

where

$$P_{k1}(a) = P_{k1}(0) - aP_{k2}(0)/\sqrt{(1 - a^2)} \qquad \text{Equation IV.12}$$

and $\quad P_{k2}(a) = P_{k2}(0)/\sqrt{(1 - a^2)} \qquad \text{Equation IV.13}$

and $\quad P_{kj}(a) = P_{kj}(0), k \neq 1, 2.$

Thus only the paths from X_1 and X_2 are affected by the value of a. It is also a straightforward matter to see from Equations 12 and 13 how changes in the value of a will affect P_{k1} and P_{k2}: they will not be particularly sensitive to a until quite high values of a are reached.

This happy situation does not persist when further hypothetical parental variables are introduced. Suppose that $X_1, X_2,$ and X_3 are parental variables and $X_4, X_5, \ldots,$ are hierarchical response variables. For the sake of argument we will assume that $X_1, X_2,$ and X_3 are uncorrelated since the general case presents no new problems. Then, proceeding as before, we can reduce X_k to

$$X_k = C_1 X_1 + C_2 X_2 + C_3 X_3 + W_k \qquad \text{Equation IV.14}$$

and obtain the relationships

$$r_{1k} = C_1$$
$$r_{2k} = C_2$$
$$r_{3k} = C_3$$
$$r_k = C_1^2 + C_2^2 + C_3^2.$$

These equations do not enable the correlations r_{2k} and r_{3k} to be determined unambiguously. Thus no paths can be determined objectively, not even those between observed respondent variables. In particular, if arbitrary (possibly negative) correlations are permitted between $X_1, X_2,$ and X_3, paths of almost any sizes can be manufactured. Whatever its merits on other grounds, therefore, the practice of using more than one hypothetical variable (a practice followed by Jencks) has serious drawbacks.

Bibliography

BANKS, O., *The Sociology of Education*, London: Batsford, 1968.
BANTOCK, G. H., *Education and Values*, London: Faber, 1965.
    Freedom and Authority in Education, London: Faber, 1966.
BELL, D., *The Coming of Post-Industrial Society*, New York: Basic Books, Inc., 1973.
BERG, I., *Education and Jobs: The Great Training Robbery*, New York: Praeger, 1970.
BERNSTEIN, B., 'Class and Pedagogies: Visible and Invisible', in J. Karabel and A. H. Halsey (eds.), *Power and Ideology in Education*, New York: Oxford University Press, 1977.
    'Social Class, Language and Socialization'. In J. Karabel and A. H. Halsey (eds.), *Power and Ideology in Eudcation*, New York: Oxford University Press, 1977.
BILLEWICZ, W. Z., 'Some Remarks on the Measurement of Social Mobility', *Population Studies*, vol. 9, 1955.
BLAU, P., and DUNCAN, O. D., *The American Occupational Structure*, New York: John Wiley & Sons, Inc., 1969.
BOUDON, R., *Education, Opportunity and Social Inequality*, New York: John Wiley & Sons, Inc., 1973.
BOURDIEU, P., 'The School as a Conservative Force', in J. Eggleston (ed.), *Contemporary Research in the Sociology of Education*, London: Methuen, 1974.
    'Cultural Reproduction and Social Reproduction', in J. Karabel and A. H. Halsey (eds.), *Power and Ideology in Education'*, New York: Oxford University Press, 1977.
BOWLES, S., 'Unequal Education and the Reproduction of the Social Division of Labor', *Review of Radical and Political Economics*, vol. 3, Autumn 1971.
    and GINTIS, H., *Schooling in Capitalist America*, New York: Basic Books, Inc., 1976.
BURGESS, T., *A Guide to English Schools*, London: Penguin, 1969.
BURT, C., 'Class Differences in General Intelligence: III', *British Journal of Statistical Psychology*, vol. 12, 1959.
COLEMAN, J. S., et.al., *Equality of Educational Opportunity*, Cambridge, Mass.: Harvard University Press, 1969.
COX, C. B., and BOYSON, R., *Black Papers 1975*, London: J. M. Dent & Sons, 1975.
CROSLAND, C. A. R., *The Future of Socialism*, London: Jonathan Cape, 1956.
CROWTHER REPORT, THE, *15–18*, Central Advisory Council for Education, Ministry of Education, London: HMSO, 1960.
DAVIE, R., BUTLER, N., and GOLDSTEIN, H., *From Birth To Seven*, London: Longman, 1972.
DEANE, P., and COLE, W. A., *British Economic Growth 1688–1959*, University of Cambridge, Department of Applied Economics, Monograph 8, 1962.
DONNISON REPORT, *The Public Schools Commission Second Report*, London: HMSO, 1970.
DORFMAN, D. D., 'The Cyril Burt Question: New Findings'. *Science*, vol. 201, 1978.

DOUGLAS, J. W. B., *The Home and the School*, London: McGibbon & Kee, 1964.
All Our Future, London: Peter Davies, 1968.
DUNCAN, O. D., 'Inheritance of Poverty or Inheritance of Race?', in D. P. Moynihan (ed.), *On Understanding Poverty*, New York: Basic Books, Inc., 1968.
EYSENCK, H., *Race, Intelligence and Education*, London: Temple Smith, 1971.
The Inequality of Man, London: Temple Smith, 1973.
FIELD, F., *Unequal Britain*, London: Arrow Books, 1974.
FLOUD, J. E., HALSEY, A. H., and MARTIN, F. M., 'Educational Opportunity and Social Selection in England', in *Transactions of Second World Conference of Sociology*, Vol. II, pp.194–208, 1953.
Social Class and Educational Opportunity, London, Heinemann, 1956.
GLASS, D. V. (ed.), *Social Mobility in Britain*, London: Routledge & Kegan Paul, 1954.
GOSDEN, P. H., *Education in the Second World War*, London: Methuen, 1976.
GRAY, J. L., and MOSHINSKY, P., 'Ability and Opportunity in English Education', in L. Hogben (ed.), *Political Arithmetic*, London: Allen & Unwin, 1938.
HALSEY, A. H. (ed.), *Educational Priority*, vols. 1–5, London: HMSO, 1972.
'Sociology and the Equality Debate', *Oxford Review of Education*, vol. 1, no. 1, 1975.
(ed.), *Heredity and Environment*, London: Methuen, 1977.
and FLOUD, J. E., 'Intelligence Tests, Social Class and Selection for Secondary Schools', *British Journal of Sociology*, vol. 3, no. 3, 1957.
HAUSER, R. M., 'On Boudon's Model of Social Mobility', *American Journal of Sociology*, vol. 81, no. 4, 1976.
HEATH, A. F., *Rational Choice and Social Exchange*, Cambridge: Cambridge University Press, 1976.
'Significant Developments in the Sociology of Education?', *Oxford Review of Education*, vol. 4, no. 1, 1978.
HERRNSTEIN, R. J., *I.Q. in the Meritocracy*, London: Allen Lane, 1973.
HOGBEN, L. (ed.), *Political Arithmetic*, London: Allen & Unwin, 1938.
HOGGART, R., *The Uses of Literacy*, London: Chatto & Windus, 1957.
JACKSON, B., and MARSDEN, D., *Education and the Working Class*, London: Routledge & Kegan Paul, 1963.
JENCKS, C., *et.al.*, *Inequality: A Reassessment of the Effect of Family and Schooling in America*, New York: Basic Books, Inc., 1972.
JENSEN, A., 'How Much Can We Boost I.Q. and Scholastic Achievement?', *Harvard Educational Review*, vol. 39, Winter 1969.
Educability and Group Differences, London: Methuen, 1973.
JONES, D. C., 'Social Factors in Secondary Education'. In vol. 3 of D. C. Jones (ed.), *The Social Survey of Merseyside*, London: Hodder & Stoughton, 1934.
KALTON, G., *The Public Schools: A Factual Survey*, London: Longmans, 1966.
KARABEL, J., and HALSEY, A. H., *Power and Ideology in Education*, New York: Oxford University Press, 1977.
KERCKHOFF, A. C., 'Stratification Processes and the Outcomes in England and the U.S.', *American Sociological Review*, vol. 39, 1974.
LINDSAY, K., *Social Progress and Educational Waste: Being a Study of the 'Free Place' and Scholarship Systems*, London: Routledge, 1926.

LOCKWOOD, D., *The Black-Coated Worker*, London: George Allen & Unwin, 1958.

LOWNDES, G. A. N., *The Silent Social Revolution*, Oxford: Oxford University Press 2nd edition, 1969.

MACDONALD, K. I., 'Interpretation of Residual Paths and the Decomposition of Variance', *Sociological Methods and Research*, 1979.
and DORREIAN, P., *Data Analysis for Social Science*, London: Methuen, 1979.

MILLER, D. I., *Social Justice*, Oxford: Clarendon Press, 1976.

NEWSOM REPORT. *The Public Schools Commission First Report*, London: HMSO, 1968.

PEAKER, W., *The Plowden Children Four Years On*, London: National Foundation for Educational Research, 1971.

QUALIFIED MANPOWER TABLES, SAMPLE CENSUS 1966, GREAT BRITAIN, London: HMSO, 1970.

RAFFE, D., 'The "Alternative Route" Reconsidered: Part-Time Further Education and Social Mobility in England and Wales', *Sociology*, vol. 13, no. 1, 1979.

ROBBINS REPORT. *Committee on Higher Education Report*, Cmnd. 2154, London: HMSO, 1963.

RUBINSTEIN, D., and SIMON, B., *The Evolution of the Comprehensive School, 1926–66*, London: Routledge & Kegan Paul, 1969.

RUTTER, M., MAUGHAN, B., MORTIMORE, P. and OUSTON, J. with SMITH, A., *Fifteen Thousand Hours*, London: Open Books, 1979.

SCHULTZ, T. W., 'Investment in Human Capital', *American Economic Review*, vol. 51, no. 1, 1961.

SILVER, H., *Equal Opportunity in Education*, London: Methuen, 1973.

TAWNEY, R. H., *Equality*, London: Unwin Books, 1931.
(ed.), *Secondary Education For All: A Policy for Labour*, edited for the Education Advisory Committee of the Labour Party, 1922, London: Allen & Unwin (first published 1922).

TAYLOR, W., *The Secondary Modern School*, London: Faber & Faber, 1963.

THUROW, L. C., 'Education and Economic Equality', *The Public Interest*, vol. 28, Summer 1972.

TROW, M., 'The Second Transformation of American Secondary Education', in J. Karabel and A. H. Halsey (eds.), *Power and Ideology in Education*, New York: Oxford University Press, 1977.

TURNER, R. H., 'Sponsored and Contest Mobility and the School System', *American Sociological Review*, vol. 25, 1960.

TYLER, W., *The Sociology of Educational Inequality*, London: Methuen, 1977.

VAIZEY, J. (with K. Norris and J. Sheehan), *The Political Economy of Education*. London: Gerald Duckworth & Co. Ltd., 1972.

YOUNG, M., *The Rise of Meritocracy*, London: Thames & Hudson, 1958.

Index

National Children's Bureau, 21
Newsom Report, 32n

Oliver, F.R., 231

Peaker, W., 72n, 161, 171
Pearl, R., 231
Plowden Report, 6, 161

Raffe, D., 124n, 177, 190, 194n
Rao, C.R., 233
Reed, L.J., 231
Renner, K., 17
Ridge, J.M., 14n
Robbins Committee, 3
Rubinstein, D., 32n
Rutter, M., 175n

Schultz, T.W., 14n

Silver, Harold, 3
Simon, B., 32n

Tawney, R.H., 3, 4, 8, 25, 35, 203, 205
Taylor, William, 32n
Thorburn, Phyllis, 14n
Thurow, L.C., 114
Trow, Martin, 24
Turner, R.H., 135, 146, 147n
Tyler, W., 174n

Vaizey, J., 125n

Weber, Max, 3
Westergaard, J., 66, 67
White Paper (1943), 27–29, 67, 104, 212, 214

Young, M., 6, 7, 8, 208